DARK PSYCHOLOGY AND
GASLIGHTING MANIPULATION

INFLUENCE HUMAN BEHAVIOR WITH MIND
CONTROL TECHNIQUES: HOW TO CAMOUFLAGE,
ATTACK AND DEFEND YOURSELF

RYAN MACE

Influence Human Behavior with Mind Control Techniques: How to Camouflage, Attack and Defend Yourself

Ryan Mace

CONTENTS

PROLOGUE

WHEN WE LOOK up to a leader as aspirational, what is it about them that piques our interest the most? Is it the way they dress, their overall charisma and kindness, the years of good work they have done, or simply the overall impact of their magnetic charm on us? It's all of these—but especially the last.

There may be any number of good people out in the world. People who are kind, respectful, and care about the feelings of those they engage with as well as the larger world around them. Yet, not all of these people reach the heights of success that we associate with "leadership."

Deep down, all of us want to be aspirational (to different degrees). You may want to be held in high regard by your immediate family, your friends and larger peer circle, your professors, colleagues, and employers. Human beings are wired to seek appreciation. Essentially, this is because appreciation engenders gratitude. We want to feel safe, loved, sheltered, and looked up to by those who matter to us.

Therefore, it can be terribly dampening if life just passes us by without us ever reaching those heights or experiencing the joys of being reliable. Not that we are inherently incapable of persuasion or influence—many of us just don't know how to wield it.

If you crave ambition, and the semblance of needing to be desired or loved or even looked up to, dark psychology is the ultimate answer. Before you think of it as voodoo and hogwash, let me ask you something very simple.

When you are in a relationship, do you not desire to be able to communicate in a way that will allow the other person to understand that they can fall back on you? Well, in simple enough terms, dark psychology will teach you how to do just that. *All* great leaders rely on tactics of persuasion, influence, and mind control to varying degrees. The difference lies in either using it for good or for bad.

Dark psychology is not something inherently evil. Neither is manipulation or exerting influence. I have come to recognize that labeling these skills as evil is the result of two main lines of thought.

First, the people who consider these traits as evil are not sure what they can be used for and are absolutely against believing that they can result in good things. Second, those who have already reached positions of influence may not be open to sharing everything they know with the rest of the world.

We want to get ahead in ways that feel "legitimate" or "fair"—but this is a very subjective way of looking at things. There is nothing "illegitimate" about using the techniques of communication that will work the best for us.

Dark psychology uses communication techniques like manipulation and persuasion to help you achieve your goals. It has earned a lot of controversy as being something that can be used to "exploit" the weaknesses of your peers, but the funny thing is, I can vouch that all of us want to be able to persuade others. Whether for their own good or because we want something from them.

The line between manipulation and persuasion is very thin. When you know how to manipulate your words and expressions to exert an influence for good reasons, there is absolutely nothing wrong with it. However, when you manipulate with the sole intent of harming others, you are on a different trajectory; one which is based on gaslighting and brainwashing.

Like I mentioned before—you have to draw that line yourself. And if you do, you will find that dark psychology is one of the most powerfully persuasive tools at your disposal. By helping you to understand how people feel and what they think, you can turn circumstances—even the most difficult ones—in your favor.

And which powerful leader doesn't do this? Dark psychology is used for many purposes. This can mean getting someone to purchase a product, convincing an audience to cast a vote in your favor, winning a tough case through mind control, or cracking a tough interview. It can also mean convincing someone to commit a crime, brainwashing people into accepting you as their God, and hurting anyone with the power of your words alone. Again—you make that choice.

There was a point in time when I, like most others, felt that "manipulation" was wrong—and allowed myself to be used by others repeatedly. The more I researched about the human mind and techniques of influence, the more I learned that there is nothing wrong with manipulation—it's just a word.

It's how you use it that counts. And it has been a key tool for success that has helped many leaders all over the world. Leadership hinges on being able to hold a sizable audience's interest—in persuading them to keep coming back for advice and help, regardless of temporary hurdles along the way.

So, in this book, my focus will be on teaching you the tools of dark psychology that you can use to exert beneficial influence while protecting yourself from inherently dangerous human traits like emotional gaslighting and conning.

It is pertinent to begin by just looking at the point of origins of dark psychology. As a concept, it is simply the study of human conditionality in the context of the psychological impulses of people who seek to exert influence or prey on others.

Each one of us has the potential to victimize and harm other living creatures, including humans. The normative powers of social values and the weight of our own conscience keep us from inflicting what we think is "harmful"—for instance, toxic influence.

There is a section of the human population that struggles with keeping their dark urges under control, and gives in to using them of free will—and this is when dark psychology becomes dangerous. When you learn to use it, you will understand why your knowledge of it is important—not just for extending your reach, but also for the safety of yourself and your loved ones.

When human beings prey on others, they either have very specific intentions, or they may do it just because "they have nothing better to do" because the mere act of inflicting harm gives them a God complex or makes them feel good about themselves. They may even consider these motivations to be completely natural, while we, on the other end, cannot fathom why they feel or act the way they do.

The point is that when people engage in "socially unacceptable" acts, they still have certain goals in mind, and they usually also have rationales that (to them) make the acts entirely legitimate. Hitler's brutal hunting of the Jews was legitimate to him, and strangely enough, to millions of other people who fell under the spell of his powers of brainwashing and gaslighting.

Be it religious dogma, political propaganda, sexual gratification, academic excellence, or any other fathomable domain of human life, you need to learn about dark psychology so that you excel in terms of influencing others *while staying safe from potentially harmful influences yourself.*

Today, if you have found your way to my book, I can surmise that you have faced a lot of difficulties in your life because of how others have treated and used you. Time and again, you have noticed that the ones who can wield influence and manipulate others get away with pretty much everything—but when trying to understand how—you've been snubbed and told that only "evil" people manipulate.

A part of you still reasons that manipulation can work as an impactful social communication tool that will help you—if you know how to use it well. Mind reading, control, and manipulation aren't immoral or "evil"—they will exist and occur as the sun rises and trees shed leaves in Autumn.

In other words, they will play a role irrespective of our "intentions." We already use these things from time to time— especially when forming an impression about others, or looking for ways to communicate that will earn us their attention or help us evade tricky situations. When you're finished with this book, you too will know how to use these techniques intentionally, intelligently, and with charisma.

This means that you'll never have to worry about being manipulated or gaslit by others. You'll instinctively know when someone is trying to use you to gain something— and be able to make a wise and informed decision about whether you'd benefit from playing along, or simply refusing to allow it.

On the flip side, you'll be able to utilize what you learn to move up the social ladder—without harming others. It is your discretion when it comes to manifesting what you learn, and influence doesn't necessarily condition itself on destroying the lives of others to get somewhere. Every branch of psychology has an element of "darkness" in it, and all of them have certain notions that can help us model our social skills.

In other words, once you get deeper into the book, you will no longer be a pawn in someone else's game. You will detect when someone has your genuine well-being and interests on their mind, and when they just want to use you.

We will go on a detailed journey where I will elucidate the shadowed, gray areas of our minds, and how you can build your mental fortresses against harmful denudation. You'll uncover essential dark psychology information that will teach you to sift out the truth from the trickiest of situations.

If you or someone you deeply care about has lived through emotional abuse or is currently dealing with it, the knowledge in this book will equip you to understand what works in the minds of the abusers, and how you can turn the tables on them.

And if you are just curious about how "evil" works, and why manipulation has a far wider and deeper context than just being relegated to the backdrop of being an undesirable human trait, this book will show you the way.

Together, we will demystify and simplify dark psychology into something that you can wield in your daily life while learning about every aspect that contributes to its core functionality.

Before we move to the first chapter, I know that many of you may be curious about the historical foundations of dark psychology.

UNDERSTANDING THE HISTORICAL CONTEXT

How did dark psychology earn this derogatory label of being something poisonous— even though it is actually useful? Well, let's take a brief trip to when psychological experiments were often conditioned around unscrupulous ethics that gave dark psychology an often erroneous bad rep.

Not too many decades back, ethical regulations involving human experiments were far laxer than what they are today. In the contemporary day and age, social and psychological experiments can only occur after crossing innumerable bureaucratic hurdles.

More importantly, they are subjected to the strict regulations imposed by the American Psychological Association—which is pedantically serious when it comes to conforming to a set code of ethical standards. If your experiments do not qualify these standards, forget publishing, you will not even be able to conduct them.

It wasn't always this way.

The Monster Study

Perhaps one of the most petrifying studies in the science of human psychology was The Monster Study of 1939. The Monster Study constituted a stuttering experiment that was performed on 22 children, all orphans, at Davenport in Iowa. Mary Tudor, a graduate student at the University of Iowa, conducted the experiment under Wendell Johnson's supervision.

The core of the experiment lay in dividing the orphan children into two groups. While the first group received positive speech therapy that exhorted and praised the fluency of their speech; the other half was exposed to negative speech therapy. The latter group was constantly berated and belittled for imperfections in speech.

Given the ethical conundrum, the study came to be dubbed the "Monster Study" because of the horror it instilled in some of Johnson's peers as to how he could manipulate and mentally abuse orphan children all for the purpose of a hypothesis. So great was the backlash that the experiment was eventually kept under wraps for fear that it would cost Johnson his entire reputation.

The world was also in a state of turmoil, with Nazi Germany running a full-fledged campaign to torture and extinguish an entire civilization of people. The Nazis were notorious for conducting terrible human experiments, which would have placed greater suspicion in the context of Johnson's activities. Since the results of the experiment never made it to a peer-reviewed journal, until today, the only evidence we have of it ever happening lies in the withering pages of Mary Tudor's thesis.

So great was the impact of Johnson's manipulation on the children that the ones who received negative speech therapy developed lasting psychological issues, with some retaining speech problems for the entirety of their remaining lives.

During the study, the researchers had four questions that influenced everything they did to the children in the course of the experiment:

- Would removing the "stutterer" label from the children have any impact on the fluency of their speech?
- Would the endorsing of the "stutterer" label impact their speech fluency?
- Would affirming a "normal speaker" label have any effect on speech fluency? And finally,
- Would labeling a previously regarded "normal speaker" a "stutterer" influence their speech fluency?

The details of the experiment were kept under wraps for the participants. Going into it, they had absolutely no idea of the intent of the research—they believed that they were going to receive helpful speech therapy. On the contrary, Tudor attempted to induce stuttering in perfectly healthy children and to see whether convincing stutterers that their speech was "fine and normal" would cause any changes.

Ten of the study participants were orphans who had been categorized as stutterers by matrons and teachers. Along with five graduate students, Tudor graded the orphans on a scale of fluency, with 1 being the lowest and 5 being the highest, and agreed with the prior assessment of the teachers and matrons.

Of these ten students, five were assigned to an experimental group and convinced that their speech was fine. The other five, however, were told that their speech was as bad as others had remarked.

The other twelve children were randomly chosen from orphans who had normal speech fluency. Six of them were told that their speech was far from normal, that they were starting to stutter, and that they had to correct this immediately. The other six were complimented on their enunciation abilities.

Mary Tudor tested every child's IQ to identify whether they were right or left-handed—there was a popular theory doing the rounds at the time that stuttering was the result of a form of cerebral imbalance. For instance, if a person was born as a left-handed child but society had taught them to use their right hand, their internal nerve impulses would backfire and negatively impact their speech patterns. While Johnson had no faith in this assumption, he went along with it.

Tudor made the children squeeze dynamometer bulbs and draw on chalkboards. It was found that most of the children were right-handed, but there were a few left-handed ones in each group. There was no visible correlation between this and their speaking patterns.

The entire duration of the experiment lasted for about four months, from January to May 1939. Every few weeks, Tudor would drive to Davenport and talk with each child for forty-five minutes under the guidance of an agreed-upon script. In her thesis, she mentions that when she talked to the stuttering children; she convinced them that in part, they'd outgrow the stuttering and speak much better than how they were speaking at that moment. She told them to pay no heed to the words of others regarding their speaking capabilities—for they did not understand that this was nothing more than a transient phase.

The non-stuttering children, who were to be branded as stutterers, received a different kind of treatment. She convinced them that the staff had concluded the children were having significant difficulties with their speech and that they were exhibiting many of the symptoms common to children beginning to stutter. Additionally, she told them that they had to use their willpower and do anything they could to keep from stuttering and that they shouldn't ever speak again unless "they could do it right."

Children's minds are often compared to wet sponges. They are quick to absorb words and signals from the external environment, which makes them infinitely more susceptible to being manipulated. So, the children, who were perfectly normal but falsely branded as "stutterers," responded immediately.

Five-year-old Norma Jean Pugh resisted any new efforts aimed at getting her to speak, although she had been speaking very freely just a month before. Likewise, nine-year-old Betty Romp refused to talk. Fifteen-year-old Hazel Potter became frustrated and repeated the letter "a" with increased frequency. When asked why she said that it was because she'd become afraid of what she was going to say next. Keep in mind—all of these children were fluent speakers before the experiment began. There was nothing in them that indicated stuttering issues.

Academics for these manipulated children began to suffer. Among them, one of the boys flat-out refused to recite in class. Another began correcting everything he said. He told Tudor he kept stopping because he knew he'd mess up the words even before he said them. When Tudor asked him how he knew that, he replied the sounds *"wouldn't come out. Felt stuck in there."*

Another orphan, 12-year-old Mary Korlaske, became irate and withdrawn. When asked if her best friend knew about her descent into stuttering, she muttered that she wasn't even talking to her best friend any longer. Korlaske would later run away from the orphanage and land at a harsher Industrial school for girls. As a corollary—she would escape from the horrors of this manipulative human experiment.

The acerbity of the experiment was such that Mary Tudor couldn't escape unscathed either. She returned to the orphanage multiple times after the experiment was over with the intent of providing follow-up care. She tried to make amends by telling the children she'd manipulated that they didn't stutter at all. The impact, while intended to act as a bandaid, raised more questions. She would later write a scathing letter to Johnson, saying that while she believed the manipulated children would recover in time, she later realized that they had made a definite impression on them.

In 2001, the University of Iowa publicly apologized for the Monster Study. An assistant professor of speech pathology and audiology, Patricia Zebrowski, discerned that the data they garnered from this experiment, terrible as it was, also constituted the largest collection of scientific data on the topic of stuttering. She also identified that the link between stuttering and the thoughts, feelings, and attitudes of the affected individual had never been apparent before—but due to the experiment, it was out in the open now.

Now—there is no contesting that this experiment came at a cost that was far too great—irrespective of the meager positives involved. The reason why I went into such depths in discussing it, however, is different. I want you to understand something. Many of you who are reading this book right now may have been led into believing or doing things that go in line with the kind of manipulation that was carried out by the researchers of this experiment. The effects may have either hurt you, belittled you, or completely shattered you.

The sad thing is—the world will always have people who will want to use their powers of manipulation and persuasion to make you feel inferior or to convince you to do their bidding. If you don't learn to identify such situations or people, you run the risk of facing the same consequences that befell the innocent children who had no issues save one—they put their faith into the hands of a manipulator.

But—and this is important—if you learn how to identify and play an Uno Reverse upon vicious manipulators by using dark psychology to your own benefit, you will be able to evade many of these dangerous situations from even happening. In some cases, you may even be successful enough to get the manipulator to do your bidding.

The secret is in learning the tools that they use as intimately as you can and using these tools for two main purposes. First, to protect yourself and the ones you love. Second, to wield practical and theoretical knowledge wisely so that you remain one step ahead when facing or dealing with a manipulator, *every single time.*

The Wave That Altered World Dynamics

In his article, *"Did A History Teacher's 'Third Wave' Nazi Social Experiment Go Too Far?"*, Lauren Coontz talks about an experiment that will forever go down the hallowed halls of infamy. Fervent chants followed as the students of Cubberley High School walked in a rally led by their history teacher, Ron Jones, in April of 1967. *"Strength through discipline! Strength through community! Strength through action! Strength through pride! Strength through insight!"*

This was the last day of the said social experiment through which Jones sought to educate his students on the dangers of a fascist, totalitarian regime. Before the onset of the experiment, Jones elucidated the gory history associated with the Holocaust (Shoah).

During the Second World War, European Nazi Germans slaughtered over six million Jews over four years—something that haunts humankind still today. Known as The Holocaust, it was the largest human genocide to ever happen.

When Jones lectured his class on the terrible nature of this genocide, the students were initially horrified. They asked the normal questions any child would when faced with information of atrocities of such an extent—how could the German citizens look on and do nothing as the Genocide happened in front of their very eyes? Why did no one raise any opposition to what was happening?

At the time, Jones was known for his unconventional methods of teaching. Given the interest of the students, he came up with the idea for an experiment. He decided to replicate conditions that existed in 1930s Germany. He would do this by engendering a sense of entitlement among a group of his students while ostracizing another group. The more I consider this experiment, the more I see why it was doomed from the onset. But I will get into that later.

On the first day of conducting the experiment, Jones took a piece of chalk and wrote the words *"strength through discipline"* on the blackboard. He delivered a lecture on the worthiness of disciplined and unquestioned obedience to a routine. He ordered his students to sit up straight during the length of the class, and when responding to questions, they were commanded to stand and deliver clear, concise answers.

On the second day, Jones added another line to the blackboard—*"strength through community."* He delivered a lecture on the merits of working together as one team and fostering a community spirit. In time, he also taught his students to salute with a hand cupped and raised next to their heads, the elbow bent at a perfect right angle. Sounds familiar? It's just how the Nazis performed the *Sieg Heil* salute.

As the experiment progressed, Jones attached the label "Third Wave" to the experiment. It was symbolic of how surfers in the ocean only ride the third waves, which are known to be the strongest. He made personalized index cards to act as membership proof for students who'd have the "privilege" of belonging to the Third Wave. All the students who earned a card that had a red X marked on the back were regarded as informants. Jones went to the extent of referring to these randomly assigned students as "Gestapo". Again—is this familiar to you? During World War II, the Gestapo was the political police of Nazi Germany, its main role being the coordination of the Jews to be deported to ghettos, killing sites, concentration camps, and killing centers—almost as if an entire race of innocent people were nothing but a sack of potatoes being tossed around at will.

What was worse? Masses of people felt honored to belong to the Gestapo. Much like how Jones's randomly assigned students would come to feel. I don't know what possible bizarre thinking pattern justified this experiment in Jones's head, but he gave the student "Gestapo" body the power to report anyone who acted in methods that went against the community values of the Third Wave.

On the third day of the experiment, Jones scribbled *"strength through action"* on the chalkboard. He delivered a lecture on the advantages of activism and asked the students to begin mass recruitment. He told them that the other policies—strength through discipline and community, would amount to no sense if there was no action to supplement them.

Jones's intentions may have been benign (though I doubt that), he may have been carried away as the mastermind of an experiment, or he may have just been doing all of it out of morbid curiosity. Whatever his initial intent, his strange actions soon paved the way for a full-fledged war-like situation at school. One of his students at the time, Sherry Tousley, asked him why they couldn't just say what they thought. At that, Jones banished Tousley from class. He did the same with all other students who questioned the ludicrousness of the experiment.

The banished students flocked to the library, where Tousley told the librarian, who had grown up in Nazi Germany, what was happening within the walls of their classroom. Alarmed, the librarian advised her to not take things lying down. At this, Tousley and her father began pasting anti-Third Wave posters clandestinely all over the school halls. A day later, all of them had been removed.

Jones was becoming addicted to the power he wielded upon the students. To his mind, he was becoming a modern-day manifestation of the glorified Dictator. He loved the command and the control he had over a hundred students, and how they hung on to his words for approval at each step. He began reveling in their adoration, how they saluted him in the hallways, and the overall attention he had begun to enjoy.

By the third day of the experiment, Jones had also begun hosting mock trials for informant testimonies. Members of the Third Wave stopped trusting their best friends— fellow students that they had grown up with and known since they were in kindergarten. Ugly fights broke out in the hallways over dominion and membership. The entire school was divided into those who opposed and those who adored Jones's unorthodox methods of teaching.

On day four, Jones wrote *"strength through pride"* to the chalkboard and told his students that the Third Wave was real—that it was happening. He went on to describe it as a national movement geared to save the country from the tyranny of the Republicans and Democrats, who could not form simple agreements on national policy or save the country's soldiers from facing further humiliation and destruction in Vietnam. The students, especially the adoring ones, believed their charismatic teacher.

Jones informed the students about an incoming rally for Third Wave members exclusively, during which the "national leader" heading the movement would make themselves known via a television broadcast to over a thousand participating schools. On the day the event was held, photographers thronged the auditorium. Unknown to the impressionable students, these "photographers" were actually Jones's friends whom he'd convinced to play "press", in other words, they didn't belong to the media, they were only pretending.

Jones positioned himself at the very front with two hundred students hanging on to his every word like bees flocking to fresh honey. He told the students to demonstrate the extent of what they had learned. The students stood up in attention and belted out the phrases they had been taught—

Strength through discipline.

Strength through community.

Strength through action.

The words began as a chant but grew louder in frequency. Then, Jones turned a 19-inch television on and stepped out of the room with the photographers and his self-appointed bodyguards (who were students). He left the television on with an auditory-visual of snow crackling on the screen.

Naturally, the whole thing imploded like a pressure cooker that had too much water in it. The students remaining in the hall instinctively knew that something was wrong. They began running from the auditorium, with some being afraid that Jones had locked them inside. Fear and revulsion propelled them out of the hall.

The lights came on and Jones once again appeared in the room. He was now apparently disturbed. A student shouted out, blurting that there was no national leader. Jones broke down in response to a "Sieg Heil" salute. He seemed to have realized the extent to which the experiment had gone—and it was indeed far too much.

He told the students that they had been participants in an experiment centered on the tenets of fascism. They had willingly participated in building a false sense of superiority—much like the "pure Germans" had done during Nazi Germany's time. He apologized for how far everything had gone and played some scenes from Nazi Party rally films from 1933 to 1935.

Jones was so struck by the impact of his own experiment that he told the students he was dismayed to find that they were no better or worse than the Germans—they were *just like them.*

Do you see the purported ease with which a whole aware and educated civilization can turn on itself, so long as a leader is there to show them the "right path?" Power is a very dangerous concept—and it is even more insidious when it is imagined in proportions that cannot exist within the limits of any civilized society.

Before we go into the third and final experiment I'll cover in this book, I have a question for you. Take a minute to think about the answer. What is it about power that makes it so slippery, yet so so desirable? No matter what we say or feel about it being unnecessary, *all of us* desire it to a certain extent, whether it lies in having a say with one person who we love or want to be with, or a whole audience, or an entire country. Why, though?

I'd say that a lot of this is kind of configured into our evolution. Human beings have been predisposed, since times ancient, to gravitate towards someone who can supposedly show them the path to salvation. There is a natural urge in societal living to establish itself according to a hierarchy. A lot of that is already done for us, so we just fall into patterns.

For instance, when we enter a corporate firm, we know that there is an organizational flow in place, and what degrees of professional respect we have to give to each level of this flow. However, there are also those hierarchical categories that work like riddles in the dark—they're there, and they're more potent than we give them credit for. The only difference is that they're not as apparent as the hierarchies that stare us in the face.

Humor me for a minute here as I enunciate a hypothetical situation. Let's say I have met another human being who just has a "hold" on me. There's something about the words they say, their view of the world and everything in it, and their core philosophies that makes me want to know them more. As I spend more time with them, I realize that I would do anything to be near their presence.

Then, they begin to withdraw. The minute I feel them moving away from me, I panic and give more and more of myself. They gratify me with the bare minimum of a few hours of presence once in a blue moon, and I, starved for their appreciation, spend all my time waiting only for those hours. This is when power becomes insidious—when it leaves you starved for the presence of the person you have elevated to a God-like status.

And, if you've known a classic manipulator, you've been in this situation. Perhaps far too many times. Well, the tables are about to turn soon. Let's take a quick gander at what power can become manifested as.

First, power can take shape in the form of rewarding, where we give the ones wielding it whatever they desire, sometimes at the cost of our sanity and well-being. Second, there is coercion, where the people wielding power use fear as a tactic to get others to do what they want. Third, power presents itself through vital information possessed by others which we'd do anything to know.

Fourth, we have legitimate power as the head of an organization or a team leader. Fifth, there is the "expert" power which comes from being the most adept at something in a situation—for instance, if a company has only one software engineer, they may wield an enormous amount of power. Finally, there is referential power which is gained via inherent charisma, status, fame, and the mere magnetism of presence. *This last kind is the one you need to watch out for the most.* The others can be pretty apparent. The last, however, can be used just as much for good influence as well as for bad.

This brings me to the third experiment that's always made me wonder—why? Why are we so susceptible to manipulation?

The Zimbardo Prison Experiment

Back in 1971, Philip Zimbardo, a professor at Stanford, undertook an experiment where he divided a group of student volunteers randomly. One group was entrusted with the role of playing prisoners, while the other group played prison guards.

Zimbardo and his colleagues were reportedly interested in learning more about the brutality that had become so entrenched in the American guards' treatment of prisoners. Their main point of concern was—did this violence originate from a dispositional context (in other words, the innate sadistic personalities of the prison guards) or a situational context (occurring due to the constant exposure to a prison environment). Regarding the latter context, Zimbardo felt that the constrictive power structure of prisons could often manipulate feelings the guards would not have otherwise, therefore giving rise to situational responses. And he was right.

The subjects of the experiment were chosen after a long process involving tests to single out the most mentally stable of the applicants. In the end, 24 men were proclaimed as the most mentally and physically stable, the least prone to or involved in antisocial behavior patterns, and the most mature. They were, therefore, chosen to participate. None of the participants knew each other prior to the experiment.

Before the experiment began, the participants were randomly assigned to two different roles—the "prisoner", and the "prison guard." Zimbardo created a make-believe prison environment in one of the basements of the Stanford University Department of Psychology. Two of the participants were categorized as reserves, and one dropped out before the experiment commenced. Ten "prisoners" and eleven "guards" remained.

Within the simulated environment, the prisoners were treated terribly—like any real-life prisoner would be. The guards arrested them in their homes with no forewarning. They were blindfolded and driven to the University. Zimbardo, possibly to make the environment as realistic as possible, barred the doors and windows, and even prepared small cells. A process of deindividuation began.

The "prisoners" were stripped naked upon arriving in the "prison." They were deloused and had all their personal effects removed from their body. They were given prison uniforms and bedding and referred to by a serial number.

On the other end, the guards were given khaki uniforms, a whistle to wear around their necks, and a billy club each. They also wore designated sunglasses so that they wouldn't have to establish any eye contact with the prisoners. They had the freedom to do whatever they deemed necessary to maintain law and order in the "prison."

While Zimbardo's official role was to observe the subjects of the experiment from the purview of a researcher, he slipped into the role of a prison warden with ease.

The guards, likewise, began harassing the prisoners hours after the experiment commenced. At 2:30 am, prisoners received a rude awakening by guards blowing on their whistles, signaling the first round of "counts." These counts served to familiarize the prisoners with their serial numbers and also gave the guards a means to exert control and influence over them.

Soon, the prisoners also began to think and act from the perspectives of jailed men. They shared issues they were facing in the "prison" and also complained about each other to the guards. Some of them began adhering to the prison's rules very seriously —almost as if disobeying them would cause dire consequences.

The guards plied the prisoners with petty orders and dehumanizing insults. As the second day of the experiment rolled in, the prisoners retaliated by removing their stocking caps, ripping off their serial numbers, and barricading themselves inside the cells by pushing their beds against the cell doors.

As a form of ruthless response, the guards used a fire-extinguisher that produced a stream of toxic carbon dioxide fumes, compelling the prisoners to step away from the doors. The guards broke into the cells, took the beds out, and stripped the prisoners of all their clothes. The ringleaders were punished with solitary confinement, and the guards ramped up the harassment.

As prison privileges, one of the three cells was marked as a "privilege cell." Three prisoners who had been least involved in the rebellion received privileges. They were given their beds back and allowed to possess precious notables like shampoo and brushes. They also got to enjoy special food in the presence of the remaining prisoners, who were not given any meals at all. This was done to remove any existing solidarity among the prisoners.

As the prisoners became more and more reliant on the guards, there was increasing derision in the latter's treatment of the former. The guards treated the prisoners with contempt, and the prisoners only grew more submissive.

Only thirty-six hours into the experiment, prisoner 8612 displayed signs of acute emotional turmoil, disorganized thought patterns, inconsolable rage, and a heavy bout of weeping. The guards told him he was weak and manipulated him into convincing the other prisoners that they couldn't leave, no matter what they tried. Consequently, he began displaying symptoms of mania. He screamed and cursed profanities and went into storms of anger that proved impossible to curb. Alarmed, the psychologists let him out.

Following a visit from the prisoners' parents, a rumor of a mass escape plan started doing the rounds. The guards and the researchers, worried their experiment would end halfway, sought the help of the Palo Alto police department. They were told to increase the harassment and double down on verbal abuse. During this time, they made the prisoners clean toilets with bare hands.

A few days later, a priest was summoned. Prisoner 819 broke down in front of him and began crying hysterically. The psychologists were forced to remove the chain off his foot and asked that he rest in a room next to the prison's yard. Zimbardo finally told him he wasn't 819. He addressed the harangued prisoner by his real name and reminded him that he was a psychologist, not a prison warden. *This is just an experiment, and those are students. Not prisoners. Just like you. Let's go.*" The prisoner was immediately okay.

Now, Zimbardo had intended for the experiment to run the course of a fortnight. However, he was forced to terminate on the sixth day given the intensity of the emotional breakdowns among the prisoners, and the surprising levels of aggression displayed by the guards.

Later on, Zimbardo regretted the experiment. He mentioned that he realized he'd gotten too far into the role of the prison warden—so much so that he'd started thinking like a prison superintendent, not a research psychologist.

The goal of the Zimbardo Prison Experiment was to prove how readily people conform to social roles that they are manipulated into believing as "necessary" or "essential" or simply "the current state of affairs." There is also an element of stereotyping here, where those uplifted to positions of coercion display the kind of aggression that they wouldn't dream of under normal circumstances.

None of the guards had innately sadistic tendencies. It was the environment and the roles—in other words, the *situational context of their manipulative positions,* that brought out a kind of bestiality from within their core. And this is dangerous because we see it happening every day.

Have you ever been told, "When we're out of the office, it's different? Inside, we're going to stick to our roles" Or, have you been part of a relationship where the significant other has always made you feel as if they love you deeply in certain situations, but completely ignore you in others?

I like to call these sly masterminds the "situational manipulators." For instance, when you are around other people, or whenever you try to bring up the topic of sharing your relationship with the world, you are met with dead, stony silence. On the other hand, when you are alone with them, they are impossibly sweet, warm, and caring.

Contextualizing This Book

It's painful to feel someone you cherish is simultaneously appreciating you one second and behaving like you don't exist for them the next. It makes you wonder if you're doing anything wrong, or if you can possibly be any better—although the chances are that you have given all of yourself, and then some. Many of us also don't realize that this is a form of manipulation. Instead, we shift the blame on ourselves and take it upon our shoulders to keep doing more until there's absolutely nothing left.

Morality itself is a concept that is rooted in deep confusion. You'll find a plethora of papers arguing about the human relationship with morality, and what it generally stands for. Why is it that something which may seem so normal to us—for instance, a live-in relationship, becomes absolutely immoral in another cultural context involving another group of people?

One way to understand this puzzle is that we have made our moral systems in a manner that allows for conflict resolution within groups. This is an evolutionary tactic that has developed over time, and is reinforced even now when our wellwishers sometimes tell us to give in and not resist something that's against our beliefs because "it will be better for us in the long run."

There's an element of indirect reciprocity involved, where you conform to the standards imposed by someone else, hoping to please the larger society around you. While we think that this can yield excellent results, most of us tend to get coerced and manipulated into behaving in ways that are just not ideal for us. Why? *Because that's what society wants.* Or so we've heard, over and over again.

Human beings naturally veer towards trying to understand what is going on in the minds of those they are engaging with. While mind control isn't something that's necessarily viewed in a good light, I'd say that most of the bad reputation it's received is because people who have employed it have intended to cause harm.

When you use mind control or even manipulation as tools to steer your course, rather than getting in the route of others, you're simply doing what everyone else does, but also being honest to yourself about it. I mean, who doesn't seek influence, power, or positions? And who can escape the inevitability of manipulation and mind control to earn each of these accolades?

These traits are natural and innate to human beings. They've been suppressed by societal norms and the weight of "doing and thinking what is morally correct"—partly because people become afraid of what they cannot control or understand.

To me, these tools are routes to building a good channel of communication. Self and collective improvement lie in finding productive ways to engage with the larger society without getting used at each step. Manipulation is a neutral word that means changing the way someone else acts.

Mind reading and mind control may sound bad, but they aren't, given that your intention lies in self-preservation without emotionally destroying others. Just like manipulative tactics are not good or bad, neither of these are. Mind reading is the ability to figure out what someone is thinking and feeling on a deep level. Mind control isn't just about being able to read someone's thoughts; it's also about changing what's in their head.

Your life will change if you improve how you talk to people, and that's why I'm here. Over the course of my career, I've learned that knowing the dark side of psychology is the one thing that can make or break your success. People who immerse themselves in these fields learn tools of communication that can change the balance of power and help them get what they want.

People who gain the ability to read minds also display greater attention and more skill in stressful social situations. They don't get carried away by a tirade of irrelevant emotions, and always delve into the larger context of things before forming any opinions.

So, you've now formed a solid idea of what human experiments in manipulation looked like back when the APA wasn't quite as stringent. I have a question for you. Now that you know the core emotional logic behind these experiments, have you ever felt like the person at the receiving end?

Did someone, or a situation, ever make you feel like a helpless orphan under Johnson's supervision? A brainwashed student blindly following the dictates of their teacher, or a helpless prisoner manipulated into being tortured by the make-believe guards? My other question is, *do you want to spend the rest of your life living these roles repeatedly?*

I sincerely hope you answered the second question with a resounding "no."

In traversing through this book, we will form a detailed idea of every aspect that makes dark psychology what it is. Not only will you learn to use it to your benefit, but you will also form a concrete understanding of whether those in your life, whether close to or distant from you, have been using these tools to harm you or drain your emotional reservoir.

The act of living is equal parts beautiful and ferocious. There isn't too much room for spending the little time we have been given, just existing for others. If you don't learn to pinpoint a manipulator or a gaslighter or anyone belonging to the proverbial dark triad (and using the tools they have acquired to cause harm), life will pass you by until one day, you wake up and think, "I did nothing for myself."

Let's change that right now.

CHAPTER 1
WHAT IS DARK PSYCHOLOGY?

IN MY EXTENSIVE years of study on the topic of dark psychology and its various nuances, I have often found it to be a smoke and mirrors situation. On the one hand, the truth behind its obviously useful aspects has always been grotesquely nullified. On the other end, the supposed harm that it can inflict has been embellished to an extent that it has resulted in labeling any curiosity about the topic as "morbid."

However, much like any other educational aspect, dark psychology is a science. It enlightens the reader about aspects of the human mind that characterize *everyone,* irrespective of the forms (latent or apparent), and the intent (good or bad). The reason why I appreciate learning something deeply, and without judgment, is this—the human mind is a fickle, but fascinating thing. Just as the workings of some minds have produced life-altering medicines, so also those of others have created warfare and armaments that have wiped civilizations clean.

What we are about to study looks to explore these nuances. Dark psychology is nothing more than a study of human subjects in their natural environments when they are operating in either insidious or self-preserving ways.

As a topic, dark psychology has long been fascinating. Many people who want to learn more about it fall into one of two groups. The first group's sole focus is on researching the core aspects of dark psychology to avoid being manipulated and abused in their relationships. The second group mastered the tactics explored under dark psychology, intending to manipulate others. You could be one of either, or you (like most of us) could be a balance of both. And that isn't bad.

It's absolutely normal to want to know what's going on in the mind of your boss when an important promotion is upcoming. In the same way, it's also legitimate to want information on whether you are being manipulated by your boss into doing things you don't want to.

Despite the burgeoning interest in the entire discipline, the very notion of some aspects of human nature holding so much power has caused some to label dark psychology as little more than party tricks. I wouldn't subscribe to that notion, given that I've seen how people who know how to master and use manipulation can play with the minds and emotions of others. It would do to remember that mere words have caused the most vociferous of wars.

To look at things from a simplistic perspective, dark psychology is an umbrella term covering different techniques that enable its users to reach within the minds of their targets, and manipulate the latter's thinking patterns and emotions to their advantage. While I'd refer to it as a science, it isn't a recognized branch of psychology in that you're unlikely to find it being taught as part of an academic curriculum. It's also not used as a professional counseling approach, given that it's not viewed as something that's innately compassionate.

Dark psychology has an element that often makes it appear as a pop culture introduction—it serves as an introduction to other, more legitimized subdivisions of psychology. It also serves to fulfill those evenings when we're bored and wonder if there are any aspects of our personalities that could link us to narcissists and psychopaths, so we end up taking some of the freely available dark psychology quizzes online.

Call it what you will, dark psychology is more than all the negativity that it has been relegated to. As you get into it, you'll find that it follows a repackaging of many "legitimate" and "out-there" psychological principles, and adds the promise of helping you advance through all hurdles with your mind as your only weapon.

UNDERSTANDING EMOTIONAL RESPONSES

The lines between a person who has gone all dark and who is essentially normal can be a hazy blur at times. This is because the ultimate end of a manipulative technique may be focused on exacting an act of well-deserved revenge, or better yet, self-defense.

When you learn about psychology, you may be mystified at how much you learn. You discover the secrets of the human brain, a very fickle and complicated organ. You learn about how it conditions the rest of your body, including how you respond to different situations—and why these responses vary from person to person.

A very specific way of understanding every human action is to view it as the sum of electrical impulses generated by neurons and passed on to other neurons. Each electrical impulse carries through our body, creating the particular thought we think, the sensation we experience, or the action we perform. In other words, we are always engaged in a constant feedback loop of processing and passing information and signals.

Different regions of your brain influence specific emotional responses within you. We may think of emotions as internal states of being that are exclusive on their own, but they are interconnected responses that result from a combination of cognitions, feelings regarding those cognitions, and the ensuing actions. So, when we think of emotions, we're not just referring to how we feel, but also how we process the feelings and respond to them.

It's legitimate, at this stage, to pause and wonder—what is the purpose of emotions? Why do they even exist?

In 1872, Charles Darwin's *The Expression of the Emotions in Man and Animals* discerned the importance of emotions for evolutionary purposes. To enable a species to thrive, there has to be the ability to survive via the passage of genetic information through generations.

Emotions such as fear or the fight-or-flight response (which readies your body to escape or defend itself from any impending danger) help keep you safe from real (and imagined) dangers that allow you to survive and pass on genetic information to your offspring. Emotions like desire and love engender the urge to reproduce and extend your species.

The human brain, therefore, functions to evaluate a stimulus, for instance, that thrill of danger you experience when you know something is just going to happen, or the charge you feel when someone excites desire within you. After it has evaluated the stimulus, it crafts an emotional response to the same stimulus. Using emotions as a stimulus, the brain dictates your patterns so that you can adapt to a circumstance, and therefore, continue to live and reproduce.

That's as simple as it gets. Against what many of us believe as extraordinarily complex patterns, our core patterns of action, thinking, and behavior follow very elementary sequences that are connected to each other. Our thoughts impact how we feel. How we feel influences how we act. And how we act once again influences the resultant thoughts that arise. From this perspective, it's remarkably easy to exert leverage on other human beings. This is where dark psychology's effects come into play.

UNCOVERING DARK PSYCHOLOGY

Dark psychology helps you to understand the most secretive motivations that work the brain's emotional responses, sometimes, even those of which the perpetrators may not be explicitly aware. When you understand what governs the responses of different people to specific situations and why they act as they do, you can wield control over them.

People who use dark psychology tactics for harmful ends know how to apprehend these responses. They can identify vulnerable targets, read them, and trap them into acting just as they want them to. When you understand the nature of human responses, however, you also become effective at preventing these master manipulators from harming you or those you love.

Master manipulators are inordinately skilled at exerting influence in secretive, unfathomable ways. Many times, you'll never realize how deep within their traps you are until it becomes too late to turn back. This is because these manipulators wield their clever understanding of human psychology to get what they want without giving a dime about how many people they break or hurt in the process, and they do it with elan.

Our primary motivation for understanding dark psychology is to uncover all the good reasons it can be used for. It can be a plausible, indeed, powerful line of defense and make you more impenetrable against the harmful impact of potential manipulators. It can also give you the skills that will bring you success when you want an elusive job or score well in a tricky interview. Just because you use the same skills that others use to cause harm, doesn't mean that you will cause harm to them, too.

Now that we have developed a keen understanding of dark psychology, let's move into a discussion of its core principles.

Principles Of Dark Psychology

I'll begin by stating something very simple, yet often overlooked. All the actions that we do are reliant on a mix of the need for self-preservation and the urge to self-harm.

Sometimes those who wield dark psychology tools and techniques do so impulsively, or without explicit knowledge that they are inflicting harm. Something within their subconscious mind tells them that acting or speaking in a certain way will be advantageous for them—and in some cases, these advantages exceed the negatives involved. They may end up thinking that the person at the receiving end is innately weak, and therefore deserves whatever treatment is being meted out.

A motivating factor as to why we become swayed by our subconscious desires could be the evolutionary instincts that operate within us. All of us have three core instincts that motivate our behaviors, and they form one whole that is known as the human "biological imperative." The biological imperative is the purpose of human life in its most rudimentary form. It is mandated by the tenets of aggression, self-preservation, and sex.

Aggression is something that all of us engage in when primal instincts become essential for protecting ourselves, what we believe in, and those who are dear to us.

The human aggressive drive has often been viewed as a subset of the *Id*, the part of our psyche that drives how we behave. The ego (rational self) and the superego (ideal self) oppose these aggressive impulses so that we can keep appearances up. Conflicts between all these subsets can create tensions within an individual, who then resort to defense mechanisms by coping.

The theory of self-psychology took shape as a subset of psychoanalytic theory. It was developed by Heinz Kohut as a way of giving credence to the core principles of self-cohesion and self-esteem that influence the human personality's function. Over the years, the principle of self-preservation has repeatedly been purported as a fundamental aspect that conditions human personality formation and overall social behavior.

It states that a subject must maintain their ties to their *self-object* if they are to preserve inner integrity. To be specific, the human personality is molded around the self's innate need for approval. While this approval can be manifested in different ways, the most important need is that of safety. This can even be necessary to the extent of conflicting with other internal instinctual or external demands.

All conflicts ultimately boil down to the preservation of the human self and its overall integrity. More than a century ago, prominent (and notorious) psychologist Freud discerned that narcissism and regulating human self-regard are geared towards acts of self-preservation. In narcissistic thinking (that is when a person lives their life by the principles of narcissism), the perception of the self, and self-esteem, are regulated by utilizing behavior strategies that are focused on enhancing worth and availability (although in superficial terms). The narcissist thrives on their self-perception of being someone who can do no wrong— and this is essentially preservatory philosophy at its most extreme.

Let me get into a very interesting theory, also propounded by Freud. This was known as the Life and Death drive, and at one point, it was widely held that these theories were responsible for our behaviors.

The Life Drive, also known as Eros, refers to human sexual instincts. This isn't necessarily perverse, for the basic continuation of life depends on a reproductive urge. The life drive, therefore, is concerned with basic survival, seeking and getting pleasure, and reproduction. It is also concerned with other instincts, like wanting to avoid pain, thirst, hunger, or any kind of situation and feelings that instill discomfort.

Now, the human life drive is concerned with all things that focus on the preservation of life—both at the level of the individual and the larger species. It urges human beings to take part in actions that will be responsible for sustenance—for instance, looking for profits, seeking relationships that offer protection and security, and taking care of one's overall health and wellbeing.

It also exerts itself through motivations that urge people to engage in acts of intimacy that will create new lives and lead to the perpetuation of a species. Behaviors that are usually associated with the life drive include cooperation, love, seeking friendships, positions of influence, and fulfillment. Any behavior that supports individual well-being while also contributing to an ordered societal existence represents the life drive.

In early psychoanalytic theory, Freud maintained that the life drive was often at loggerheads with ego forces. The latter made up human logic, which could often function as a curb upon desires. Later on, he developed a theory that the life drive was opposed by a death instinct that was almost always self-destructive or Thanos.

The concept of the death drive was first introduced in Freud's "Beyond The Pleasure Principle." His notion was that human beings are morbidly driven towards destruction and death, for the ultimate aim of all life manifests itself in death. Freud believed people can channel this inherent death drive as an "aggression" towards others. They can also direct this internally, which (if unchecked) can trigger dangerous self-harm practices or even suicide.

The theory of the Death Drive was built upon Freud's clinical observations. He noted that those who experienced traumatic events often tried to revisit or recreate them, perhaps because of the alterations in thinking patterns on more fatalistic lines. For instance, he noted that soldiers returning home from the First World War would often revisit the horrors of the war in their dreams, and wake up feeling as if they were really back in the middle of combat. He concluded people nurse a subconscious desire to perish, but that the instincts engendered by the Life Drive temper this desire.

Many aspects of these theories have been severely contested, yet they spoke to certain basic tenets of the human mind. We are always on the lookout for relationships that will sustain us, and give meaning to the time that we have been granted on this Earth. Therefore, as we grow old and begin to lose people near and dear to us, many of us feel that life has become purposeless. The innate urge to be connected, to feel safe, is derived from a deep-seated appreciation drive. And it does not matter if we are socially outgoing or reclusive. All of us want these connections—sometimes, with a few notables, and in others, with larger communities.

In the haste to form these connections, however, it becomes important to know what we are getting ourselves into. Finding genuine relationships is well and good, but seeking damage and repeatedly falling into its tortuous claws simply because our urge for equating the Life Drive to being appreciated becomes synonymous with "winning" the affections of dangerously manipulative people is not conducive.

And there is a reason for me to say this. In my own interactions with people, I have repeatedly noticed patterns where people with an innate urge to please get used by people who know how to manipulate these urges. For instance, I refer to a case of a friend —let's call them Xerxes.

Xerxes grew up in a troubled home. By the time he had reached young adulthood, his very notion of validity was mandated on "winning." In his mind, he had formed the concept that the only relationships that mattered were those with people who initially told him they didn't like him. He'd get involved with these people, his sole motivation being the need to *change their minds.* To him, meeting someone who would not be attracted to him and convincing them he was actually likable became a challenge.

While working hard isn't a bad thing, it becomes dangerous when you fall into the charms of people who manipulate you for the sake of causing harm. The moment they find they can get you to do pretty much anything in return for a pat on the back or a few words of praise, they can make you run around in circles for the entirety of your life. And that's just what happened to Xerxes.

It took years of unlearning to step away from this vicious cycle. So, in the most balanced of people, the life and death drives will operate with equal force. No one drive will exert too much influence over the other. But for most of us, there's an imbalance. Some of us are always fatalistic, always waiting for things to go wrong (and therefore living in constant doubt and fear), while others are always looking for different ways of acquiring appreciation, whether the routes are scrupulous or otherwise. Both drives are very inherent in dark psychology, which is essentially all about understanding the very human needs of fulfillment and appreciation.

Dark psychology can be summed up with five fundamental principles.

First, it is universal. Every human being possesses an innate possibility for resorting to dark psychology traits like manipulation, and every human being can be violent and predatory if they face situations that are too testing or take them to a point where they feel that violence is the only way to preserve themselves or those they love dearly.

Next, from a generalized point of view, it is a study of human thoughts and feelings, and how they use their perspectives and understanding of the larger society in their treatment of other human beings. This is because our thoughts operate in cycles of self-actualization. Our thoughts and emotions affect each other profoundly. Thought cycles can trigger a lot of emotions—for instance, worrying about upcoming interviews can cause fear.

How we appraise our lives impacts how we feel. For example, if we have an innate fear of ghosts, we may become paranoid when we watch a horror flick, and this may lead to emotional distress.

Finally, dark psychology recognizes a range of human behaviors, where some are worse or more evil compared with others. This range can often be reliant on how cruel or Machiavellian the intentions behind a certain action were. When you understand dark psychology, you learn to control or restrain harmful traits from emerging, while also knowing that you can employ it for useful purposes.

Examples Of Dark Psychology

As we go deeper into studying dark psychology, we will aim to understand the thoughts, emotions, and perceptions that compel people to exhibit predatory behavioral patterns towards each other. Most human predatory actions are purposeful. In other words, 99.99% of humans who behave in predatory ways have specific reasons in mind.

The remaining small group, however, constitute the most dangerous kinds of people, ones who harm others for no viable reasons. For the former group, the assumption is that they act because of certain motivations. These motivations may or may not be rational to all of us, but they are completely rational to this group. They have specific goals in mind, and in their perceptions, getting to these goals needs them to act in ways that fall under the tactics of dark psychology.

A tiny fraction of the human population, however, prey on and torture their victims for inexplicable reasons—except perhaps personal gratification, religious dogma, or pure predatory instinct. In some ways, we all possess dark sides—all of us have different shades within us. We are not monochromatic. None of us are completely good or completely evil. For our purposes, we will consider something as evil from the perspective of what the motivations are.

I'm going to present two hypothetical situations here—and while they sound dark, take some time to mull over them. In Scenario One, a man's child has been kidnapped, and the perpetrator has called the family and told them if they want to see the child alive, they have to commit an offense. They have deliberated all other scenarios, including involving the police. However, the only route left is to do what the perpetrator has asked. Left with no choices, they commit this act. Now, this is also a choice. They could still choose to not do what the perpetrator asks, and lose their child forever. But, from this perspective, if they cannot do that, could you still label them as evil? I could not.

I'd say they engage in an act that is the product of an evil circumstance, yes. But that is not enough for me to simply consider the act and say, "these people are evil." In this case, if they have been manipulated by a perpetrator to engage in an act of manipulation themselves, both acts are parts of dark psychology. But the first act of manipulation exhibits the harmful side of dark psychology, where people use what is dear to someone against them. The second act of manipulation is more circumstantial and situational, and, therefore, is also amenable.

Why is the first kind not amenable? Largely because people who harm for the sake of pleasure cannot stop unless they undergo a divine change of heart. Which brings me to my second hypothetical scenario. In Scenario B, a male serial killer attacks young girls and leaves their defiled bodies for policemen to find. His modus operandi is to use his charm to befriend them, take them to secluded places, and kill them. He even has his specific form of branding his victims after he kills them, his intent being to let the world know that no one except him is capable of an act of such a vile nature.

Each act that he commits has a tenet of manipulation in it. This form of manipulation, however, rests in the perpetrator enjoying the coercive nature of power and purposefully using it against people who are innately vulnerable or in vulnerable situations.

These manipulators know how to spot victims, how to brainwash them, and then use them for their own benefits or for fulfilling morbid fantasies.

Take Richard Ramirez or Ted Bundy. Even as light was shed on the horrific crimes they committed, they received fan mails or attracted the attention of young women while attending court proceedings. A predator can charm the socks off people regardless of what situations they are in—and that is specifically what makes this kind of manipulation (that is, the kind that isn't dependent on situations or circumstances) so dangerous. The ends never justify the means, and they only cause harm for the sake of their own pleasure.

It is important that you learn why dark psychology plays an important role in both these scenarios. First, if you can identify someone who is resorting to any harmful tactics because of situational manipulation, you will reach out and offer comfort or help. Sometimes, this can be instrumental. In the second scenario, awareness is important *just because it is.* Because you don't want to land up as prey to manipulators of this caliber or deviousness.

So, while I've presented two extreme scenarios to you, as I said, not everyone is using manipulation to cause harm, whether out of necessity or pleasure. Sometimes, it just occurs as a by-product of circumstances or something that your profession needs you to do. Let's take a look.

For the first scenario, let us assume you are a realtor. The market you're working in is intensely competitive, and to be successful, you have to convince people to spend a good amount of money. Investing in property is a huge thing for most people because of the resources and commitment involved. However, the job is one where the more expensive the house you sell is, the bigger your commission will be. And to move ahead and earn a name in this profession, you must earn those commissions.

The most important thing here is to persuade people. So, you decide to learn the tools of the trade. This involves understanding the core of persuasion tactics, and how you can influence your clients with not just your words or aesthetic sense, but also your body language.

Your goal remains the act of selling houses, but sometimes, you know your success is hinged on persuading clients to settle on properties that are ever so slightly upwards of their original maximum price offered. This is nothing more than dark psychology in play, giving you the tactics you need to wield this kind of persuasive power on the clients.

In the second scenario, let's take it that your success at getting a promotion relies upon giving a successful performance at the year-end review meeting. You've done well with all the questions, but then, the supervisors ask you something that you aren't quite confident about. You know that if you try answering this question and get it wrong, you'll lose your chances of getting promoted. Rather than risk that you rely on the art of deception and mind control instead, and sidestep the tricky question by distracting the interviewers' attention towards something that will be immediately more important to them. In this instance, too, you are using dark psychology tactics to evade a touch-and-go situation.

Finally, in the third scenario, let's say that you really like someone. You've been wanting to talk to them for ages, but they always seem to be too distant, too far off for you to strike up a conversation. So, you study techniques of persuasion with the simple intention of coming across as someone more confident and self-assured. Rather than manipulating the person, you learn things that will make *you* more interesting to them.

In many relationships, I've seen my friends complaining about how people change over time. The point isn't that they've changed. Rather, when the relationship was in its infant stage, they were probably being more staged versions of themselves. They were using dark psychology techniques to come across as "interesting" people who would gel well with you.

However, many cannot keep being interesting over an extended period because they become complacent. They think they don't need to keep up with the persuasion tactics once they've secured the attention they wanted. Sometimes, they may be right. But in others, life itself becomes a long-drawn-out sequence of mastering manipulation and persuasion techniques repeatedly.

You may wonder here why do I keep talking about manipulation and persuasion in the same breath? There are so many people and platforms out there which will tell you they're not the same, right? So why am I saying just the opposite thing? Well, let's look at two Merriam-Webster definitions.

The first is for the word "manipulate." It means to either "manage or use skillfully," or "to control or play upon by artful, unfair *or* insidious means, especially to one's advantage." Now, let's look at what is meant by the word "persuade." The dictionary says it means to move "by entreaty, argument, or expostulation to a belief, position, or course of action."

Now, study each of the scenarios we just talked about. Are you persuading the people on the receiving end, or are you manipulating them? Yes, your own benefit plays a major role. But you also know that if those at the receiving end buy the house, give you the promotion, or engage with you, they will benefit from your time and resources. You are using manipulative means with persuasion.

The difference is a very thin line—that of utility. People who are completely and wholly manipulative can think of nothing to save their personal gain. Most of us, otherwise, are just mixing manipulation and persuasion as we go along. Success comes when we can do this by mixing with skill.

When I say all of us, I also refer to the effect of dark psychology on play at bigger-than-individual levels.

Dark Psychology Is Rooted In The Contemporary Age

Today, dark psychology tactics are used across professions intending to ensure success and furthering organizational values. In this section, we will look at how dark psychology is being used across the consumerist age, and in ways that aren't necessarily harmful. The contemporary consumerist mindset is reliant on tactics native to dark psychology. To get a perspective on using these tactics to secure deviant ends, we'll also look at how religious cults have employed these tools for unscrupulous intents.

Our aim will be to understand how dark psychology tools can be used to further organizational or individual gains that promote self-sustenance without destroying others, while also realizing how some institutions use these tools with the primary intention of harming and brainwashing large sections of society.

The Manipulation Of The Consumerist Age

A business cannot be successful if tools of persuasion and manipulation aren't applied with skill and intent. As part of an innately consumeristic web industry, we are all facilitators in a worldwide business chain that hinges itself on successful end-user manipulation.

Producers are increasingly focusing on tools, such as advertisements and branding, to persuade people into purchasing or needing things that may otherwise be purposeless from a survivalist point of view.

Let's face it. No one needs Louboutins to survive—but many would like to have them as a symbol of status. The feeling of power associated with such purchases comes from the business heads convincing you that your home looks better with expensive purchases. And that cannot be done without some successful manipulation involved.

The business owners and producers call the purchases "users"— even the ones who are buying the most expensive things. When you buy branded products because you want to have a sense of superiority, you are, ironically, contributing to the success of the advertising business, which pushes branded products as "superior" because they know it will feed into your mindset. So, the quality may be like anything you would find in a local, responsibly sourced product. But since the latter does not have "brand fame," it isn't as appealing. These goods may not bring food to your table or get you more sleep at night, but a mere, "your look isn't complete without so-and-so handbag at your side" might be enough to convince you that you need this handbag to be "complete."

With the proliferation of technology and how simple it has become to use it, all users take businesses to bed with them. Think about how this works in real life. Before going to sleep, the minute we open one of our social media channels, we're flooded by advertisements that claim to have solutions for everything—from completing our wardrobe to getting rid of bad breath. It's a very competitive consumer-oriented world out there, and all businesses learn that technology is one of the easiest tools of manipulation.

Likewise, when we wake up, we check our phones for tweets, notifications, and updates—sometimes even before we're properly awake. We get swayed by colorful ads popping up and wonder if purchasing the item showcased so beautifully in the ad will make our day go a little better. It probably won't, but the ensuing dopamine rush (even if it is temporary) is enough to carry us over for the next few hours.

We never stop to think that we are being manipulated by the businesses who know just what our sleeping and waking cycles look like, and can modulate technology to catch us at our most vulnerable times.

Famed game creator and professor, Ian Bogost, refers to these technologies as "habit-forming" and discerns that they have become the virtual cigarettes of this century. You don't quite realize when your days become completely dependent on them.

Our moral compass hasn't quite caught up with what technology has made possible. A more addictive environment has been created by the widespread availability of the internet, which can transmit more personal data at quicker rates than ever before. The primary target of these industries is the nature of human addiction.

The Ethics Of Consumer Manipulation

Now, many of these industries actually target user behaviors that may be useful in the long run—in which case, manipulation becomes justified. When the business is making something that will result in a healthy habit, the means may justify the ends. So, if you receive convincing advertisements telling you why meal tracking or getting a virtual jogging buddy is helpful, and these advertisements are convincing enough to make you invest in the products, they're not doing anything bad because they're motivating you to do something useful for yourself.

Also, some businesses just want to appeal to the side of you that wants to let loose and have fun. If the maker of an addictive product isn't necessarily creating something that improves the user's lives but entertains them, that also doesn't fit into the category of causing explicit harm. Take the various OTT platforms that are constantly updating you on exciting new shows, and why your life depends on how many of these you can watch.

Personable characters, exciting twists that make up for the otherwise stale plotlines, and *advertising* that exists for months ahead of the show's release, all come together to tell you that this is a show you absolutely "need" to watch. There is manipulation involved here, but it isn't harming you if you are conscious of how much time and resources you're spending on these OTT platforms.

There are certain instances where the use of manipulation in marketing becomes essential because it draws people out of their entrenched comfort zones. Have you felt persuaded into reading a book you'd never consider, or getting up to try a workout when you'd rather be in bed, or trying on an outfit that you'd shy away from—all because of the way an advertisement of the related product has made you feel?

These advertisements often target your confidence levels and encourage you to dive inside. As such, we become programmed to avoid situations that may come across as challenging. This can make us averse to accepting or embracing any recent changes. Clever forms of manipulation highlight the pains of remaining in these comfort zones. For instance, take this cleverly marketed text that describes why you should travel.

> "I urge you to travel as much and as far as you possibly can. Work long shifts and save your money. Don't spend on the latest iPhone. Throw yourself out of the comfort zone you have become stuck in.

> "Discover how other people live, and realize that the entirety of the world is a much bigger place than the small borders of your hometown. And then, after it all, when you come home, yes, home may still be the same. And you may go back to the same people and work the same job, but deep inside you, something will have changed. And trust me, that changes everything."

The person who wrote these beautiful lines remains anonymous. Yet, these lines have been used again and again (to the extent of being overused in some cases) in various marketing agencies and products that belong to the travel industry. This, again, is an industry that thrives on human emotion.

The very soul of countries that are reliant on tourism depends on manipulative marketing like this, which urges someone who may otherwise dislike traveling, abhor sand, heat, and mosquitoes, to pack their bags and go somewhere tropical, that while aesthetically stunning, will include all the things that they essentially dislike.

So—and I say this with utmost nonchalance—this game of convincing end users to buy products that may only remain on their shelves or locked in cupboards isn't necessarily abusive or coercive. If we were in the same businesses, we would probably invest in similar technologies and look to draw in potential customers via the same tools. Since the industry itself is so cutthroat, successful manipulation could be the key point of differentiation between a company that makes it, and one that tanks.

For instance, Weight Watchers is probably one of the most successful mass manipulation products to exist out there. The customer's decisions are *always programmed by the system designer.* It's not like they're giving you the freedom to make choices. Rather, they're conditioning you into believing that by doing what they want, you're acting of your free will. And most of us don't question the morality behind such deeply manipulative tactics.

Obviously, the businesses that can convince users to buy products that may not be essential for survival are the ones that will continue to thrive. The human consumerist market is increasingly depending on one quality that isn't anywhere near the basics (food, water, and shelter). This is *desire.* Desire itself is a product of manipulation because it involves our minds making us want things we may not be able to afford, or may not even need.

Using Manipulation As A Business Owner

The world of manipulation is essentially one that you cannot escape from. If you are a business owner, its effects don't just impact on your individual self, but the success of your entire enterprise. However, you get to make the choice of keeping this manipulation ethical.

Marketing deception is a given if you own your own company. To build a following of devoted customers, offer them goods, and earn their loyalty will always need you to manipulate their thought patterns to a certain extent. The problem isn't whether or not you manipulate, but how you manipulate.

The most successful businesses I've known are well aware of how they manipulate consumers via their marketing efforts. They don't feel bad about it, and you shouldn't either. Because it has the potential to have a beneficial effect on your target audience when done correctly. Amazon is an excellent illustration of this. When searching Amazon, have you ever discovered a book that you immediately fell in love with?

Then there's the matter of Facebook. What if you discovered someone you now like and respect because of a Facebook advertisement that appeared in your newsfeed, highlighting only good qualities about them and their product? Manipulation is like a designed experience that has been crafted for influencing and changing behavior.

While we become uncomfortable when someone explicitly tells us they're trying to get us to do something we wouldn't dream of doing otherwise, we're all indulging in it from time to time. This means that manipulation isn't all bad. If it were, the many multi-billion dollar industries that have made fortunes from getting users to willfully submit to manipulative tactics would be reduced to dust by now.

Since our minds often work at a subconscious level, they take in and filter large amounts of information before presenting these information chunks in viable forms to your emotions. And this is important because, given the amount of information we handle on a day-to-day basis, we wouldn't be able to survive unless the brain, operating at the subconscious level, received information, processed it, and made assumptions about it.

So, when you are scrolling through Facebook or YouTube, you may not have a clear cognizance of what's happening. You take the messages in like you're supposed to, but you may not question their validity. It's impossible to cross-verify every nugget of data being fed into your mind, so you go on autopilot, forming beliefs and convictions that are more innate than conscious.

Marketing has built its walls around this gospel. The reason why global brand giants like Coca-Cola have become so huge is because of their omnipresence. It's everywhere, from your phone screens to billboards, to advertisements in between songs and shows, to being plastered in newspapers.

In some countries, Coca-Cola has also made a master stroke in terms of advertising—for instance, in the Indian market. In India, Coca-Cola has become synonymous with bringing the family together because of its "Share A Coke" advertising. The implication of this ad is masterfully simple and evocative. It shows that the soft drink brings families together to celebrate good times.

In doing this, Coca-Cola targets core sentiments true to the Indian consumer market centered on family values. This is an example of successful manipulation. The company inherently understands that if users can view the brand as something connected to the things they hold dear in their lives, they'll form attachments to it.

On an entirely other, but related trajectory, consider the 2016 U.S. election. Plenty of manipulative tactics were used, and conspiracies were constructed on the back of these tactics, including the "fake news" conspiracy. Political groups rallied support by targeting specific clusters of people and enhanced this support by adding a "truthfulness" to statements that may not have been true at all. Their target (and an effective one, at that) was the very human trait of perceiving perceptions as realities.

This isn't a novel concept. For ages, religious institutions, governments and companies have targeted population "bubbles". As people, we have inbred tendencies to attach ourselves to these bubbles depending on shared beliefs, peer circles and age groups, interests, religions, professions, and so forth.

The stakes, however, are more competitive than ever. Anyone who has access to the right algorithms (which are as simple as having access to online platforms like Google and Facebook) can target, manipulate, and mold these population bubbles. Amazon can give you timely reminders from past purchases.

Other online shopping sites can send you email reminders asking why you've left a product that "you wanted so much" in your cart. They can tell you that these items are fast selling out and that you have good taste (in other words, generate renewed interest). Likewise, the media can manipulate you into believing the legitimacy of certain campaigns over others, and politicians can manipulate you into forming perceptions and prejudices.

When done correctly, marketing manipulation may be beneficial for you as a business owner. But, like with other wonderful things, if you put it in the wrong hands, it can rapidly become bad. You need to know how you can ethically use manipulation for marketing yourself, your ideologies, or your products.

At the onset, you have to know your product or whatever you are offering at a deep level. Does it bring about any transformations in the end user? Is it targeting an aspect of their health or mood? Will it have a genuine and largely beneficial impact on the users who are attracted to invest in it? Have faith in what you are marketing at an individual level. If your product becomes something you wouldn't dream of using in your own life, it's not ethical manipulation.

At the next level, you need to know who the product will be helping. An intimate understanding of your audience will help you to build a genuine base. Try to look into what the problems or your users are, and how your product can help counter these problems. Most of the wildly successful businesses are always trying to target a specific emotion in their audiences. Either they want to appeal to their artistic instincts, or their urge to escape the realities of life, or simply to help them become better versions of themselves. Whatever it is, your product should have a clear answer for the target audience's core desires.

If your end desire is to help your audience with what you have to offer, a degree of manipulation is necessary to help them figure things out. It helps you to be relevant to the solutions that they are looking for, both at the subconscious and conscious levels. Other than that, omnipresence and intimacy are key tools to ensuring that the manipulation you should (and must) engage in ensures profits for your company while also benefiting your users.

Manipulation In Sales

Just as manipulation is an unavoidable part of business, so also it plays an important role in sales. A salesperson's biggest challenge lies in defeating the inner voice in a potential buyer's head that tries to reason with them against buying the product the salesperson is trying to sell.

All users will have this voice. For instance, let's say that I, as a user, walk into a store and find the most perfect pair of expensive earphones that promise to cancel out all white noise. I pick them up, revel in how they feel like they "belong" in my life, and then I hear a voice exploding inside me which begins battling with another voice.

While one keeps saying "look at how good these look on me," the other voice asks, "do I really need these?" On one hand, I think, "this is just what my life has been missing," while also thinking, "my partner will kill me if I come home with these."

I *know* that my old pair of earphones will work just fine. At this point, a salesperson who has been watching my internal battle from the side approaches me with a few succinct words. He tells me about some useful reviews and lets me listen to some music on the earphones, displaying the extent of its "noise canceling" features.

And then comes the icing on the cake. He tells me they're holding a sale, and these headphones are 20% off for only today. He tops this off by saying that they have only five remaining. I panic, thinking that if I come back tomorrow, neither will I get the sale price, nor will there be any left to purchase.

He makes the product a notch above "being amazing." He makes it *indispensable.* So I end up buying the headphones, willing to take the angry tirade from my partner. Heck, I have noise canceling if I need it. Now, I am a rational being. I know that these "sale offers" and "it'll be sold out soon" statements are all part of a marketing gimmick.

I end up being willingly manipulated, anyway. I know it won't be the end of the world if I don't get the headphones, but I *want my life to include them.* And so long as they aren't destroying my life or making me spend money I don't have, it's okay.

When salespeople use tools that signify urgency, exclusivity, and scarcity, they hijack the brain's rational reasoning abilities and instead urge the brain to fast forward into taking immediate action. The very art of persuading someone to purchase something is inherently manipulative—but it need not be deceptive.

In sales, manipulation entails persuading potential customers to act in favor of something that truly interests them. There is a shift in priorities from "I'm interested, but maybe I'll get this later" to "I'm interested enough to get this right now." So, as a buyer, you move from a phase of "considering" when and if you'll buy that thing or service that interests you, to actually purchasing it.

If you go over various shopping platforms, you'll find no dearth of these sales tactics. They can take the shape of sales offers that expire after a certain date, testimonials and case studies, discounts for being a special customer, and displays of inherent value.

Clever salespeople will also create urgency based on your need— if you have been thinking about toothpaste and have made one search online about the safest brands, you can be certain that over the next few days, you'll be bombarded with chemical-free paste sales ads across various social media platforms.

Hypothetically, let's say that you've been planning to get healthy by beginning an exercise regimen. You could do something as simple as going outdoors for a run. But many of us feel more comfortable driving to a gym and spending copious sums to run on a treadmill. If you ask them why they'll probably be unsure of the answers themselves. They'll come up with justifications like they can run faster when the speed is automated, or they like being in the presence of a company.

In reality, these are ways of rationalizing the money spent on becoming a gym member. We nearly always follow through on commitments when there's a financial cost involved, simply because we feel we should get what we can from the value invested. And this is a good thing. While the gym manipulates you into believing that your membership is the roadmap to your best health, the money you spend takes you closer to realizing that ambition.

Therefore, manipulation can provoke you into taking action on things that work out to be in your best interest. However, if you become part of a campaign that promises you washboard abs (from a state of having never worked out) in ten days—that's deception.

When the market's actions are hinged on claims that aren't true, they become deceptive and harmful. And there's no dearth of these either. There are programs out there that promise to make you lose 30 pounds in 10 days, enable you to look 20 at 70, and give you enviable career skills in 2 days.

Manipulation in sales becomes a problem when you promise to offer something that you cannot possibly deliver within the stipulated time, or convince buyers to purchase dubious products by saying it will help them when it will do just the opposite. This includes all the magic pills that claim to make you lose weight in a week with two pills a day. This kind of marketing is also manipulation, but it is the dangerous, unscrupulous kind.

The difference between manipulation as it is and deceptive manipulation has to do with what is being offered. In deception, there is a vast difference between the claims and benefits being offered and what is actually received. If you sell something that does not deliver on the promises you've made or at least a part of them, you're being deceptive. On the other hand, if you're nudging someone to purchase something that they already desire, and that will add a form of real value to their lives, that's manipulation.

Being deceitful is pretending to be ignorant or excusing your terrible actions to yourself. The good thing is that in order to sell successfully, you do not need to breach ethical limits. When you're speaking the truth, you're more likely to close sales. In reality, the most successful sales methods are those that are based on truth and objectivity. There is no need to resort to illegitimate methods of marketing if you are delivering real value to the individuals on the other side of the trade.

According to David Ogilvy, the father of direct sales, "The client isn't stupid, she's your wife." Trying to trick her only works the first time; doing it a second time will fail miserably. Deception isn't beneficial for anyone: you, your customers, and your company all suffer as a result of it.

So. Manipulation is a *tool.* Deception is a *lie.* The former will benefit sales, but the latter will only cause harm in the long run—both for the users and your product.

The Impact Of Manipulation On Law

It turns out that even professions like law (especially from the context of how lawyers must have a hold over the courtroom to induce favorable decisions) are not exempt from manipulative tactics.

When it comes to understanding the context of manipulation in terms of legal practice, Machiavellianism becomes pertinent. This is a pejorative that stands for the inherent willingness to do anything that is needed for getting to the desired end. Lawyers do have to operate according to an ethical code that is supposed to act as a shield against extremes of manipulation.

However, the effectiveness of this ethical code has been the subject of a lot of controversies, much like the efforts of the organized bar to enforce ethical rules. A responsible lawyer needs to understand ethical manipulation—and not go to an extent where manipulation could qualify as abuse.

Lawyers have to operate within a cultural framework that is rife with manipulation, power, and, at extreme levels, deception. The role of an advocate is to operate within the limits of each of these. The philosopher Plato had a poetic way of looking at it when he discerned an advocate function by *enchanting* the minds of courts of law.

While we'd like to believe that nothing is more important than the naked truth, in these courts, *conviction* always plays a more significant role. Truth is important, but what's more important is to deliver it in a manner that is more convincing than lies. If the lies become convincing enough, they may be enough to sway favor.

Manipulation of other human beings is inescapable, and it is an inevitable part of the professional lives of lawyers. There are moral limitations, but aside from these, all lawyers manipulate symbols, concepts, events, institutions, words, and people. If you practice law without manipulating the conditions of your surrounding environment, you won't earn success, irrespective of whether you think that's the more "ethical" way to go about things.

We are constantly manipulating (or trying to manipulate) in discovery, interviews, investigations, pleadings, and negotiations. While it is impossible for effective advocates to avoid manipulating people, it is highly possible for them to make their tactics fall within the limits of their (and the overall societal) moral compass, depending on how far the case and their own conscience will take them.

Manipulation in legal practice becomes more apparent when an issue goes to trial. Advocates of both parties will resort to dark psychological tactics in their attempts to persuade a judge or a jury to believe their respective accounts. Everything—from their body language to how they tackle the opinions and evidence presented by their opponents, and their manner in answering or avoiding questions—becomes a skilled game in convincing decision-making to rule in their favor.

In criminal law, a person cannot be charged if the evidence brought in by the prosecution is not incriminatory unless there is a majority consensus that the evidence gathered is beyond a reasonable doubt. More often than not, defense attorneys will use body language to instill doubt in the minds of the judge and jury to get the case dismissed. Likewise, the prosecutor will apply the same methods to convince everyone of the defendant's guilt and move for them to be punished. It's a game of being able to convince with confidence—and that is not possible without manipulation.

A lawyer may possess all the theoretical knowledge in the world, but if they cannot present it in a palatable form that will turn the legal jurisdiction in their favor, it will be a waste. To be very candid, a good lawyer is one who can win a losing case. One of the most important skills needed to do this is manipulation. The lawyer *must* know how to turn the tables in their favor by interpreting and presenting the law in a manner suiting their client's needs.

Market And Currency Manipulation

You'd think that the world of finances is skewed enough as is— but wait. Manipulation is literally one of the most important things at play here, and it can turn an entire financial market in favor of just a few layers of society.

Market or stock manipulation refers to the manipulation of a financial market for one's personal gain. It occurs when people can influence the rise and fall of securities. There are several ways by which stock prices in the market can be manipulated.

Deflation of the price of a security is achieved by placing a large number of small orders at a price lower than the present market price of the same security. Investors take this as a signal that there is something untoward happening with the company. This negative perception compels investors to sell their securities and, therefore, push stock prices lower.

One of the many ways of inflating a security price is by placing equal numbers of sell and buy orders for the same security at the same time with the help of different brokers. The orders work to cancel each other out. The large volume of the orders that have been executed presents an impression to the investor that there is increased interest in the security. They become convinced that there will be future price appreciation, so they buy the security. This pushes the stock price higher.

Market manipulation tactics are concerned with spreading false information through online channels that have a lot of investor traffic. The overflow of this information on messenger boards, in combination with legitimate market signals, encourages traders to go forward with dubious trades.

One such technique of market manipulation is known as pump and dump. This is used to inflate security prices artificially. The manipulator sells out of security, and the followers are left with overvalued security. The other technique is poop and scoop. Here, the stock prices of a large or medium-cap company are artificially deflated. The manipulator purchases the undervalued shares and makes a profit.

Legitimate institutions, including central banks and individual governments, are involved in a type of market manipulation known as currency manipulation, making it distinct from other forms of market manipulation. Even while currency manipulation isn't technically illegal, international bodies like the World Trade Organization have condemned it as malpractice.

Currency manipulators might face penalties from trading partners. The value of a country's currency may be devalued or inflated under a floating exchange rate system. Trade imbalances may be addressed by lowering the cost of exports and making imports more costly by issuing government bonds or creating money.

Countries also use currency manipulation as a way to weaken their currencies so that they can boost their surpluses. This practice has been on the rebound in the post-COVID world. The pandemic has sparked flows of capital out of developing and into developed economies. Renewed currency manipulation exemplifies attempts to divert these flows to the largest economies, particularly America.

Different nations manipulate their currency values by buying and selling within currency markets with the sole intent of making exports cheap and imports expensive. In 2020, eight countries were on the radar for being currency manipulators—Hong Kong, Guatemala, Israel, Korea, Switzerland, Singapore, Taiwan, and Thailand. The Treasury Department of the United States stated that Vietnam, Taiwan, and Switzerland met its criteria for currency manipulation in 2020.

Politics And Dark Psychology

The connection between politics and dark psychology is a no-brainer. Politics is basically getting people to side with a particular person, ideology, or party. It is rooted in the ability to successfully manipulate people into believing those who are in positions of power or seeking the same.

At the onset, let's look at some instances of political phenomena where manipulation is likely to play a significant role. Imagine, for instance, a candidate tarnishes the image of their competitor by using innuendos. These can be of a colorful variety, ranging from the competitor being soft or dubious on issues needing a stern stance, to being likely to engage in policies that can culminate in the outbreak of communal unrest and wars. This is one of the commonest ways by which political parties turn tables in their favor. It's commonly known as political mudslinging, and boy is it effective.

Political mudslinging doesn't have to take place in a conversation or in a direct confrontation between two competing clients. Lobby organizations, campaign advertising, cold calls, and surveys are all examples of ways to smear opponents.

A typical practice among media conglomerates is to have financial relations with significant financial institutions (such as the mainstream media and social media sites). Large pharmaceutical businesses, military contractors, and technology firms are also part of these financial institutions' portfolios. These financial powerhouses are free to engage in open lobbying of elected officials and party leaders.

Big media conglomerates have a tendency to focus attention on the candidate or party that best serves their interests and those of financial institutions. Because of this, they focus their ire on the party or candidate that might harm their interests.

Mainstream United States politics has often relied on subtle or direct character attacks between competing candidates. The metaphorical implication is of two grown adults throwing mud at each other, essentially engaging in smear campaigning. A prominent example I can recount dates back to the 1796 presidential election. The *Gazette of the United States* came up with a mysterious essay accusing candidate Thomas Jefferson. The implications were he was intimately involved with an enslaved woman (outside his marriage). Upon investigation, it was found the essay's author was the incumbent Treasury Secretary, Alexander Hamilton.

One can question the moral aspect of all of this—but it should be understood that politics and morals rarely go together. Most of us, when we're looking for leaders, don't stop to think about whether they're being "moral" or "ethical." Our concerns are larger, and at times, more necessary within the context of societal demands. *Will the candidate be able to solve our issues? Can they take a stand? Will they do what it takes, no matter what?* These questions become paramount when we look for someone to lead.

There have also been times when candidates have successfully avoided perjury by maintaining they didn't know a claim to be false. They would say they "thought" this claim was true and that the public deserved to know it because it was in their best interest. So, if a promising candidate has been slandered for "having an affair" by another candidate, let's say the promising one proves their competitor was lying. When they face the competitor, he simply says he thought what he had repeated (that is, news of the affair) to be true. To be frank, this can be a genius move. It's very difficult to cross-verify the potential awareness (or lack thereof) about something being true or false, and mudslingers are known to use this dubiousness to their advantage.

During the 2020 presidential election, for instance, Hillary Clinton faced a defamation lawsuit against Tulsi Gabbard. Clinton had stated on a podcast that she was a "favorite" of the Russians, without explicitly taking her name. Towards the end of the podcast, the host discerned Clinton's belief Gabbard would be a third-party candidate supported by Donald Trump and the Russians. Gabbard denied all the accusations and filed a lawsuit for $50 million against Clinton. She had to later drop the lawsuit. Clinton's vague comments and her cleverness in not mentioning a specific name meant it was extremely difficult for Gabbard to prove she was talking about her.

Another instance of political manipulation lies in candidates vilifying their competitors for taking a stance they deem as "publicly inappropriate" or "not in the best interests of a section of people" (read potential voters). When they get elected for this very reason (that is, for assuring people they won't do what their competitors did), they support the very policies they'd insulted their competitors for possessing.

They go back on their promises. A recent study of pledges from the Conservative party's 2017 manifesto showed promises considered more vital by voters *were less likely to be fulfilled*. A commitment to reduce net migration to below 100,000, for instance, was broken repeatedly. This is related to a different kind of political manipulation that dates back to policies used by some of the most feared leaders of all time—Hitler, Mussolini, and the like. In these instances, a potential leader resorts to xenophobia and garners support for aggressive military or restrictive immigration policies by manipulating the population into believing they should stand up for themselves first.

Another clever political manipulation tactic lies in rival party leaders appealing to their members in the legislature to investigate their opponents on corruption charges. These charges may be completely baseless, but their pertinent stance lies in the mere act of investigation instilling the seeds of doubt in the majority opinion. A dominant party can also resort to redrawing electoral districts so that voters from opposing parties fall within a district cluster smaller than the opposing party's proportion of the electorate.

It's not just parties who resort to political manipulation. Legislators can attach a damning amendment or clause to a piece of legislation they don't like but have been forced into making. Their tactic rests in turning this amendment into something so unappealing voters have no choice but to call for its rejection. A chairperson can, likewise, resort to political manipulation by arranging votes to maximize the chances of getting the outcome they will prefer.

Now, all the instances we just covered are examples of political manipulation in a narrow sense. But, society itself is constantly employing political manipulation, wherein it tries to turn opinions in certain ways. For instance, a beauty advertiser can use psychological appeals to make potential consumers feel less than confident about particular aspects of their body that said advertiser claims to have a miracle cure for. If we extend "politics" to cover interpersonal and broad social interactions, everyday forms of manipulation also become political.

A little child using the appeal of enormous eyes or tears to convince their parents to buy a toy they'll play with for a week becomes rudimentary political manipulation. A group of adolescent children uses peer pressure as a tool of manipulation to ensure conformity with group norms. In intimate relationships, one spouse manipulates the other into guilt-tripping so they can come to a consensus on certain things. The list could go on and on, but you'd stop and ask here, how much of this is manipulation, and how much is just instinctively human nature?

In 1957, Robert Dahl defined manipulation as an act where person A has power over person B if they can get B to do something they wouldn't otherwise do. So, from a simplistic perspective, manipulation is but a tool of power used by those who wish to and know how to wield it.

The distinction between manipulation and coercion, or manipulation and persuasion within the context of political power, remains a tad elusive. This problem becomes more profound since manipulation can be used to illustrate two very distinct strategies for influencing someone to do something. I'll explain using an example from Joel Rudinow in 1978 to drive my point home.

Let's take a hypothetical person and call him Henry. Henry meets the admitting officer of a psychiatric clinic and says he has had a terrible fight with his spouse. He claims if he isn't admitted, he will get drunk, brawl, do something untoward, and either end up in the emergency ward or in jail.

The psychiatric clinic is already overburdened with patients, so the admitting officer refuses Henry's request, saying he isn't qualified to be someone with serious mental health issues. A mere fight with his partner doesn't label him as someone in need of psychiatric help. Henry threatens to jump off a bridge if the officer doesn't comply, and leaves the ward in a rage.

An hour later, he comes back with a group of policemen, who report he did, indeed, try to jump off a bridge. They suggest he be subjected to overnight observation. Henry is admitted. Perhaps without question Henry has successfully manipulated both the ward officer and the policemen into getting what he wants. This is a case where manipulation is applied in two different ways to earn the desired results. On the one hand, Henry manipulates the police officers into believing he could commit irreversible self-harm. On the other hand, he manipulates the admitting officer by *arranging* this entire situation in a way to ensure he gets what he wants. He doesn't just influence the state of mind (of the policemen), *he also manipulates the situation.*

Both these kinds of manipulation—psychological and situational —occur within politics. Are you familiar with the Willie Horton ad or the Daisy ad? Both of these infamous political advertisements have used forms of manipulation to sway audiences.

The Willie Horton ad was used during the 1988 election campaign between George Bush (Sr.) and Michael Dukakis. The ad showed an African American murder convict committing additional crimes of violence while being laid off because of a Massachusetts program—all while Michael Dukakis was the governor.

The Daisy ad was used in a political campaign between Barry Goldwater and Lyndon Johnson. It depicted a small child counting some flowers moments before a nuclear explosion. A voiceover hinted Goldwater was likely to begin a nuclear war.

Both advertisements are manipulative and fall within the domain of psychological manipulation. Other manipulative tactics like dividing opposite coalitions, engineering vote orders to sway outcomes, gerrymandering, and dividing opposite coalitions are clear instances of situational political manipulation.

Take gerrymandering. It doesn't work by changing anyone's decisions. Rather, it manipulates rules in a way that the manipulators get exactly what they want. Electoral district boundaries are politically manipulated with the only intent of creating leverage for one party, socio-economic class, or political group within a constituency.

Another psychological-political manipulation tactic we may not be aware of is using fear to get to the minds of the electorate. A study published by the American Journal of Political Science has found that politicians often use fear as a way of manipulating people into approving policies they wouldn't otherwise side with. Fear as a tool of manipulation becomes likely when audiences don't understand the gravity of an issue or are unlikely to realize its overall impact.

Since both psychological and situational manipulation is rife within the gambit of politics, it becomes difficult to clearly state, "I'm not manipulating the people to get what I want, I'm just persuading them to do what's best for them." We all know the politician's definition of "what is best for us" may actually be the furthest from what's truly best for us.

Cult Practices And Manipulation

One of the more guileful uses of dark psychology tactics has to do with how it is used by cults all over the world. In cults, especially the destructive kinds, a group leader works to systematically brainwash its followers into a state of complete and unquestioned obedience. The cult leader becomes synonymous with, and in some cases bigger than, God. Their voice is the ultimate command. Several dark psychology tactics are used to isolate people, break down their social relationships, and even relegate them to societal fringes where they become outcasts and cannot seek help or clarification from the larger society. They become forgotten and are often viewed as "oddballs" or "eccentrics" by the outer world, with most people feeling that the safest thing is to leave them alone to their devices.

Personal needs become secondary to the leader's whims and wishes within these cults. Any urge to work towards familial or personal welfare often gets termed as "selfish" and punitive. Cult leaders draw in followers because of their innate charisma and their ability to use seduction techniques like brainwashing, mind control, and overall isolation. Cult members are reduced to obedient robots who have no voice or feelings of their own.

Look at the Peoples' Temple of the Disciples of Christ cult. Jim Jones, the cult leader, used a plethora of dark psychology tactics to build this cult. On 18th November 1979, he convinced about a thousand of his cult members to consume drinks laced with cyanide. Those who didn't want to consume were forced to do so by inducing fear of what would happen if they didn't comply. *All of them perished.*

And of course, as long as we're discussing manipulation in cults, how can we forget religious manipulation?

The Religious Conundrum

With the intense appeal to human emotions like fear, devotion, and redemption, manipulation tactics can become more embedded in religions than we realize. Many religious practices are concerned with using manipulation to keep people in line. These practices are designed to help people come together in the faith of sharing a common purpose and goal. The mandate is they have to act in ways that will ensure the maintenance and perpetuation of this goal or purpose, even if these actions may not always be conducive to self-interest.

Religion can be manipulated, and grotesquely so, to control the words, actions, and even the thought processes of large sections of society. There is no other justification why terrorism in the name of religion still has so many devotees and aspirators worldwide.

In the ancient history of the world, a time came when Christianity was at the helm of all religious faith. This did not come via simple addressing of the needs of Christianity's target audiences. On the contrary, Christianity flourished by creating a kind of need that no one, until the time it became established, realized as something important.

Barring Jews, most peoples of the ancient world subscribed to a form of paganism. They believed in many gods—state gods of

Rome, family gods, local municipal gods, forest and mountain gods, and wind gods. Everything in nature had a spiritual connotation attached and was, therefore, worshipped. Earth gods ensured crops flourished, and animal gods were kind enough to let livestock reproduce. Atmospheric gods caused rain and sheltered people against storms. Then some gods protected people from sickness and disease, maintained social stability, and even helped them win wars.

The established belief was that these divine spiritual beings granted their blessings in exchange for sacrifices and worship. These sacrifices rested in prayers, annual festivals, and appropriate rituals. If the gods were not taken care of via these methods, it was thought that they would reign chaos on the Earth. So whenever there was a period of strife, such as epidemics, draughts, military defeat, or economic collapse, they believed failing to appease the relevant gods had led to these conditions.

The fundamental belief was that gods were principally active (whether for good purposes or bad) to worshippers in the present moment. No one had the concept of worshipping for some distant future aim. There was no perception of an eternal reward until Christianity took birth. Unlike pagan religions, the Christians claimed that there was one God, and he was not to be worshipped by sacrifices, but by belief.

Anyone who did not believe in things that were intrinsically "Christian" would be doomed as a transgressor to God. The Christians also spread the notion that punishments and rewards weren't just reserved for mortal life. There was an *after*life and this afterlife could be eternal heavenly bliss or everlasting torment in hell. This was a novel concept in religion, and many people skittered to it like moths to a flame.

The concept of living for something beyond the temporary and transient age of life was, in short, illuminating. It gave people a purpose to live, a purpose that transcended beyond routine drudgery. In short, the Christians birthed a dire need for salvation that was hitherto unknown. Then, they argued only they had what it would take to meet this need.

Now, you could label this in different ways. You could find many justifications, but the result remains the same. The success and the mass conversions that followed happened because of the influence these dictates had on the minds of people. Not too many of them stopped to question things. And this isn't just a case with Christianity.

In several other religions, like Islam, for instance, all power and authority are centered on one man, one vessel of the ultimate and divine power. Redemption lies in living your life as this one man has asked of you, regardless of whether or not you like it. They say it is in your best interest, *so it must be.*

Religion is a need for human progress and survival because it serves as a method of regulating behavior and enforcing rules. The absence of a guiding authority figure would lead to anarchy and disorder. Fear of rejection from an afterlife, the denial of nirvana and the possibility of reincarnation as an inferior person, or even the possibility of being struck by lightning while standing still are some of the reasons why some people are afraid of disobeying religious tenets.

Fear is a powerful motivator in all of them, regardless of the cause. When individuals feel fearful, they are more susceptible to being persuaded by others, which enables the propagation of religion as a system of perpetuation.

And finally, to conclude this chapter, I'll mention in passing that the very OTT platforms we spend a major chunk of our contemporary lives on are successfully manipulating the socks off of us. I'll discuss this in detail in a subsequent chapter, but for now, let's get into a riveting case study.

A Case Study On OTT Manipulation: Netflix

The world of entertainment has become an extremely diverse place following the proliferation of OTT platforms. These over-the-top media services offer programs and films for the viewer's pleasure, based on monthly or annual subscriptions that users have to pay.

The dystopian drama Squid Game has become one of Netflix's biggest-ever series with over 110 million viewers tuning in to watch each episode.

So, out of the many programs airing on Netflix, how did so many people become fixated on watching the same show? The answer lies in the algorithm, a computer program that builds and propagates personalized recommendations based on individual and community-specific data.

Streaming platforms, including Netflix, have reshaped the way we consume media. This has been partly achieved by increasing the variety and the quantity of music, film, and TV options. From life within the womb to aliens and what kind of food they like to consume, nothing is "too undoable" for the television world any longer.

A significant aspect of our cultural landscape is automated, rather than being left to our understandings and inherent perceptions based on individual experiences, social circles, or backgrounds. These algorithms aren't just responding to what they perceive as "our tastes," they are literally shaping, influencing, and creating them.

Cultural transformation also has another important trajectory. For the purposes of making content manageable, streaming platforms have come up with organization via categories that label cultures under watchable "genres". The new normal on these platforms is to enable people to develop a world view via labels, genres, and categories—a world view that can be so nuanced that it exemplifies our very identities and sense of belonging.

How many times have you felt like you didn't belong because you couldn't understand the hype behind a show that was loved by millions of others? This identification of where you belong based on your love (or derision) of a popular show or film has become entrenched with the snowballing of OTT platforms.

About five decades ago, you could have chanced upon a music label or a specific genre by visiting a record shop or through close friends. Today, the very ability to stream music through different channels has brought genre and music classification to what can only be visualized on a grandiose scale.

The more the availability, the more we consume. Spotify alone boasts over five thousand genres of music. Listeners have the power to make their genre labels when they create fancy playlists. So, as consumers, we are constantly bombarded with new categories and labels, each manipulating us into acting and receiving entertainment in certain institutionalized ways.

In many ways, the mushrooming of these categories has resulted in specific and eclectic tastes, which means we get to pursue roles that are fundamentally fluid. The personalized recommendations, in turn, transform and shape this fluidity.

For instance, YouTube keeps recommending videos I've never heard of, and it isn't until I've viewed them that I'm left to wonder at the manipulative marvel of it all. Spotify brings year-end personalizations that can introduce you to music genres you'd have never heard of before, prompting you to search and learn more about them.

How can we cope when we're presented with this very unfathomable level of options? Where do we even begin? Well, that's where the algorithm comes in. OTT platforms like Netflix use these algorithms so our attention gets diverted and channeled in specific directions.

When you open such platforms, you'll also be met with prompts on the lines of "if you can't decide what to watch, let us choose for you." On top of that, sections like "trending" or "top 10 today" give you an irresistible urge to see what's so great about a show for it to attract millions of viewers. As soon as you open the OTT app, the personalization process commences.

The very specific categories that we get hooked on are actually categorized and stored as metadata codes on the backend of these platforms. They form the core of personalized recommendations, and they influence what we consume.

We'd like to believe we choose what we watch—but if you get into it, *we don't*. I realized this on the seventh day of mindlessly watching hapless bakers mold cakes into hyper-realistic shapes— something I'd never even thought of as an essential part of my daily life until, well, it became so. So, if we visualize Netflix as a vast archive of different TV and films, the way it is structured through metadata influences what we discover within it.

The thousands of categorizations on Netflix are so niche-specific that you will probably find something to get hooked on. You have your conventional documentaries, romance, horror, romantic comedies, and reality television, but you also have oddly targeted niches like "camp movies" or "father-son relationship TV shows" or "TV programs featuring a strong female lead." Squid Game has earned its fame in multiple genres—Korean, drama, and TV thrillers. Altogether, it's safe to assume that Netflix's metadata and the resultant categorizations are shaping the entire identity of your internet cultural consumption.

The personalizations on the homepage employ algorithms that showcase certain genres and specific shows to each of you. Because all of this is dependent on the internal metadata, we may not even know what categories are being served to us.

At any rate, we're unlikely to wonder why Netflix or any other OTT platform seems to know what we want to watch when we're sitting in front of the television or our laptop or phone screens, bored out of our minds, stressed, or with plates full of food.

Squid Game's success is an instance of how algorithms can work to reinforce something that's bound to become popular once it catches on. Once something becomes a trend, algorithms can manipulate more attention to make these blossoming trends go full-blown viral. Netflix works to get this done too, signaling which programs are popular or trending in our localities and communities.

With so much digital manipulation guiding the very core of what we watch, you may now stop to think—who is in control? Well, as everyday consumers, we aren't quite there yet when it comes to understanding the workings and potential of these algorithms. The digital classification of cultures could block our minds to certain voices, and this can be limiting or harmful.

Social media has made the spreading of misinformation via the use of vibrant colors and "relatable messages" a very real and dangerous phenomenon, and unless we can understand and act on what we watch consciously, we do become subjected to a global cultural manipulation game.

To an increasingly growing extent, our very social connections get shaped by the cultures that we consume—so what we watch becomes synonymous with who we interact with. The mounting questions, and the ones I will close this chapter with, are twofold.

Who decides what the labels are? What gets put into those shiny categorization boxes, and therefore, what we ultimately end up listening to, reading, or watching?

In the next chapter, we're going to look at the elusive dark triad. I know this term sounds pretty ominous, but it's simply a classification of the kinds of personalities making up dark psychology. All of us may exhibit traits that meet some criteria exhibited by the dark triad personalities—but these traits are minute. Whereas, in dark triad personalities, their very essence is defined by the specific dangerous quality that is inherent to their natures.

Knowing what makes up these personalities will make you more aware the next time you see these characteristics on display. After all, our goal here is to increase your awareness of the many forms in which you can be manipulated. This understanding will remain vague unless you learn about the dark triad personalities.

CHAPTER 2
THE ENIGMA OF THE DARK TRIAD

I'VE OFTEN WONDERED, what is it that makes the mind of a notorious serial killer like Richard Ramirez? How do you end up justifying the heinousness of your acts by simply passing them off as being done in some form of divine (or in this case, fiendish) light? Turns out that Ramirez was a complete narcissist, so consumed by his own image and notoriety he devoured all the attention that came from being a merciless serial killer. He even enjoyed the "Night Stalker" label given to him by the media.

During his court proceedings, he made it a point to groom himself in all black clothes and sunglasses, and waved to female groupies who were fascinated by his nature and wanted to be with him. Yes, you heard that right too. Tons of women, especially young and naïve, were enamored with the Night Stalker. He had a veritable fan following among these groupies, including women who wanted to marry him and hopefully make a saint out of the devil.

The point here is, that it's pretty difficult to change someone who's been labeled as a narcissist unless they undergo a major change of heart. Which brings me to ask—what's the first thing that crosses your mind when I refer to the "dark triad?" Does it sound very Hollywoodesque? Or does it sound like a cult you'd encounter in a docuseries or a thriller? Actually, the dark triad is a core concept tying together the very understanding of everything that makes dark psychology, well, "dark."

You'll soon discover that all dark psychology's other themes are derived from this one: the "dark triad", home to the three most deleterious and harmful affective personality traits. We'll do our best to bring these personality characteristics to light and truly comprehend them in order to better prepare ourselves for them.

BROADLY UNDERSTANDING THE DARK TRIAD

Let me begin this section by asking you a simple question—*are people inherently good, evil, neither, or both?* I'd say that we each have traits qualifying as a bit of all of these characteristics. In some of us, traits that are conventionally considered "good" exceed the negatives. In some others, there's a balance. And in yet others, the behaviors and characteristics which are predominantly "evil" become synonymous with the entirety of who they are. To not get into an existential or philosophical debate, it is perhaps best to say the qualifications vary from personality to personality. There is no one-size-fits-all approach to classifying all of humankind.

With this being said, psychologists have been able to identify certain predominant behaviors with what constitute major "red flags." I'd say that a negative quality becomes a red flag when it becomes one of the dominant traits you associate yourself with. A thief may be a wonderful person at heart, but if they are predominantly stealing, that becomes synonymous with their core identity.

So, these red flags come together to make up the dark triad. The three dominant traits making up this triad are narcissism, psychopathy, and Machiavellianism. These dark personality characteristics are completely distinct from each other, but they can overlap and coexist inside the same individual.

PERSONALITY TRAITS

Individuals manifesting the dark triad personality and its subtypes display tendencies towards criminal activities and violence. Even if they don't become socially unacceptable, they often veer to the suburbs of what is the norm, and tend to lack any empathy, be self-serving, and dominantly (sometimes cruelly) manipulative.

Personality traits are constructs used by psychologists to understand differences in the way people think and act. They do this by assigning people to specific traits depending on their dominant behavioral patterns. The people who get assigned to a particular trait are usually expected to behave in ways common to this trait consistently, over time, and irrespective of any changes in their surrounding circumstances.

Psychologists usually refer to a template comprising five personality traits—otherwise known as the *big five*. These are openness, conscientiousness, agreeableness, extraversion, and neuroticism. After analyzing the behaviors of people, psychologists score them low or high on these core traits and build an outline of their core personality type.

The Dark Traits

Negative human behaviors are linked to certain dark traits. This doesn't necessarily link them to specific external displays or actions like greed and deception, because dark traits are linked to broader definitions of particular categories.

Dark traits, in non-medical terms, are personality types displayed by people who are generally considered antisocial. While you could find a lot of things to be against your ethics, in broad societal terms, antisocial behavior lands itself under three main dark trait characteristics.

Narcissism

The origins of the term "narcissism" date back to the works of the Roman poet Ovid in his *Metamorphoses* (Book III). Here, it can be found in the first-century prose of Narcissus and Echo. This term would eventually become something highly specialized and psychoanalytic.

In Ovid's mythology, Narcissus comes across as a handsome youth who rejects the advances of many lovers, including Echo, a nymph. Echo's name came from being cursed to echo only the sounds produced by others. Following Narcissus's rejection of Echo, the Gods punished him by dooming him to fall in love with his own reflection over a pool. Upon finding that the very object of his love could not return his passions, Narcissus eventually pined after his unfulfilled romance and died.

Narcissism boasts a complex and rich literature of clinical psychoanalytical history, starting with an entrenched focus on abnormal self-focused sexual tendencies. In 1898, Havelock Ellis was the first psychologist to use the term "narcissus-like". He linked Ovid's myth to auto-eroticism, a condition where the patient was sexually attracted to themselves.

Later on, Freud employed the terms "ego libido" and "narcissistic libido" to signify self-love interchangeably in *Three Essays On The Theory Of Sexuality*. These early deductions of narcissism were largely very immature and relied on the notion that sexual gratification was essential for the survival of the self. The clinical definition today is far broader.

Ernest Jones included two more characteristics to define the concept of narcissism. He identified an inherent "God-complex" to exist within narcissistic personalities. These personalities, he discerned, came across as inaccessible, aloof, overconfident, auto-erotic, self-important, and exhibitionistic. They also displayed fantasies where they'd be omnipotent and omnipresent figures. Jones's studies revealed his understanding that narcissists needed to be "unique" for nothing was as offensive to these personalities as the notion that they resembled someone else.

Jones's depictions of narcissistic personalities are remarkably close to what we currently understand them to be. Around the same time he came up with his theories, Freud published his landmark essay *On Narcissism: An Introduction,* where he dealt with the topic on a developmental basis.

Freud conceptualized narcissism as a phase of maturation common to the healthy development of all children. He viewed it as a complimentary trait to the egotism of the self's inherent instinct of preservation. So, his theory was that before children could grow up and become attached and develop intimate relations with others, they go through an adaptive phase of *primary narcissism* where they are largely egocentric and unable to accept the perspectives or reasonings of others.

Healthy development would occur when children, upon maturing, departed from this primary narcissism and invested their libidinal energies in people other than themselves.

According to Freud's economic model of love, each of us has a finite amount of instinctual vitality that can only be allocated to a single activity at a given point in time in our lives. As a result, as children mature and progress from primary narcissism to external love, their self-preservation instinct undergoes a natural and necessary decline.

In a healthy relationship, the libidinal energy of both parties is invested in each other, yet neither party experiences a loss as a consequence of this investment. In certain cases, when external love objects are unable or unwilling to reciprocate the love displayed by individuals, the rejected individuals retreat to a pathological condition of narcissism known as secondary narcissism. This becomes a compensating technique so that the self remains loved, even if the means grow ugly or deviant.

In 1925, Wälder published a case study—the first of its kind—of someone who displayed narcissistic personality traits of a disordered variant. Wälder's patient was a scientist who had an unusual attitude of superiority. They could not empathize with others and felt that they differed from the rest of mankind.

The patient displayed an unhealthy obsession with engendering self-respect and did not have any feelings of guilt. By Wälder's testimony, the patient was also extremely logical, and analytical, and gave preference to thinking for the sake of it, rather than being concerned with emotional manifestations. Their sole interests lay in self-perpetuation and applying scientific theory to understanding human civilization, with no emotions involved. Wälder's case study has a significant impact on how professionals view narcissism as a mental illness today.

Of the three dark traits deemed as antisocial and making up the core of the dark triad personality, narcissism is most misunderstood and misdiagnosed. This is because many of us make the overgeneralization that any form of selfish behavior is "narcissistic."

If this were true, *all of us would be situational and circumstantial narcissists, because the mere act of existence deems selfishness from time to time.* The actual definition of narcissism goes a little deeper than mere human selfishness.

Narcissism, as it should be understood, is a concern with the self to uniquely extreme levels. Everyone can be guilty of putting their needs ahead of others sometimes, but narcissists will do this like it is their bread and butter.

Psychologists attempt to understand if an individual is a true narcissist by marking them on a four-part scale called the Narcissistic Personality Inventory. This scale measures an individual's propensity towards self-absorption, their sense of superiority and authority, and how likely they are to exploit other people for their own gains, irrespective of the hurt they may cause. Narcissists often face difficulties building and maintaining relationships, since this would mean they'd have to consider needs external to their own.

You could say that a narcissist is someone who loves themselves to the point of refusing to believe that anything existing outside the realm of their own interests can have any possible validity or importance.

Recognizing A Narcissistic Personality

When someone has a narcissistic personality disorder, they are particularly resistant to modifying their conduct, even when it is causing them issues. They have a proclivity for placing the onus of failure on others. Their heightened sensitivity means that even the smallest disputes or perceived slights are seen as personal assaults by these people.

In many cases, those in the narcissist's life choose to comply with their demands rather than deal with the harshness and rages of the narcissists themselves. By learning more about narcissistic personality, you can identify the narcissist in your life, defend yourself from their power plays, and set healthy boundaries.

One of the most defining characteristics common to all narcissists is their obsession with being absolutely powerful. In their eyes, no one can possibly level their superiority. There cannot be any rival to the greatness of who they are. No one can match them. The mere notion that someone can be "better" than them is absolutely unthinkable. They will tend to seek praise and validation wherever they go, to the extent of absolutely shunning people and situations that aren't conducive to their inflated sense of self-worth.

Another common characteristic of a narcissist is the belief that they are inherently superior to others. Having self-confidence isn't enough. The narcissist's universe revolves on the dichotomies of good/bad, superior/inferior, and correct/incorrect.

The narcissist is at the top of the hierarchy, which is really the only position where they feel comfortable. Narcissists must be the finest, the most correct, and the most capable; they must accomplish everything according to their own rules; they must own everything, and they must have total power over everyone.

Being the worst or the most erroneous may also give narcissists a sense of superiority since it makes them feel better about themselves. As a result, they believe they are entitled to a sense of relief and compensation, as well as the right to damage you or demand an apology to "put things right." Vulnerable or covert narcissistic personalities function just this way.

Narcissism is characterized by excessive self-importance. Grandiosity is more than simply conceit; it's a false belief in one's own magnificence. Narcissists feel that only other "special" individuals can understand their uniqueness or "specialness." In addition, they're just too amazing to be anything but exceptional. At all points in time, their only concern lies in associations that will extend their sense of self.

As well as thinking they're better than everyone else, narcissists want praise and admiration for their superiority, even when they have done nothing to merit it. When asked about their accomplishments and abilities, they will often embellish trivialities or flat-out lies.

Also, if you listen to them speak about their jobs or personal relationships, you'll hear nothing but praise for their accomplishments and praise for the individuals they've been blessed to have as friends or partners. Everyone else is only a supporting actor or actress in their show.

For a narcissist, validation is only valuable if it is received from others. But even if you keep validating them, it will feel as if nothing that you say or do will ever be "enough." This is because they are constantly seeking to invalidate you by telling you and reminding you how little you do for them.

People belonging to this personality type never think that anybody can love them, no matter how many times they are told they are loved, admired, or praised. It may be surprising to learn that narcissists are insecure and afraid that they won't live up to their lofty ideals.

Without constant acclaim and acknowledgment, a narcissist's feeling of superiority slowly deflates until it bursts. It's not good enough to get a single compliment. Those who are narcissistic need to be surrounded by others who are eager to feed their desire for affirmation. These are very one-sided connections.

Only what the narcissist needs from the devotee matters, and not the other way around. Moreover, if the devotee ever shows signs of diminishing attention or appreciation for the narcissist, the latter sees it as a betrayal.

Narcissists seek special attention because they believe they are unique. They believe they are entitled to nothing less. It's as though they're certain that they should have anything they desire.

They also believe those around them should immediately comply with their wishes and whims. All they are worth is that. You're worthless to them if you don't foresee and satisfy their every demand. And if you do have the audacity to go against their wishes or ask for anything in return, brace yourself for hostility, wrath, or frigid treatment. Prepare yourself. Their delicate egos want continual attention and validation from others, yet despite how much they get, they always crave more.

I'll give you a very real-life example. In North Korea, the word of the Supreme Leader Kim Jong-un has traditionally been upheld as the closest thing to God. J0ng-un's personality has been the subject of curiosity for many researchers, and the repeated results of many studies have revealed him to be ambitious/self-serving (narcissistic) and outgoing/gregarious (histrionic) with a secondary antisocial pattern. Traits that are dominant, sadistic, passive-aggressive, and borderline exist in minimal quantities alongside the two predominant traits.

Leaders sharing Kim Jong-un's personality type are the likeliest to engage in political antics defined by a cold and indifferent conscience, deception, and fraudulence. They prefer using their inherently gifted tactics of guile, manipulation, and cunning rather than force to get what they want from others. Studies have likened Kim Jong-un to being the consummate con artist, so versed in the art of manipulation, that he doesn't need to possess any other traits requiring physical action.

So, North Korea would be an ideal example of a country that is completely under the control of a narcissistic personality. Those at the helm of affairs command god-like reverence from their people and punish anyone who would dare to hone a thought, or concept, or carry out an action going against the formal state doctrines.

Machiavellianism

Machiavellianism is one of the dark triad personalities, the others being psychopathy and narcissism. These traits, through the proven test of time, have been glamorized in books, films, and television—although they're hardly as "appealing" if you have to deal with them on a daily basis.

The word "Machiavellianism" owes its origins to the Italian philosopher Niccolo Machiavelli, the author of the political treatise *The Prince*. This treatise is a controversy unto itself, with lines implying no matter what the means are, the end always justifies them, particularly among politicians.

Machiavelli was a Renaissance philosopher who believed living a life where you are feared by others is better than one where you're loved. He also felt if you need to injure someone, the extent of the injury should be such that the victim should never be able to take revenge on you. Over time, these descriptions have naturally become definitive of a personality disorder exemplified by cold selfishness.

Niccolo Machiavelli And The Prince

Niccolo Machiavelli (1469—1527) was a historian, diplomat, writer, and philosopher belonging to the Italian Renaissance period, and he's been touted as the founder of modern political science. He was a senior official in the Florentine Republic for a long period and had diplomatic and military responsibilities. He wrote his most well-known work, *The Prince,* in 1513.

"Machiavellianism" has become a widely employed negative term that characterizes politicians of the kind Machiavelli upheld in *The Prince.* Machiavelli termed immoral behaviors like killing innocent people and dishonesty as normal, even essential in politics. In certain cases, he went as far as endorsing these deviant practices. The book became notorious when readers claimed Machiavelli was professing evil and providing villainous recommendations to help tyrants retain their positions of power.

Over time, "Machiavellian" became a philosophy associated with deviousness, political deceit, and the nuances of *realpolitik.* *Realpolitik* designates a system of political principles where decisions get mandated on practical considerations over moral or ethical issues.

The Prince, from a generic perspective, is an entirely political treatise concerned with the crowning of a new prince, rather than the traditional target audience concerning a hereditary prince— which was the norm of the time. In order to retain power, the hereditary prince had to balance the conflicting interests of many institutions to which all people had grown accustomed.

By contrast, the new prince had to face more difficulties when ruling. He had to stabilize the source of his newfound power and build a political structure that would endure changing times and situations. Machiavelli felt that stability and security's social benefits could only be achieved via a route that caused moral corruption.

He thought leaders had to distinguish between public and private morality if they were to achieve success. A ruler's concern had to extend beyond the limits of reputation and encompass the willingness to act immorally if situations demanded it.

Machiavelli may not have been a Machiavellian personality himself. He was more of a political theorist, responding to the troubles of the time. As an objective theorist, he felt occasional demands for brute force or deceit, exercised methodically, where necessary. This included exterminating entire noble families if they dared to rise up in challenge against the prince's authority. He believed violence was entirely essential to stabilize power and build new legal institutions.

Also, he believed force should be used for eliminating political rivals, bringing resistant audiences to submit to authority, and purging the community of any potential competitors who could be strong enough to challenge the king and take his position. Machiavelli became infamous for such preachings and therefore earned himself the adjective of being Machiavellian.

The Prince is often touted as one of the first works of modern philosophy, particularly in the contemporary context. The effective, bland truth was considered more important than any kind of abstract, far-fetched ideal. Perhaps part of the reason it was so difficult to digest was in how the truth stared us in the face. Many leaders today possess traits that are essentially Machiavellian, and at times, necessary for them to retain their positions of power. And I'm not just referring to leaders from the perspective of national politics, but even leaders in the places we work, socialize and engage in.

Machiavelli's core ideas have had a profound impact on political leadership throughout Western nations, perhaps amplified by printing press technology. During the first few generations following Machiavelli's passing, his main devotees lay in non-Republican governments. A historian once noted that *The Prince* had found great favor with Thomas Cromwell of England and also influenced Henry VIII's turn to Protestantism. A copy of *The Prince* was also kept by emperor Charles V and the Catholic king.

In France, *The Prince* earned a mixed reaction at the onset, but soon, Machiavelli's influence pervaded Catherine de Medici and the St. Bartholomew's Day massacre incident. In the 16th century, Catholic writers deemed Machiavelli as a supporter of the Protestants, although ironically, the Protestants themselves found him to be Italian and Catholic. He influenced both Protestant and Catholic Kings.

Modern materialist philosophy began developing through the 18th century. This philosophy was largely republican and more in line with *The Prince's* original philosophy. Machiavelli's realism and his extortion in using contemporary innovations to dominate over and manipulate others got far more credence than his emphasis on politics and war.

Scholars have suggested that Machiavelli's strong preference for the republican form of government had a significant impact on the political thought of America's founding fathers. When they attacked the growing aristocracy, they felt Alexander Hamilton was building with the Federalist Party, and Benjamin Franklin, Madison, and Jefferson adopted Machiavelli's republicanism.

This is so far as the political context of *The Prince* goes. But, on an entirely different trajectory, the treatise has also paved the way for the study of a complete personality trait, also known as Machiavellianism. Someone who earns the label "Machiavellian" is traditionally considered to be a trouble-maker. And this doesn't mean they simply seek out situations of trouble, rather, they take pleasure in making mountains out of molehills. A Machiavellian personality does not have a discernible moral code and is cunning and sneaky.

Machiavellianism As A Personality Trait

During the 1970s, psychologists Florence Geiss and Richard Christie discerned Machiavellianism as a personality characteristic that mandated deceit, manipulativeness, and a view of the external world that is largely calculating, cold, and cynical. A Machiavellian personality places strategy above all else. When they see a goal in sight, their only concern lies in the skillful realization of this goal. It doesn't matter what they need to do for this to happen. They're largely unconcerned with the feelings of other people.

Machiavellian personalities have no qualms about using unscrupulous tactics, including manipulation, for getting what they want out of people and situations. For this reason, people may consider them to be unemotional. Interacting with a Machiavellian personality may be very confusing at the onset. They come across as charming and engaging, yet very elusive. No matter how hard you try, you never feel "close enough" to them because of their dire lack of empathy.

Unlike narcissists, Machiavellian personalities can seek their goals without needing to become the center of attention. Rather than constantly putting themselves up for display and adoration, they're perfectly fine with working in the background and pulling the secret strings, so long as the outcome is just what they desire.

Machiavellian personalities use people to their advantage without bothering about the emotional consequences. Their emotional experiences are largely shallow. As a result, while they may have relationships, most of these are dysfunctional and abusive. They also find it remarkably easy to walk away from someone who no longer serves their purposes. Many of them remain out of touch with their inner emotions for a large part of their lives.

Now, as a concept belonging to the domain of personality studies, Machiavellianism has earned a lot of interest. People who exhibit traits considered Machiavellian display intense interpersonal manipulation, which includes the use of deceit, flattery, and lies to get to their goals. They also adopt traditionally amoral viewpoints to promote their own goals.

Machiavellian personalities may also be unable to identify or label their own emotions and feelings. Alexithymia, which is common to Machiavellian people, is the absence of words needed for expressing feelings and emotions. People with this condition not only have trouble expressing their emotions, but they also cannot differentiate their emotional state from their physiological or physical states of being. Additionally, they lack imagination and creative spirit and cannot introspect most situations.

Anhedonia, another characteristic linked to Machiavellian personalities, comes through as an inability to experience any pleasure along with diminished sensitivity to difficult situations. These traits are also common in people with depression and anxiety disorders.

Machiavellian individuals can read the minds of others, and they can comprehend social situations very easily. This helps them manipulate these social situations to serve their inner motivations. Research also suggests Machiavellian personalities possess better mind-reading abilities and remain detached from the external population in general.

Their emotional disconnection is comparable to alexithymia and anhedonia. Detachment of this nature may also be seen in people who suffer from schizophrenia, anxiety disorders, and depression. For this reason, it's important that you look for other traits before judging someone to be Machiavellian—mere emotional aloofness isn't a qualifier.

Individuals with Machiavellian personalities are as far off from empathy as they can be. Empathy lies in being able to understand situations from multiple points of view before determining their correctness or invalidity. There has to be a distance between the two people involved in the situation so that there's no conflict between person A's internal feelings and the feelings experienced by the other person.

Empathy itself has two components—cognitive empathy, which implies identifying and understanding the emotional circumstances of others, and affective empathy, which lies in sharing others' emotional states. Multiple works of scientific literature studying human personalities have found negative connections between Machiavellianism and empathy. Some, however, suggest that cognitive empathy is still possible for a few of them—and this may not be great news. Why? Because a skilled Machiavellian can understand emotional traits in others and exploit their vulnerabilities to get what they want.

How Do You Spot A Machiavellian Personality?

Empirical research suggests that all Machiavellians display certain dominant traits in social settings.

First off, they perform well in situations where rules tend to be ambiguous. This means that while they may not be inherently creative, they enjoy creative spaces because of their penchant for chaotic environments. Wherever there is scope for creation over orderliness, rules and regulations tend to be a little unclear. Machiavellian personalities can make use of such situations to propel themselves to positions of leadership. Established norms and procedures may be too difficult for them to follow.

A Machiavellian personality can never exhibit a full range of emotions. So, they can appear very detached from normal situations. If something really distressful (in the general context) happens, we would become nervous and display anxiety. Machiavellian personalities only show signs of anxiousness when circumstances do not go their way and they cannot achieve their goals. It doesn't matter if the world outside is burning. If that's what they wanted, it's fine.

Machiavellians can perform well in competitive environments, so you may find them to be friendly and outgoing initially. They use soft tactics for gaining support and commitment. Over time, this becomes their method to get things happening the way they want, and if you cannot do that, you'll likely earn their wrath. They also rely on making others feel guilty to get to their ends—something they share with narcissistic personalities. They may also go to the extent of engaging coworkers or people around them in risky behaviors (think liaisons and covert romantic relationships) to suit their own means.

Machiavellians are people who have a strategic approach to life and are known for their tendency to focus solely on their own self-interest at all points of time, as well as their willingness to exercise ruthless power and cruelty. They also have an acute awareness of the importance of their public image and the way others perceive them.

As a result, Machiavellian individuals consider any possible repercussions of their actions only from the perspective of how these affect them or what they're seeking to gain. "How will this profit me, and how will my brand persona be impacted?" is what defines every thought they think and action they exhibit.

The first obvious trait you need to watch out for is manipulation. Machiavellian personalities are long-term planners who love to strategize. They pride themselves on being able to read people and uncover the things people are most afraid of or vulnerable towards. Then, they work to use these fears or vulnerabilities against these people. They have no scruples about breaking or bending rules, faking empathy, or tricking people.

A Machiavellian person can come across as someone who's completely charming until you're under their spell. Once they've properly ensnared you, they can become exploitative and bully you to keep conforming to what they want.

Next, a Machiavellian personality will always believe that the entire world runs on self-interest. They lack the ability to form close relationships and rarely trust anybody other than themselves. They're always going to choose power, fame, and money over emotions and relationships. This means that Machiavellian personalities can be notorious for their extremely disloyal natures, and can overrule social pacts or bonds based on trust.

Machiavellians recognize the importance of information. They're unlikely to share information with other people unless it is in their best interest to do so. They can also manipulate innocuous information and present something entirely different from the original messages to you. This typifies their craftiness at sourcing a kind of information and manipulating it or using it out of context.

People bearing Machiavellian traits are very ambitious. They like to wield control and manipulate others to realize their goals. In 2016, a study revealed that these personalities can be evident in managers or leaders who are abusive and aloof. Power has the potential to act as an amplifier, drawing out the inherent behavioral patterns, beliefs, and emotions that are associated with a Machiavellian personality.

Finally, a Machiavellian will more likely be an intensely competitive individual. They consider the entire world as their adversaries and will only be team players when that is conducive to their advantage. They tend to be sensitive to power dynamics operating in social contexts and can alternate between competition and cooperation, depending on what they need to achieve.

Christie and Geis, in their *Studies In Machiavellianism*, built a test called *Mach IV*. They based this test loosely on portions taken from *The Prince* to understand what traits would be the most characteristic of Machiavellian personalities, and what wouldn't be as profound. The test has 20 questions, with the total score being 100.

People scoring over 60, with more affirmative answers to questions highlighting cynicism, manipulation, and deceitfulness, are high-machs. They are the least empathic of all Machiavellians, and also the most deceitful.

Callous, manipulative, and selfish people may share certain genetic commonalities. However, external influences, such as the kind of environment the personalities grew up in, their home life, their relationships with their primary caregivers, and their ability to gel with society during their youth may also play a determining role in the appearance or development of Machiavellian tendencies later in life. A poor start in life can shape any child's future path negatively—and this applies to Machiavellianism as well.

Because Machiavellianism evolved from the need to display these qualities for survival, it might be considered a kind of maladaptive coping. Though individual Machiavellian roots may not begin in infancy, many imprinted traumas originate there.

Psychopathy

There is a tendency to look at psychopaths as people who are devoid of any character or moral persuasions whatsoever. While many think this to be a sign of the times, certain sections of the population, or rather, certain people, have *always* functioned according to this tenet. For as long as human beings have lived on this planet, there have been some who've just come across as emptied souls. Theophrastus, the Greek philosopher Aristotle's student, was the first to write about such people. He referred to them as *"the unscrupulous."*

Is Psychopathy A Recent Thing?

In ancient times, therefore, psychopaths were people who didn't have or couldn't feel the ordinary human connections binding us all. This meant they also lacked the inhibitions posited by these connections. You and I may want to leave our professions aside and become people of the underworld, but the mere weight of the social connections we keep and adhere to will stop us from even thinking about this possibility. For psychopaths, it wouldn't be a dilemma at all. They possess no conscience, and as a corollary, no empathy.

Psychopathy has existed throughout human society and has often featured in many myths and historical tales. Greek and Roman mythology, for instance, is askew with mentions of psychopaths,

Medea being the most well-known among them. The Bible, notably the Old Testament, is also rife with mentions of characters that can only be understood as psychopathic personalities.

The merciless King Shahyar, Shakespeare's psychopaths (think Richard III and Aaron the Moor), and Ximen Qing in the well-known Chinese epic Jin Ping Mei are all examples of psychopaths in popular culture. Alex DeLarge from The Clockwork Orange and Hannibal Lecter from Thomas Harris's literary creations are two contemporary instances of psychotic individuals who have enthralled humanity.

Historically, psychopaths have been found to come from the ranks of ordinary people. In one of his works, the American psychiatrist Hervey Cleckley wrote about routine patients who seemed to display extraordinarily psychotic tendencies and were therefore thoroughly incapable of living a normal life. In the same breath, Cleckley also studied patients coming from higher strata—physicians, psychiatrists, and scientists, and found that while they were also psychopathic, they had an easier time navigating through society harboring grandiose delusions, impulsive tendencies, and remorselessness.

Psychopaths also existed in various preindustrial societies—so they are not typical of certain cultures or related to what many of us consider as the malaise of contemporary societal times. The Yorubas, a tribe indigenous to Nigeria, refer to psychopaths as *aranakan*—meaning people who always go their own way regardless of how they impact others, and who are full of malice, uncooperative, and bullheaded. Inuits use the term *"kunlangeta"* to refer to psychopathic personalities who thrive on tendencies like lying, cheating, raping, and stealing.

Current Context

Over the years, the label *psychopath* has often been loosely used by several professions and people around us—the police system, prosecutors, victims, probation officers, parole and prison officials, and judges. The meaning of the label itself has been oversimplified to just refer to a personality that is "incorrigible." In most instances, psychopaths have made up the small cohort exemplified by patients who have notably been resistant to all forms of rehabilitative treatment.

The real understanding of psychopathy, however, demands far more nuances, beginning from the onset of psychological symptoms that emerges early during the impacted individual's childhood, and extending to all the aspects of their current life that it negatively impacts—including social performances and relationships with friends, family, school and work.

Symptoms of psychopathy manifest themselves through a complete lack of empathy, guilt, or remorse; extreme impulsive behavior; irresponsibility; and shallow affect. As far as mental disorders go, psychopathy is more common than we'd think it to be. It is twice as common as anorexia, bipolar disorder, schizophrenia, and paranoia, and about as common as eating disorders like bulimia, obsessive-compulsive disorder, personality disorder, and narcissism. The only kinds of mental disorders more common than psychopathy are related to depression, post-traumatic stress disorder, and substance or alcohol abuse and dependency.

When it comes to criminal rehabilitation, people are often faced with the conundrum of nothing quite working out—however, this is even more true with psychopaths. They are twice as likely to be imprisoned for violent crimes as criminals who don't have psychopathic tendencies. They are also more adept at securing early releases by faking "good behavior" while spending time in prison. Once released, they will return to their life of crime, and in most cases, will amp up their violence and reactive tendencies to even more dangerous levels.

The defining characteristic of psychopaths is their unusual proclivity to act cruelly or aggressively towards other living things, including, but not limited to, people. While Machiavellians may look to causing harm for their own sake, psychopaths may harm for no good rhyme or reason. To them, "I just felt like it" may be as good a reason as any for bullying, trolling, or assaulting others.

A psychopath's brain isn't the same as yours or mine. They have smaller prefrontal cortexes. Your prefrontal cortex regulates impulses, behavior, and influences planning. Psychopaths also have a deformed amygdala, which is key to feeling emotions like guilt, sadness, and fear.

Psychopaths like the opportunity to stir up trouble. Keeping things interesting is essential since they become bored rapidly. They might start a fight and then play the victim. At the same time, their actions cause chaos in other people's lives while they remain unmoved.

As a result of contact with a psychopath, you may begin to doubt your reality. Assume the psychopath informs you while at work that a colleague has been making disparaging remarks about your appearance. Confrontation with the individual is encouraged. When the dust settles on a nasty argument, you recognize that the other individual was provoked in the same way you were. At the helm is the psychopathic colleague, probably laughing at the two of you squabbling over a make-believe issue that never existed in the first place.

Psychopathy has a lot in common with narcissism. However, it is traditionally far more exploitative than any of the other dark triad personalities. There is a mix of ruthless selfishness and remorseless boldness in people of this trait. They may come across as careless individuals because of their natural love for taking risks. They lack inhibitions and, as such, aren't bothered about the repercussions of bending or breaking rules.

How Do You Spot A Psychopath?

As with the other dark triad personality traits, you have to look out for some key characteristics to understand whether someone is displaying any psychopathic tendencies. To begin with, consider whether their charm or affable persona is just an act—or something that seems largely superficial.

In other words, a psychopath will not come announcing their true nature to you. Just as a skilled actor can play any role, a psychopath will use a mask of normality to appear pleasant. They can be huge extroverts, drawing people to them like moths to the light. They may have stable jobs and experience high rates of success.

Imagine a life that's completely devoid of any kind of anxiety, fear, or guilt. Some of you may think this sounds wonderful—but wait. These emotions make you human, and without them, you'd lack the ability to differentiate between right and wrong. You'd do whatever you wanted without worrying about being questioned or feeling shameful. Social consequences wouldn't bother you. And you wouldn't give a dime about the social wellbeing of others. You'd probably know the rules society runs by, but you wouldn't care, since you're above these rules.

If you know someone who blatantly touts all societal rules and feels that emotions are nothing but pesky hindrances, there's a chance you are dealing with a psychopathic personality. And they're pretty hard to single out because of how convincing and charismatic they appear at first glance. People generally gravitate towards those who are self-assured, and a psychopath may not be many things, but they are definitely confident about who they are. They are unlikely to be loners, like control and power, and enjoy leeching off of people.

It naturally follows that psychopaths don't care about the pain they may inflict on others. Psychopaths understand "emotional behavior" clinically—in that, they can study how and why people get emotional, and copy the same actions that bereaved or vulnerable people employ to manipulate others. Know a frenetic cult leader or dictator who could convince you to commit murder? You probably know a psychopath.

In order to make you see them as the victim, psychopaths master the art of playing on your fears and vulnerabilities. As a result, you become more susceptible to damage in the future. As long as the victim mindset is used as a psychological resource, you should be on the lookout for this person's true character.

Psychopaths have little to no control over their impulses. They desire stimulation and even thrive on it. So, they may get bored living life like the rest of us, and look for stimulation via deviant activities like overdrinking and causing a ruckus, humiliating people, starting fights, shoplifting, drugging and raping vulnerable human beings, or torturing innocent animals.

Psychopathic actions are characterized by complete irresponsibility. They don't feel the need to help or be responsible for others. If they feel like a job isn't doing it for them, or even a relationship, or an academic course, they'll leave it with the clear-cut notion that what they're leaving behind is spoiled seconds, only good for losers.

A curious trait about psychopaths is their physiology differs from non-psychopaths. The conducting power of their skin is lower, as is their resting heart rate. Additionally, changes in their heart rate are different from others. Situations that elicit reactions from the rest of us may not affect them at all. While their partners or family members may be freaking out over something, they remain calm. On the other hand, when they're involved in acts of violence, their heart rate goes up and they experience excitement, even intense pleasure.

There's a good chance that psychopaths come from a history of juvenile delinquency. Common threads exist between those who become psychopaths in later life and acts of crime during childhood. These crimes include excessive aggression towards others. In addition, juvenile psychopaths are unlikely to respond to punishment or stress, like other youths of the same age.

Take a look at the personal ethics and moral code of the people around you. They are likely not a psychopath if they seem to have some kind of morality. As a general rule, psychopaths lack a sense of right and wrong. They'll do everything to get ahead, and they don't give a flying fig if someone is injured in the process. Psychopaths don't have the emotional capability of functioning according to a code.

Another thing you could consider is—when someone is being backed into a corner because their lie, tricks, or deceit has become far too apparent, how does their apology feel? A psychopath may put on a show to meet the demand for an apology. Since their emotional impulses are blunted, they'll not do a great job of it. They'll feign surprise and ignorance, and say things like "I'm surprised this would even hurt you," or "Don't you think you're being too sensitive?" or "We've already discussed this, why do you keep harping on the same point?"

A psychopath will utter a variety of falsehoods, from the tiniest to the most elaborate, in order to confuse and deceive you. Yet they continue to choose lies even when the alternative is easier. This doesn't create embarrassment, which is surprising. They are proud of their deceptions. If you think you've got them, they'll just move the facts around to make it seem like they're telling the truth.

In addition, psychopaths won't act surprised by a deception. In all likelihood, they'll reverse situations to make things seem like you're responsible for everything going wrong, and that you're the source of all the trouble. You would walk away from a conversation with them feeling like a failure, thinking you had tricked a completely honest individual into doing bad things. On the contrary, the psychopath is secretly enjoying how they've led you to believe you're the villain, when, in reality, you're the victim.

ARE WE ALL DARK?

At this juncture, you may be wondering—*what if I belong in the dark triad? What if some of my traits are common to what I just read?*

I'll clarify this at the onset. Yes, to certain degrees all of us possess traits that aren't "all positive." But not all of us belong to the dark triad, no.

Indeed, this has been a subject debated time and again. There are theories out there that believe all of us are self-serving to certain degrees, and I'm inclined to agree.

When we're faced with imminent danger, few of us will consider what we need to do to make it. A maneater prowling in front of us may just be hungry or in need of food, but we won't think before pulling the trigger since, well, *the food is us.* Does that make us antisocial? Or are we just trying to survive? Turns out, there's more to it than simple close-ended answers.

In terms of pure, blunt psychological information, narcissism is a personality characteristic that touches all of us to a certain degree. It exists on a spectrum—which is true of all human characteristics. So, all of us belong somewhere within this spectrum. The good news is this is one huge umbrella, and self-centeredness, to a certain degree, is *good for you.* You'll have people who care deeply about you, but when it comes to allegiance, you're the best bet you have. A measure of self-centeredness results in confidence, ambition, perseverance, and the ability to make decisions that won't harm or endanger you.

However, if you take any personality trait beyond a certain level, it becomes pathological. Consider someone who only lives for other people. Anytime they feel like they've disappointed someone, they cease functioning normally and clam up. Can you imagine how exhausting, and pathologically reprehensible that life becomes? Other people shy away from those who do too much and a guilt factor comes into play. They end up blaming the perpetrator for their feeling of inadequacy and the situation snowballs.

I knew a girl who sacrificed a great job to go to a foreign city. Her reasoning was fine at the time she left. She wanted to be with her partner and hoped her educational qualifications would help her get a job in the new city. Two years later, she'd not managed to secure a decent job and was hanging on to her partner like a life raft. To her, he was a child who needed constant care and attention. She saw that as her role, to be a mother figure. In truth, she was using that as her excuse for not even stepping out of the house to look for work opportunities.

Well, as you can imagine, it got too overwhelming for him after a while. He didn't need mothering, he needed a partner.

So yes, you may begin something with the best of intentions, but if you add twenty spoons of sugar to a cup of really well-made tea, it'll still be undrinkable. It's as simple as that. Therefore, a person who is very high in the narcissism spectrum has what we call an NPD or a *Narcissistic Personality Disorder,* which is qualified as a mental illness.

Self-diagnosis of tough individuals is becoming more prevalent as narcissism and the problem becomes more widely discussed. Many folks nowadays claim to know someone who has a narcissistic personality disorder, even though it is very rare (between 0.5—1 percent of the overall population or one in every 100 people). This appears to be especially true at work, where interactions may grow particularly hot and contentious.

Disliking someone because of a mental condition is unethical and unfair. When you're angry, you may spout phrases like "my boss is totally nuts" or "she's a raging narcissist," but pathologizing others can be harmful. Besides further stigmatizing people who actually have mental health diagnoses, labeling someone as having a psychiatric disease trivializes the seriousness with which narcissistic personality disorder may be.

So long as we have mere narcissistic traits without going overboard, we're only bound to be mildly selfish from time to time, and usually when self-preservation comes under excessive threat. A person with a narcissistic personality disorder, on the other hand, follows a deeply ingrained pattern that is nothing short of pervasive. Their sense of self-esteem is as fragile as a piece of glass exposed to high temperatures, and they always mask it with an air of unbearable superiority. Interact with them long enough, and you'll find that your days and nights are a constant play of praising and catering to their inflated egos, and wondering why nothing seems enough.

In your larger environment, you need to be especially careful before going and attaching a "narcissist" label to somebody. But this also means that you should be on the lookout when someone comes across as intrinsically damaging in important contexts, for instance, in the workplace. Why? Well, people with narcissistic personality disorder attract lawsuits because they can't handle criticism and respond in harsh ways whenever it comes to them.

Also, narcissists are very drawn to power, but always supplement in with an exhausting need to be admired and extremes of unethical behavior. When you marry these traits to a complete lack of empathy, such people can completely destroy workplace morale.

We discussed the general traits you need to look out for. The Diagnostic and Statistical Manual of Mental Disorders by the American Psychiatric Association provides a more "clinical" way to know whether someone has NPD. The criteria for diagnosis include an overwhelming need for admiration and constantly seeking external approval; a deep-seated sense of entitlement coupled with extremes of condescension; an inability to understand the feelings of other people; largely superficial relationships; and constant, unexpected mood fluctuations. It's as good as existing alongside a ticking time bomb.

People with NPD are likely to engage in thinking patterns and behaviors that are completely unreliable and unwarranted. They'll thrive on making false accusations and manipulating facts to gain attention. Rules and boundaries matter zilch to them. And, the only love in their lives (save themselves) will be towards tactics like public shaming, blame deflection, and gaslighting.

Understanding The Difference Between Narcissism and NPD

We already know narcissism translates to being overly preoccupied with themselves or desiring praise and appreciation from others to the extent that it impinges on healthy relationships and setting proper boundaries. If left unchecked, too much self-attention can hinder normal social function.

Otherwise, we can safely assume that *all of us* need to be praised and admired at some level or the other. These needs can even occur differently during different stages in our lives. For instance, during our school-going years, praise and admiration may be sought via academic excellence. When our parents, teachers, or other caregivers talk favorably about our abilities, it makes us happy, and it motivates us to keep working hard, to some level, so that we may continue to get praise.

As we mature into adulthood, this need becomes transformed into something that's more physical. We seek appreciation based on how we look, carry ourselves, speak, and so forth. We also desire approval from different people depending on situations and age.

Melody Wildman, in her article labeled *"I'm a professor of human behavior and I have some news for you about the 'narcissists' in your life,"* writes that narcissism is a personality trait possessed by all of us to different degrees. Likewise, she agrees with the predominant notion that a degree of self-centeredness is productive. When we look at the mirror to ensure we're in good shape, keep healthy boundaries in our relationships, or do things from time to time to keep our sense of self-preservation intact, it's fine.

When we talk of "narcissism" in general, we talk about something that's more extreme. The levels we'd link narcissistic behavior to include unusually high margins of selfishness, arrogance, and insensitivity. And these margins aren't necessarily pointing to "self-preservation." Rather, they come by way of the person naturally possessing them because that's all they know about life and living. This is NPD, and it bears a formal diagnosis.

Narcissism is a human characteristic that almost everyone exhibits now and then. It is possible that you have a propensity to inflate your own significance, or that you are envious of your coworker's accomplishments. This doesn't necessarily mean you have NPD. Even I get worked up thinking others are ahead of me in life. That doesn't make my anger plausible for a diagnosis. There are other instances in life that may cause the nerves to jitter like teeth in cold weather.

At times, we forget to look at the situations of others close to us because we're too wrapped up in our own lives. We keep making up excuses to seem better or to get out of tricky situations. We know friends or have siblings who're always trying to be the family pet. Early on in their lives, a close friend of ours developed the notion that manipulating and deceiving others is the only way to earn appreciation in life.

We know someone whose ego is extremely inflated from a childhood presupposition instilled in them by their parents (the "my child is a genius" rhetoric). All of these traits are narcissistic and exist somewhere in the spectrum, but for those with NPD, these are permanent fixtures. There's no cure just years of therapy to reduce the effects.

A parent who has NPD, for instance, will always try to single out a child as "special" based on which of their children will suit their needs the most. They'll assign lower status to other children. Even with the children they favor, they'll constantly alternate between excessive adulation to over-shaming them. The children will feel a perennial need to keep satisfying their caregivers because there's a good chance they'll be too afraid of what happens if the parent isn't in their best mood. Narcissistic caregivers will also nurture contempt for the child's needs—affection, emotional support, or validation.

NPD parents will look at their children as extensions made to support and validate their own existence. To ensure this happens, they will try to manipulate and control all behavioral patterns of their children. They will devalue children who shy away from what they deem is right. For instance, if the child grows up to join an employment or study in a university that doesn't validate the parent's ego, they'll likely cause trouble.

The same applies if they get involved with people the parent considers "beneath" them. A mother with NPD, for instance, may keep pointing out flaws with her daughter and berate her in the attempt to feel superior.

It isn't unusual for parents to consider children as commodities to a certain extent. When I say commodities here, I don't mean that they consider their children as clothes or cupboards. Rather, all parents, being humans, would have honed ambitions at different points in their lives. It isn't possible to fulfill all these ambitions in one lifetime.

So, when they have children, they form a belief, often subconsciously, that their children will do what they could not. When the child chooses a life path that veers away from the weight of these expectations, the parents are bound to feel anger and disillusionment, even disappointment. But in most cases, parents make their peace so long as their child is happy and thriving in the line they've chosen for themselves.

They accept the child's right to make their own decisions and live life on their terms without consciously looking for ways to sabotage their plans. The same can't be said of NPD parents, who will constantly remind the child, both verbally and through actions, of how much disappointment and hurt they've caused the family. Nothing the child does will calm an NPD parent who feels the child has let them down.

Someone with NPD will not treat you like this just once or twice. Their interactions and discussions with other individuals are likely to follow a set of patterns. A person who is trying to create good self-esteem could, on the other hand, rely on the support of others. Without regular reinforcement or praise, a spouse who seems insecure does not necessarily have NPD.

When you enter a relationship with a partner who has NPD, you may notice an unusual amount of devotion at the get-go. They may tell you they love you within days to weeks, gush over how wonderful you are, and keep emphasizing they've known no one as good as you. They will try to charm you and treat you as someone special and deserving of their attention until you go and do something that doesn't fit their expectations of what's right or doable. Over time, you'll notice they're constantly angling for compliments when you're not offering them.

You'll find yourself being the brunt of hurtful words on a daily basis. When you try to stand up for yourself, they'll say they were joking and you shouldn't take them so seriously. They'll also ask for regular validation of how attractive and endowed they are, and never bother with offering you any support or attention (unless you decide to leave). Every time you make a mistake, you'll be mocked till you can't take it anymore.

When you try to call it quits because you've just about had it, a partner with NPD will threaten self-harm or refuse to let you go by promising you will never be happy with anyone else, and if they can't have you, no one else should. They'll ask friends to convince you to stay, call you incessantly, and show up with expensive gifts. You'll find yourself caught between contradicting tirades of "You're never going to find anyone else" to love affirmations like "You're the one; I can't live without you."

A Hypothetical Scenario

Let's look at what happens when your partner is someone with a narcissistic personality disorder. In this scenario, your partner has just returned from work. You are about to go out. You've already let them know you've made plans to meet a friend the night before.

They respond by telling you, "But I just got home! Wait till you hear how my day went! I'm about to get a promotion this week, but I think my talents deserve a better company and pay grade!"

You say you'd love to hear about their day later, but you need to rush now since your friend is waiting. This shouldn't be an issue at all, because they already know you'd made plans. But, the moment they hear your urgency, their attitude takes a 360-turn. They launch a subtle verbal tirade. "Why do you care so much about this friend? Don't they have any other friends? Why do they only want to spend time with you? I'm your partner, and I am much more important. You're supposed to keep me first."

You try to stay calm. You remind them you'll be back soon, and you can spend the entire night conversing about their day. They're not about to back down from accusing you. "Maybe I'm not going to be here when you get back. Why should I waste my time with someone who'd rather be with their friends? You never have any time for me." With this, they leave you in silence.

This could very well be a situation where you're handling someone with NPD, particularly if you come back home to the same kind of resistance, and this scenario happens time and again.

On the other hand, what happens if you come back home and find your partner is sincerely apologetic? They tell you, "I'm sorry I reacted so terribly. I should have considered your feelings. I thought you didn't want to hear about my day and got angry."

In this case, while your partner may need to deal with self-esteem issues, they're not affected by NPD. Individuals who have NPD will *never* be bothered about how their actions make you feel unless they're afraid you will leave them. Then too, their statements will come across as superficial and remind you of how lucky you are to have them. It'll hardly ever be a situation where they stop to consider how you'd be feeling.

Regardless of what you may think, the best kind of diagnosis is one that can be given by a professional. If you're afraid someone close to you is exhibiting traits similar to people with NPD, consider getting in touch with a licensed psychiatrist for a proper evaluation.

Healthy Narcissism Is Also A Thing

Now that we know what dangerous narcissism looks like, the good news is not all narcissism works the same way. Healthy narcissism helps you recognize and accept your intrinsic value. It is a kind of self-love that allows you to keep yourself first in situations that demand a bit of selfishness. When you have healthy narcissism, you understand you have unique abilities that make you special but don't assume they make you better than everyone else in the world.

Healthy narcissism can come across in someone who says they deserve better when they're passed over for a promotion they truly deserved. It involves desiring recognition for a job done well; taking pride in the trust they earn from those close to them; and recognizing their inner intelligence, creativity, and other talents. Essentially, this is healthy because it helps you preserve your inherent value.

A few narcissistic tendencies may be seen in most people at some point in their lives. When that's the circumstance, it is possible to become conscious and try to change these habits so that they do not become disruptive. People with NPD may find it more difficult to get this understanding on their own, although it is workable with the help of a qualified therapist.

When you accept the consequences of your conduct, seek to comprehend the emotions and wants of others, and explore other, healthier ways of meeting your needs, it may be easier to become self-aware of narcissistic qualities. Regardless of whether someone you know has some narcissistic traits or NPD, they can improve in various ways. But, unless they're ready to put in the work, this change is unlikely to materialize.

THE DARK TRIAD IN POPULAR CULTURE

How many of you enjoy a good drama-cum-thriller where the protagonist is nothing short of a dark triad personality doing what they do because "they want to right all the wrongs in this world?"

I grew up marveling at the emotional coldness of Dexter Morgan. There was something about his personality I couldn't put a finger on, but it was so attractive! When I was old enough, I realized that the character had conveniently manipulated me into believing he was doing a good job killing hapless wrongdoers and playing God. The deeper we get into the analysis of his role in the beloved series *Dexter*, we see him as a wolf in sheep's clothing.

In the first season, viewers discover hallmarks of what would later become Dexter Morgan's covert profession of choice—a serial killer ridding the world of criminals. In his youth, he has a penchant for murdering innocent neighborhood pets. Animal cruelty is a common trait associated with psychopathic tendencies since it reflects a dire lack of empathy. As with most other personalities belonging to the dark triad, Dexter is also impossibly charming and very likable. He conceals his inner urges to murder with ease.

What sets the character apart from other psychopaths (in real life) is their intelligence. A psychopath who's as violent as Dexter was portrayed in the series generally comes from a poor background and little to no education—which usually translates into a life of petty crime and doing menial jobs. However, if a psychopath or any other dark triad personality is handed the right tools growing up, they may well bully and manipulate their way to the very top of their chosen path—be that the path of a CEO or a serial killer.

The question is—how far is a dark triad personality willing to go to stay concealed? In the series, Dexter's self-analyzing capacities are a tad odd for someone who is psychopathic. We have known serial killers who have displayed the same kinds of self-appraisal, for instance, Jeffrey Dahmer regretted his actions, while also thinking that he couldn't have stopped them. Herein is a very striking comparison. Dahmer likened himself to a monster who needed to be put away. In the same way, towards the end, Dexter had the self-realization he'd have to protect the ones who loved him from himself.

Some psychopaths can compartmentalize their tendencies. Research has indicated the presence of an empathy switch in some criminals with psychopathic tendencies, meaning they can feel deeply for a few people, while not caring if the rest of the world is up in flames.

The actor portraying Dexter's role himself felt the most profound characteristic of the serial killer was his ability to stay calm under pressure. This inherent calmness when everything around them is crumbling is a key reason why we feel so fascinated when we consider the minds of psychopaths. Unlike us plebeians, they can work with absolute impunity, not giving a tinker's curse about what people think. While we live in an age of constant surveillance, this kind of freedom is refreshing, even if it isn't ours.

The primary antagonist in Korelitz's 2014 book *You Should Have Known* and the 2021 television miniseries *The Undoing* is Jonathan Fraser. When his spouse, Grace, and son, Henry, find out that he is on trial for the death of his lover, Elena Alves, the narcissistic psychopath, begins to play mind games. And it's compelling to watch his thoughts play themselves out.

Through the ages of popular culture and its various nuances, we humans have been fascinated by individuals who are masterminds of intrigue, deception, and manipulation. The same can be said for how so many of us are attracted to Joseph Goldberg from the Netflix Series *You* or Fraser from *The Undoing.* Fraser himself is among the newest in a crowded room of iconic dark triad characters, from Iago, a purely Machiavellian figure in Shakespeare's *Othello,* Lord Varys and Cersei in *Game of Thrones,* the narcissistic Kathryn of *Cruel Intentions,* or Regina George in *Mean Girls,* to Satan themselves in Milton's *Paradise Lost.*

It's not that the roles of dark triad personalities only play out in notoriously dark and deadly courtroom thrillers or drama shows and films. They can also feature in romantic comedies and stuff that's sugar-sweet otherwise. Take Hugh Grant as Daniel Cleaver in the very beloved *Bridget Jones's Diary* films. The role of Cleaver was a take on Jane Austen's character, Mr. Wickham, from the cult classic *Pride and Prejudice.* You could say, in making these characters the notorious individuals we read of and mused about, the authors and filmmakers were largely inspired by traits making up the dark triad of personalities.

Many of these characters display traits that would link them to Machiavellianism, one of the three dark triad personalities. People displaying these personalities are motivated by duplicity and acting in ways that will perpetuate their personal gains. They also display risky behaviors in acts of intimacy. While such traits do occur in other genders, for instance, the character of Love Quinn in the Netflix drama You, Jenna Maroney from 30 Rock, or Amy Dunne in Gone Girl., they are largely dominated by men. Regardless of your sexual orientation and gender, you will encounter someone belonging to the dark triad of personalities at least a few times in the course of your life.

The Attractiveness Of The Dark Triad Personalities

People with narcissism and psychopathy may not be attractive to most of us as friends or love partners, but for some reason, we find ourselves drawn to those who possess both. Moody vampires and mean girls are both discriminatory tropes conveying desirability traits in today's popular culture. Although I can't imagine the thought of a vampire sucking life out of me to be appealing in real life, I keep falling for shows and books that predominantly blossom romance between innocent young girls and narcissistic vampires who are over a thousand years old.

Recent studies have shown that those with "dark" personality qualities are physically more alluring than others. Knowing what appeals to them can help us figure out why people with certain personality qualities are so good at taking advantage of others.

A psychologist from Durham University, Dr. Gregory Carter, specializes in the study of narcissism. His research is largely centered on why we find the people displaying the dark triad personality traits to be so attractive. Basically, he wants to know why individuals who we know are awful to us, who we know we can't trust, who are completely self-obsessed, are the stuff of so much obsession, both in real life and popular culture.

You're not alone if you've searched *"Why can't I stop falling for bad guys?"* or, in fact, if you've ever penned the iconic lines *"Why am I drawn to individuals who are awful for me?"* while tearing your hair out wondering whether something is wrong with you, and not the people you choose to be with. Carter believes the dark triad personalities largely attract women, in particular, young women.

Let's quickly recap the predominant traits of each dark triad personality type. Narcissists thrive on an inflated sense of self-worth and self-love. They consider themselves to be better, more beautiful and intelligent, and more of "everything good" than anyone else. They love competing so long as they're likely to win. The limelight is their favorite place to hang.

Machiavellian individuals largely live off of interpersonal manipulation. They tell others what they want to hear with the covert aim of maximizing their own benefits. Finally, psychopaths are characterized by an absolute absence of empathy. They lack concern about the feelings of others and engage in all kinds of social deviance simply because it makes them feel good about themselves.

A man belonging to the "dark triad" is one who goes down the hall of dark fame as the proverbial "bad boy," or, in a more modern context, "fuccboi [sic]". There's no end to social media posts and the burgeoning styles of florid articles that highlight how you can spot these men. For instance—"10 signs you're dating a fuccboi", or anything to this effect.

The *Urban Dictionary* describes the modern "fuccboi" as a manipulating tool who will do whatever it takes to benefit himself, irrespective of who he's screwing over in the process. If there's a scandal around him, he's going to be in the center of it— but he'll find a way to skirt around the blame and ensure the brunt of all of it falls on some hapless innocent's shoulders.

In this scenario, it so happens that nice guys do finish last. But with the dark triad, all forms of attraction are generally short-lived. No matter how hard you fall for someone who has a dark triad personality, they will always strike and move on, meaning they'll do enough to get you to be ensnared, and either destroy you before leaving or leave because they can't destroy you.

We can wonder what makes them so attractive. Carter believes that narcissism, and other dark traits, bear an overwhelming superficial charm that is very attractive to be around. They dress well, they peacock, and they have a body language that makes you want to talk to them, to know more about them, and essentially, fall in love with them.

When we speak of smooth body language, we refer to someone who's remarkably self-assured. You'll notice them from a distance, a charming smile on their faces, a relaxed posture, and fluid movements. You'd marvel at how composed and cool they are, and how they can hold eye contact without fidgeting or twitching. This makes them very appealing, because you immediately think, "here's someone who owns who they are. They'd make good mates." Deep within, these people may burn with insecurity and the need for validation, but you'd never guess.

And you're already in your primal instinctual mode, which considers the term "mates" not from the perspective of love or relationships, but from a more procreative level. The good first impressions dark triad personalities make leave you desiring to procreate with them, simply because they look like people who can hold their own in all situations.

They come across as people with high value, and you think they'd make brilliant partners. Machiavellians and narcissists seek positions of leadership and may be highly successful, which makes them all the more attractive. Because of their desire for high status, they are prone to portray themselves as important individuals, and they do this very convincingly.

In the beginning, it may be impossibly difficult to resist the narcissist, Machiavellianst, or psychopath's allure. When someone is physically appealing, they tend to have a host of other favorable attributes instantly associated with them, which is known as "the halo effect." When we see someone's physical attractiveness, we naturally assume that they are also more compassionate, intelligent, and self-assured.

First impressions are critical, and a visually appealing veneer is a powerful tool for accomplishing this. Even more effective is the combination of physical attractiveness with self-assurance and humor, and it appears that those with unscrupulous personalities are also more successful in this.

So, if you are attracted to a dark triad personality, know you aren't alone. First off, they're truly convincing as go-getters and come across as individuals who will love and care for you "just as you deserve." They will go after you as hard as they can. Remember, these personality types enjoy the thrill of the hunt, so they're going to have a ball chasing and manipulating you into a place of vulnerability.

However, as time passes, and the mundaneness of a long-term relationship settles in, they'll likely be frustrated. This doesn't mean they'll voluntarily break up. Many will seek to keep you around while playing elsewhere. After all, why should they be constrained to sleeping with just one person when they have the universe worshipping at their feet (at least, that is what they believe)? Many will also turn the tables to create such scenarios where you take the onus of breaking up on yourself.

One thing we may not consciously be aware of is the proliferation of these dark triad men in social media apps geared towards dating, especially ones based on validating one-night stands. These apps, particularly in dense urban areas, appeal to dark triad men because of the viability and apparent availability of potential victims. Since the sea is literally full of fish, they're even less inclined to put up pretenses about being devoted to a single partner. The anonymity with which they can carry out their lecherous acts works as an added godsend.

So, why do we go on with the hopeless "If I show them how much I'm willing to do, I'll *make* them love me." narrative? Now, this narrative has become increasingly hackneyed, in part because of how popular culture keeps portraying vulnerable young women who give up promising careers to stay with abusive partners. You scream and yell at them from the other end of the screen, wondering why they can't see what you can.

However, allow me to ask you something. Would you be able to get out of there quickly if someone came into your life promising you sunshine and safety and showering you with a love like you've never experienced before, only to turn into a cold-hearted manipulator a few weeks to a few months later? For most of us, *it's not that easy. Or simple.*

We end up blaming ourselves for the changes we see in these manipulators. We think they're becoming cruel and cold because *we* made mistakes and drove them away from us. Regardless of how cruel or inhuman the dark triad personality becomes, because of how dependent we've become on them, we keep holding on to the thread of "it wasn't like this at the start."

Plus, abusive personalities often confuse their victims by promising change. I've known this in the course of my life as well. The husband beats up his wife, and when the wife tries to leave, he breaks down and says he'll never do it again. The wife thinks he won't survive on his own and stays on. So it goes on, in a vicious cyclical pattern.

Dark triad personalities are also remarkably difficult to call out about their indiscretions, manipulations, and blatant lies. The only time you'll see a narcissist in their truest devil state is if their ego is under terrible threat. God help you if you find a loving partner or a good job and make them feel like you'll do just fine without their presence in your life. That isn't acceptable to them.

Another thing that constantly draws us to dark triad personalities is their ability to dish it out. Oh, it's so refreshing to be near someone who has a sharp sense of humor married into relatable sarcasm. We identify the issues with this far later, when every lie we try to call them out on becomes a self-deprecating joke.

So, if you ask, "why didn't you tell me you were meeting a female colleague over dinner?" You may well hear a response like, "your husband's career is in the hands of the fragile female ego. Trust me, it's not something I'd want, but it seems my bosses think I should wear some frocks and drink cosmos at night." You brush it off, laughing. The dark triad personality has a secret ball, confident they've lied and omitted themselves out of a tricky situation. To them, the very act of living is like reading a script and doing it well.

Let's step away from this for a second. In the literary works of Shakespeare and Milton, the moral dilemma of designating boundaries to what is good and evil, to the stubborn notion that all of us have Satan inside us, the rating question remains—what makes someone a predominantly dark triad personality? Sure, we may all like being selfish occasionally, but that doesn't mean we're all narcissists, does it?

You can breathe. It doesn't. Genetics and nurturing play a very important role in who becomes a majorly dark triad personality. Coupled with heritability is childhood trauma—for instance, abusive parents to excessive exposure to bullying or harmful external environmental situations.

Most of the characteristics of dark triad personalities are concerned with an immense amount of self-preservation traits, which naturally stem from growing up in situations where deviance was one of the major routes to survival. If you grow up in an environment where you have to lie, cheat, steal or kill to get what you desire before it goes to someone else, you'll come to a point where you naturally become, well, a master manipulator.

Men with varying levels of the Dark Triad qualities were rated on their attractiveness by college women in a study. The physical qualities of the men remained the same, but the three psychological attributes they had differed greatly.

Individuals with a higher score on the Dark Triad Attributes were found to be substantially more appealing than others. Mostly, the men who scored high in narcissism, Machiavellian characteristics, and psychopathy were seen as such by the women rating them. In other words, the raters weren't in the dark. They knew full well they were singling out dark personality traits as the more attractive of the participants, yet they consciously chose to do it, anyway. Why? I'd say they felt that with enough love and attention, the "bad boys" would become gentlemen.

There lies the conundrum. Manipulators who have intrinsically come to see deviance as the only means of surviving may not necessarily consider their acts to be morally sound. Indeed, they may not even understand what we mean when we speak of moral soundness. But there's no denying the skills they've learned are useful and have served them well. So, if they're succeeding in life because of how dark they are, the question is—*why would they stop? And why would you think you could make some change in their way of life?*

If these behavioral tendencies bring success, dark triad personalities will continue to perpetuate them. They'll have a script ready for all of it. The first date. That interview. The promotion meeting. The break-up talk. The convincing, manipulation, and deceit. You'd give them an Oscar for screenplay if you could. You'll likely never know they're beyond any rehabilitation because *they'll never give themselves away,* at least not consciously. Each new target will present a new script for them, one they'll eagerly take on, and likely carry out with elan.

As long as the overall feedback remains positive, they'll keep acting as they always did.

The research done by Dr. Carter considers why the dark side of our nature is so physically attractive. To an extent, this can explain our age-old fascination with arch-manipulators and heartbreakers. We go into these relationships thinking, *"So what if the rest of the world couldn't change them? I'll do it. I'll prove everyone wrong."* Ah, but it's not that easy. If it were, the world would be a funnily quiet place to be alive in.

It may be beneficial to take your time while deciding whether or not to create an opinion about someone you've just met. More than five centuries have passed since Machiavelli's *The Prince* began doing the rounds. Yet, people inspired by his masterwork continue to dangle our hearts on strings of thread. We pine over bad boys in films, books, and TV. We rally into obsessing over dark romance tropes, where a dominating storyline continues to be an alpha bad boy and a sweet, innocent damsel who'll stay with him no matter what hell he sets loose. It's art imitating life, not the other way round.

While we continue to fawn over the mysterious charm of the dark triad personalities, maybe, after reading this book, you will approach such relationships with more carefulness. Popular culture often shows a reformed narcissist in the end. The bad boy becomes a doting father who can't possibly love anyone save his wife. The serial killer becomes a model citizen. The rapist says sorry to his victims. Unfortunately, sometimes, the dark reality of life is that none of these happen, and dark triad personalities continue to exist in the shadows of notoriety because that is what *sustains them.*

Maybe some will truly change and give you fairytale endings. But then again, maybe not. In *Othello,* when Iago finally gets arrested, it's not before he has destroyed pretty much everyone around him. Including causing the deaths of Othello and Desdemona.

Washington University's Michael Strube and Nicholas Holtzman have displayed interest in studying the relationship between physical appeal and the tendency to veer towards narcissists, Machiavellians, and psychopaths. Their work is concerned with understanding whether these traits are predisposed to successfully enhance their possessor's outward charm.

To put their theories to the test, they called upon a hundred and eleven college students. Every student was photographed upon arrival. After the initial photographs were taken, they were asked to change out of the clothes they'd worn, and put on a simple t-shirt and gray sweatpants. Women were told to remove all makeup, and pull their hair back into ponytails if it was long.

Students were photographed once again in this *au naturel* state. The researchers produced both sets of pictures to strangers who were then asked to rate the participants on a scale of physical attractiveness. This gave the researchers the ability to determine to what extent every student could increase their appeal because of makeup, accessories, and flashy clothes.

Next, Strube and Holtzman studied students' personalities and their tendencies towards the dark triad. They asked students to rate themselves and asked them for the email addresses of their friends, who were then also told to rate these students. The combination of peer and self-ratings was then used to get personality scores.

The dark triad score was distinctively linked with how they looked when they were in their made-up states. The participants with dark personality traits were not more physically attractive than others when their outward instruments (with which they'd design themselves to be more appealing) were taken away.

These findings are in line with existing research showing narcissists are relatively more popular, especially on account of first impressions. In 2010, a study collected information on the personalities of students and made them do brief introductions to each other. The students then filled out surveys where questions were built around what their first impressions of each other were.

It was found students who scored high on the narcissism spectrum were inherently more likable to a majority of the participants. They were well-dressed, with confident body language, and displayed likable facial expressions. These findings discerned narcissists can easily carry and present themselves in ways that impress others instantaneously.

Interestingly, some of us are in positions of a disadvantage because of how we are wired. *Emophilia* is a condition where we fall in love too fast, often, and easily. Those of us who display high levels of emophilia are more at risk of being attracted to individuals who belong to the dark triad, possibly because we're unlikely to test the waters before plunging in, head-first.

There's nothing intrinsically wrong with love at first sight, but impressions, especially complete ones, take an age to form. Those with low levels of emophilia will usually take a lot of time to know and understand the proper nature of someone before even considering falling head over heels for them. In other words, those of us who believe in the "love at first sight" philosophy are prone to be easily seduced by those who belong to the dark triad, because we mistake their very cunningness as charm and the propensity to love and protect us.

As time goes on and you become deeply entrenched in a relationship with a dark triad personality, you will notice their popularity fading over time—at least in your own eyes. This process can take ages, because of how skilled these personalities are at making it seem like everything going wrong is because of your ineptness. Interpersonal exploitation being a trademark of these personality qualities, people closest to them will eventually catch on and begin to shun them. Most individuals avoid long-term relationships with persons who have unpleasant personality qualities, whether in fiction or in real life. And now we get to the point where you'll see a gap between the way dark triad personalities really exist in the world and the way the media portrays them to us.

Here's another fact that may be alarming at first, but not if you make conscious choices in your relationships. Your notion shouldn't be "I want to change my partner and make them better." It should be—and this may need you to work on yourself —"I want a partner who will support my decisions to work and function as an independent individual without me needing to mother him."

Coming to the fact. It's been proven people with antisocial personality traits have a reproductive advantage over the rest of society. The genes linked to high levels of deviancy bear a strong correlation with the genes related to desires for early parenthood and parenting multiple children. In other words, not giving a hoot about the rest of the world can well be translated into a prolific urge to procreate and produce many kids.

Dark triad personality traits like psychopathy are connected to the inherent need to live a fast life. These personalities act on impulse and love taking risks. A natural outcome is they can start producing early on and have more and more children as they grow older.

When you combine the initial attractiveness and physical appeal of these personalities with impulsive behavior, a devil-may-care attitude, and high sexual drive, you get a situation where they're not only winning from an evolutionary perspective but essentially *thriving*. The genes that make up the core of their systems have the potential to get transferred to their children in time. It can be uncomfortable to think about, but it's evolution working as it always has.

Now, evolution doesn't quite worry itself about things like justice, political truths, honesty, or morality. It isn't concerned with our social states, it's too busy perpetuating our existence. This means that traits facilitating attraction, and to an extent, reproduction, will probably be passed on—irrespective of whether those who possess them are reincarnations of the devil himself.

The bland truth is very few dark personality predictions in popular culture come across as completely inhuman or unlikeable because people won't be able to take it. They need to have a golden heart, a moral compass, a love for selective people, or deadly intelligence that's extremely attractive. And, of course, a magnetic personality. If every dark personality trait looked and spoke like Joe Goldberg in real life, too many of us would be trapped in poisonous relationships with no saving grace in sight.

Moving on, we'll go into talking about a trait, sometimes manipulative, at other times, purely convincing—but almost always extremely useful. This trait is persuasion, and you *need it* to survive well. All successful people have a powerful ability to persuade others. Is the public appreciating your ideas? How effective are you at persuading others that the universe can be a better place because of the work you are doing? Are you able to get the aid and resources you need to succeed?

At the heart of this, there is the notion that you must be able to communicate the key ideas and importance of your message without boring the audience. Persuasion is all about understanding and convincing your audience there's no one as good at a particular task or quality as you. And, given how competitive our current age has become, trust me when I say it is necessary. More in the next chapter.

CHAPTER 3
THE CHARM OFFENSIVE: PERSUASION

LET'S do something a little different at the outset of this chapter and begin with a case study. Follow along, and at the end of the study, you decide who'd be the most successful persuader.

We begin with a hypothesis where two men are introducing themselves to two women. For purposes of the study, let's name the men Adam and Hayden. In the same way, let's call the women Lili and Coraline.

Roll first scenario. Adam is a youthful man, good-looking and kind. He's preparing to meet Lili at a lunch date after being introduced to her at a mutual event the previous night. He's developed a liking for the young lady and wants to make a lasting positive impression.

To maximize impact, Adam takes time to shave and shower, styles his hair, and wears flattering clothes. He greets Lili outside the restaurant and holds the door open for her to go inside first. He notices she's wearing pretty red heels and compliments her on them. As they wait for their starters, he begins a conversation on the most recent episode of *Money Heist*. At the party, he overheard Lili enthusiastically discussing the main character of the program, and he had the idea of centering his first chat around Lili's enthusiasm for this character.

So, they discuss theories surrounding the protagonist and appreciate each other's takes on him. From there, Adam comes to a place of comfort where he asks Lili about her interests, hobbies, and background. They talk about mutual friends, and he lets her know a funny story about one of them. The date ends on a pleasant note, and Adam leaves the restaurant feeling satisfied.

Roll the second scenario. Hayden is a strapping young man, keen on impressing a girl he'd met at a mutual friend's party the night before. The girl's name is Coraline. As with the first scenario, he likes her charisma and beauty and wants to make a lasting impression on her.

Now, Hayden doesn't like to take risks. He's done a lot of background research on the art of influencing people, and he's found some foolproof methods. They include smiling a lot, showing genuine interest, calling a person by their name often, being a good listener and encouraging the person to converse about themselves, and using various methods to make the other person feel important.

Hayden understands people are bound to be persuaded by those whom they inherently like. He also knows people are drawn to those they can relate to—so, a degree of similarity, be it in personality traits, lifestyle, opinions, or overall background, can be very helpful. Lastly, he recognizes the importance of maintaining eye contact and offering heartfelt compliments.

Armed with this knowledge, Hayden searches for Coraline's profile and finds her pages on Instagram and Facebook. He studies the pictures and captions and makes note of the things she likes and dislikes. In one post she's dressed as one of the Professor's crew from Money Heist, with the caption, *"Long live Tokyo!"* In another post, she shared a picture with a false beard, and the caption *"Bearded men are so hot!"*

Hayden begins planning the date. He considers every aspect carefully—from choosing the restaurant, cleaning up after himself while maintaining his beard, delving into theories about Money

Heist and its character Tokyo, and everything else he's studied. Hayden also happens to know physiological arousal is a thing that can be induced by dilated pupils. Seeing someone with dilated pupils may make them seem more attractive—and dim lights, in general, tend to enhance physical appeal.

At the restaurant, he chooses a booth with dim candle lighting. Everything on the date goes according to plan, and Coraline is both pleased and excited at the prospect of having met a man who shares so much in common with her. She makes the promise of meeting him again and follows through with it the very next day. She can't take her mind off the man who understands her likes and dislikes, word-for-word.

I'm going to stop here and ask you to look beyond the apparent "creepiness" of the second scenario. Many of us may feel it's wrong to look someone up before meeting them. Then again, in the digital age, where we make entire plans to hook up based on filtered photos we see online, is it really so wrong to study someone's profile before going forward? with something— especially when there is an urge to make a good impression? I have a feeling if all of us could be this dedicated or persuasive, we would. Yes, there's nothing wrong with the first scenario either, but the amount of persuasiveness is far higher in the second one.

With the first, you're letting life pass you by and to be your genuine self. With the hope that it's going to be enough. And, in many cases, it will be. What if you're in a more challenging situation that needs you to have serious background information, though? What if you need to know what you're getting into if you hope to be successful at it? These are instances when you'll need to be a Hayden, not an Adam. Because what Hayden has is a distinctive advantage—*he is extremely persuasive.*

A DEEP DIVE INTO PERSUASION

The twenty-first century is a time of ideas. The capability of persuading those around us, and being able to influence hearts and minds into acting in certain ways, is notably one of the greatest skills of this century. We're in an economy where knowledge is becoming increasingly commodified, and everything is viewed from the lenses of competitive value. It is the age where being able to persuade the world your ideas count is most important. Merely possessing good ideas won't get you anywhere. The world has to know, see, and feel your ideas making the difference they are seeking.

Some economists believe persuasion alone does the heavy lifting for generating a quarter of the total yearly national income of the USA. Globally, economies are migrating from agrarian to industrial to ones relying on knowledge, and to be successful, people in nearly every career have to hone the skill of convincing others to take action.

Persuasion plays out in the simplest aspects of our routine lives. Politicians persuade people to cast votes in their favor. Job candidates persuade interviewers to hire them over other applicants. Entrepreneurs persuade investors to help with their startups. Our caregivers persuade us to choose one career over another. Leaders persuade employees to take certain plans of action. Salespeople persuade customers to buy their products over a competitor's—the list is endless.

There was a time when persuasion was considered a soft skill, but that isn't the case any longer. It has grown into a fundamental trait that can help you sell your products, market yourself as intensely employable, build brands, trigger movements, and inspire the world at large. It has become so important that the billionaire, Warren Buffett, displays a public-speaking certificate from a Dale Carnegie course in his office—it is the only diploma on display there. He has told business students repeatedly that improving communication skills can be the difference between being unsuccessful and boosting employability and professional value by 50%.

The power of words and ideas has built the modern world, where entire industries, like the burgeoning influencer industry, are entirely reliant on the shoulders of people with ideas and the power to persuade the rest of the world about the salability of these ideas. Over two thousand years ago, the Greek philosopher Aristotle wrote of a method to master the art of persuasion in his *rhetoric*. Plenty of great communicators since have used Aristotle's methodologies to deliver some of the most influential presentations and speeches—some of which we will remember till the end of time.

The Saxon Clincher

I will digress for a minute to draw your attention to one such eminent speaker—Abraham Lincoln. All of us have our own opinions on those who shaped the course of history, but what we cannot contest is the enormous hold these people had over humanity at large. Indeed, one of the most significant acts Lincoln carried out during the course of his presidency lay in delivering the Gettysburg Address.

On 19th November 1863, Abraham Lincoln gave a speech at Union Cemetery following the Battle of Gettysburg. The intention was to mourn the loss of soldiers who died in the vicious battle, but it went on to achieve far more than that. The Gettysburg address was one of the most important speeches to be given during the civil war, and it was suggestive of all the United States was struggling with during that time. Lincoln was effectively able to touch upon the emotions of the majority population at the time, to the extent that his address continues to live in many hearts to this day. Why? Because it gave people *hope.*

So, when Lincoln said, "all men are created equal," he undoubtedly heralded an age of free expression, and with it, immense controversy. He goes on to say the deaths of those who fought in the battle would not have been in vain but would herald in a new age of people where the government would be by and for the people, and exist forever.

A wonderful little book called *Farnsworth's Classical English Style* highlights one useful persuasion tool modern aspirators of leadership can take from influential stalwarts like Lincoln. Now, the English language is a marvel in itself. Unlike many other languages that have their roots in ancient culture, English has grown up as a hotpot of words from different groups that have found their way to the British Isles over time.

Much of the original English language was made out of the language of invaders entering Britain around 450 AD from regions like Saxony and Anglia. Six centuries later, the French invaded and brought their own language to the Isles, and this was derived from Latin. New French competed with the existing old English, resulting in modern English that carried aspects of both. So, words that have purely Anglo-Saxon traits usually appear very direct—for instance "get", "need", and "want". On the other hand, words that have French origins feel flowery on the tongue —"acquire," "require," and "desire."

What Lincoln would do was heavily mix two kinds of words to deliver maximum impact. He liked to begin his words with a touch of Latin-influenced English, and then move into ending with a predominantly Saxon finish. Consider the words from this speech, for instance.

> *"Either the opponents of slavery will arrest… it is the course of ultimate extinction… its advocates will push it forward… lawful in all the States, old as well as new."*

These lines are taken from his "House Divided" speech, which he begins in a formal style. He uses words like "opponents," "extinction," and "advocates" which are all Latinate. He closes the speech with fourteen straight single-syllable words, and almost all have an Anglo-Saxon origin.

This could be the key to your next maximum-impact speech. More complex, ornate Latinate words are good for demonstrating experience and expertise on a topic. They make you come across as erudite. But too much of it can overwhelm your audience, for sometimes, it isn't about the most beautiful word, but *delivering something that is both simple and profound.* At the end of your speech, when you move to use plain words, you create a situation where people know you aren't just good at what you do or think, you also know how to sell yourself to the world at large.

STEPPING INTO THE DARKER SIDE

In itself, persuasion can be understood as a process by which a person's behaviors and resultant attitudes are influenced by someone else. The power of being able to persuade can help you argue on behalf of or against ideas, influence decision-making, and herald actions that will have significant impacts on you and those in your immediate vicinity.

The Greeks were the first to use rhetoric and elocution as a means of persuasion, and they set the bar high. The Assembly was an audience to every trial, and the strength of the speaker was relied upon by both the defense and prosecution.

Every compelling argument, according to Aristotle, consists of three essential parts. The first is *Ethos,* which elucidates the knowledge, credibility, stature, authority, and expertise of the one who is speaking. The second is *Logos,* or the appeal of reasoning, cognitive and critical thinking, and logic.

The final trait is *Pathos,* an appeal to human emotions which influences the non-thinking, non-cognitive motivations behind decisions and actions. In short, the core of persuasion is a marriage between three traits—credibility, logic, and emotions.

Yet, there is a different kind of persuasion out there in the world. And this one is called dark persuasion. Influence may be referred to as persuasion. A person's views, attitudes, intentions, motives, and/or actions may be influenced by a speaker. Furthermore, it is often abused for personal advantage. According to Immanuel

Kant, reasoned persuasion is the only ethical approach to attempt to influence others or their conduct.

Anything else is morally and ethically wrong, he says. Persuasion cannot be irrational in this circumstance. If we are given an option, how can any aspect of persuasion be dark? The distinction between persuasion and dark persuasion is a matter of intent. Someone who isn't very good at persuasion may approach a friend and ask them to do something without giving it much consideration. They may even care about engaging in predominantly righteous acts for the greatest number of people possible. With a dark persuader, this is not the case. They have a distinct goal in mind, and they know precisely what they're doing and where they're going.

The idea of persuasion and manipulation that is prevalent in dark psychology has some parallels. Because both of them are used to influence the victim's intentions, actions, attitudes, and beliefs, they are regarded to be complementary. If you think about it, this makes a lot of sense. How would you classify something as manipulation, not persuasion?

It's widely held that one is more legitimate than the other, but persuasion isn't as altruistic as we'd like to believe. When our employers persuade us to work overtime, or we are persuaded to choose a course or path in life that doesn't appeal to our intrinsic natures, we can't really say it's altruistic for us.

In our day-to-day lives, we use many forms of persuasion for the purpose of accomplishing a range of goals, but one of the most significant of these goals is to bring together persons who have different points of view. To alter a person's perspective about a certain thing, idea, or event in their professional life, for instance, one strategy that may be used is the persuasive argument.

During the course of the procedure surrounding dark persuasion, the other person's ideas, emotions, or facts will be communicated to you in the form of written or spoken statements. To accomplish one's personal objectives is another common driver behind the use of persuasive techniques.

One may argue in favor of a trial as a selling point during a presentation for potential customers or during an election campaign. However, despite the fact that none of these are seen as being in any way positive or negative, they are used to give some kind of impact on the listener. One approach to thinking about the concept of persuasion is the act of using one's own personal or institutional resources to influence the perspectives and actions of other individuals.

The art of persuasion can be practiced in a variety of ways, including the use of logic and reason to sway people's opinions through systematic persuasion and the application of emotions or behaviors to sway people's opinions through heuristic persuasion. Both of these methods are examples of persuasion. Mind control may take many forms, but one of the most common is persuading others to see that one particular viewpoint is the most legitimate *for the good of everyone concerned.*

We end up believing we are doing something to help everyone, but in reality, we're only fulfilling the interests of a small cohort of skilled manipulators. For instance, during a conversation on politics, you can attempt to convince the other person to see things from your point of view. The act of listening to a political campaign will persuade you to vote in a certain manner. There is a significant amount of convincing that takes on whenever someone is attempting to offer you anything new.

The majority of people are completely oblivious to the fact that they are being controlled in this manner because of the overwhelming "it will be good for you if you do it" or "your future self will be happy" perspectives offered by those skilled in the teachings and methods of dark persuasion. You know you have a problem on your hands when someone attempts to convince you to believe in concepts and views that are in direct opposition to the ones you already hold.

There are many approaches to persuasive communication. Even if they don't want to do it intentionally, each one of them will make an effort to shift the target's perspective in some way. When a politician makes an appearance on television on Election Day, they are attempting to persuade the public as well as the voter to cast their ballot in a certain way.

When you see an ad on TV or online, the company behind it wants you to buy that product. All of these ways of trying to change someone's mind are aimed at changing what they think about the victim. To get the person to change the way they think. Dark persuasion has nothing to do with morality. The reason isn't always moral and sometimes isn't moral at all. If good persuasion can be understood as helping people help themselves, then dark persuasion can be seen as a way for people to act against their own best interests. People sometimes do it reluctantly because they know it might not be the wisest option, but they want to stop the constant attempts to get them to change their minds. Sometimes, the most skilled dark persuaders can lead people to believe they are being smart when they are actually doing the opposite.

If you've seen films like *The Wolf Of Wall Street,* you'll notice how entire professions like stockbroking completely rely on the art of dark persuasion. Stock brokers know that the best investors are the ones who can be persuaded into believing their investments are going to yield huge payouts in the near future.

However, once their money is in the system, it keeps moving in cycles. The brokers are skilled enough to ensure the investors don't withdraw the cash, and they keep earning lump sum amounts in commission. All through the mere persuasion tactic, which motivates people to think they're doing something amazing.

Dark persuasion also has a different result than positive persuasion. When persuasion is positive, there is an element of mutual benefit involved, regardless of how big or small it may be.

So, even if someone may be getting hoodwinked into doing something, there will be a degree of benefit for them.

The persuader, of course, reaps in the rewards of being able to persuade someone to act upon their will—but there is a positive for everyone involved. This means that there is no situation in which the manipulator is the only one who gains.

On the other hand, in dark persuasion, the hoodwinked person has nothing to gain from being influenced to do something. They end up becoming the victims of an act where they continue to give or lose a large number of resources and their mental health, with the false supposition of gaining something substantial in the process.

The results of dark persuasion are very different from one another. The persuader always comes out on top, either right away or because of his twisted need to control and have an effect. The person who is persuaded goes against their own best interests. Lastly, the best dark persuaders not only hurt the people they try to persuade, but they also hurt other people. Take a bad influencer who tells someone to kill themselves so they can collect on their insurance. The persuader not only gained monetarily, but the victim also died, along with hurting everyone who was ever concerned about their wellbeing.

Therefore, what are the primary goals of these nefarious individuals for whom persuasion is nothing short of a dark enchantment? There is a wide variety of styles and formats for persuasive arguments. There are some people who will go to great lengths to convince others to behave in a manner that will be to their advantage.

There are certain individuals whose acts are driven only by malice. They stand to gain nothing financially by persuading anybody, yet they do it nevertheless because they take pleasure in causing their victims misery and anguish as a result of their actions. Some people prefer the feeling of control that they get from using dark persuasion.

People who fall back on dark persuasion as a way to get what they want are largely indifferent to or unable to comprehend the impact of their acts on others. They can be complete narcissists who believe the only requirements which can possibly matter are their own. On another spectrum, they may have serious mental illnesses like sociopathy, which renders them incapable of comprehending the emotions or feelings of others.

It is impossible to have a healthy connection when both parties in the partnership are under the spell of evil influences. Both sides try to control situations, and both sides are only concerned about their own well-being. The connection becomes psychologically abusive if the partners keep abusing one another for their own ends.

For instance, one partner may not allow the other to take up the job they want or even step out of the house. They keep persuading the victim of how dangerous the world beyond the four walls of the house can be. In return, the victim keeps abusing themselves and forms a toxic dependence on the relationship.

Components Of Dark Persuasion

When it comes to persuasion, various elements should be kept in mind, just as with other forms of control. These components aid in determining exactly which persuasion is most effective.

There are several ways in which persuasion might take place. Persuasion can take place without the use of hypnosis, hypnotherapy, or any of the other methods of brainwashing, telepathy, or manipulation. Persuasion can be observed in a variety of contexts, including conversations with people you know, online interactions, and broadcast media, such as radio and television. Nonverbal and verbal approaches can also be used to persuade others, although verbal methods are far more effective.

In itself, persuasion can be viewed as a symbolic process by which persuaders communicate their message in a free-choice environment in an attempt to influence other people's views or behaviors. The victim is usually permitted to make decisions of their own free will, which makes persuasion strategies unique in that they aim to change the victim's will to that of the persuader in the long term.

The person being persuaded can choose how they want to believe, if they really want to make a purchase, or if they think the evidence is strong enough to change their minds. The key here is to deliver an argument so convincing that the victim will believe it is in their best interest to comply with the interests of the persuader, although they are being duped into believing they are exercising free choice. Persuasion has a number of components that help us better comprehend this complex issue.

Traditionally, persuasion is viewed as a symbolic process of exchange via which a certain set of people, typically the recipients of a thread of communication, are convinced to change their thoughts, attitudes, and behaviors regarding one or multiple issues. This necessitates the presence of a symbolic element. In other words, persuasion employs words, sounds, and images to deliver a message to a victim.

You may question the logic behind this, but it's actually quite simple. For a person to be able to convince another person to change a perspective that may otherwise be a core component of their way of thinking, the former will need to prove to the latter why they should act according to the former's recommendations instead of their own.

This can be done by using mediums like vocabulary, tone, speech, sound, and visuals to make an argument proving the case of the former, that is, the person who is trying to persuade. Images offer visual proof and are among the most effective ways to show evidence necessary for persuading someone to choose one route as opposed to another.

Next, persuasion has to be a deliberate act in influencing others to perform or think certain things, whether they want to or not. Necessarily, one would not use persuasion unless they are trying to implement some kind of change in the ones they are trying to persuade. To be able to make someone else believe what the persuader does, the latter will employ a range of particular strategies. It could be as simple as presenting conclusive proof or sitting down to a friendly debate with the knowledge that the evidence they have will surely change the mind of the one being persuaded. It could also rely on insidious and deceptive forms. In most cases, the person being persuaded will feel as if they are exercising free will in coming to their final decision for or against the topic of interest.

For this very reason, persuasion can only work if the evidence at the hands of the persuader is presented in a very palatable form. This makes the art of persuasion extremely subjective. I'll explain why. Let's say a salesperson is trying to persuade a client to go for a car higher than the budget they came prepared with. Now, the salesperson can go on arguing different causes as to why the client should go for the higher budget car, but a time will come when the client will get annoyed with their persistence and tell them off.

However, if the salesperson is able to show the client some salient features depending on the latter's taste and style of preference and make these features the highlight of their persuasion tactic, they are far more likely to be successful in persuading them to make the expensive purchase. But this tactic may not work if the client has no desired features in mind and only wants a simple model for daily travel. In this instance, the salesperson will really have to think and come up with an alternate persuasion strategy that will target a latent interest the client may have, which is sometimes entirely subconscious. Let me illustrate.

Salesperson: Why are you looking to purchase a car right now?

Client: It's more for my wife. She enjoys traveling in comfort, and her workplace is pretty far from home.

Salesperson: That's great you're buying something for your spouse. Is she generally fond of these smaller models?

133

Client: She loves sedans, but I'd say they're out of my price range.

Salesperson: You'd be surprised at just how affordable some sedans can be! Plus, our showroom has models that give great mileage and don't use as much energy. You can also consider easy loan options with meager interest rates. Your savings, in the long run, will make every penny worth investing. Would you like to take a look before you make up your mind?

This tactic has a good chance of winning the client's mind because it's targeting someone close to him, not just his own interests. While the salesperson is subtly implying that he will save more money in the long run. He is also telling him that he can undoubtedly afford to buy the sedans showcased so long as he takes a loan. The client, already wondering whether he's making the best choice for both his budget and his wife, may think this is hitting two birds with one stone.

This brings me to the art of subliminal persuasion.

Subliminal Persuasion 101

In simple language, subliminal is something that exists beyond the realm of ordinary and explicit human consciousness. Those with a dark disposition who are determined to succeed often communicate in ways that are difficult to decipher. The practice of transmitting subliminal signals has been referred to as the "dark art of persuasion" for a number of years. People often connect subliminal messages to schemes involving politicians or advertising, and they assert that the alerts are used to affect our ideas and actions in some way.

One of the most essential aspects of hidden signals is the fact that no matter how diligently we look for them, we will never be able to become consciously aware of them. The use of subliminal messaging is popular in the advertising industry, as advertisers attempt to capture more of your hard-earned dollars by delivering messages to your subconsciousness. As an example, casinos in

Ontario, Canada had to disable slot machines that temporarily displayed pictures promoting more gambling in February 2007.

The next point that we need to know is that those who believe in cryptic messages think that they are a prevalent and long-term means of communication that has been developed to make people respond and do things that they usually wouldn't do. In other words, they think that subliminal communications are the real deal. When James Vicary convinced people (via subtle advertising tactics in films) to consume popcorn and drink Coke in the year 1957, it became the most well-known example of subliminal advertising. Advertisers may benefit from such an influence if it is successful, but customers who wind up paying for things they don't need suffer greatly. Subliminal advertising has been outlawed in several nations as a consequence.

The idea that there are people out there using the power of subliminal messages to appeal to our subconscious is even more dangerous. You may have heard the words "conscious," "unconscious" and "subconscious" being tossed around at random when we talk about how our minds work. All of them point to one notion—our minds, and the resultant behaviors of these minds, are not as rational as we'd think them to be.

Our internal abilities to control our thoughts, experience emotions the way we want, or synchronize all movements *are subjected to the whims of the subconscious.* This is why some things hurt more than they should, forgetting painful relationships takes more time than we have, and some of our movements happen suddenly and at random.

Sigmund Freud came up with his three-level mind model, by which the mind has three components to thinking. The first is the conscious mind, which defines all our ways of thinking and actions occurring within the realms of pure awareness. So, when we consciously look at the petals of a rose and admire its beauty, we are completely in control of what we are doing.

The subconscious denotes all kinds of automatic and reflexive reactions which we do without thinking twice, simply because we've done them at times in our past, to the point of them becoming ingrained in our minds. For instance, knowing how to swim years after having learned it for the first time. Or, driving a car a decade after we got our license and finding nothing has changed. Finally, the unconscious discerns all memories and past events which do exist at the backs of our minds but are largely inaccessible. For example, pinpointing that exact feeling we had when we first learned to walk, or to say our first word.

We have executive control over our minds because of our conscious minds. We can think, assess, feel, and experience with full awareness thanks to our consciousness. Consciousness is not the same as our subconscious. Many people are suspicious of subliminal messaging since they are based on the idea the human mind may be influenced by hidden information in audio or video advertisements. Seeing or hearing anything for as little as one-fifth of a second may have an impact, and seeing a subliminal message or hearing a single phrase is all it takes.

Subliminal signals having negative connotations are more likely to be seen and retained by the human eye and mind, according to research. "Agony," "murder," "despair," and other negative emotions are more likely to be registered by your brain than phrases having good emotional connections, according to British research cited by CBS News. Using subliminal signals to make viewers or listeners feel anxious may be regarded as a bad result.

When it comes to information processing, our subconscious is often far more potent than our conscious mind. If someone is attempting to influence your thoughts or behavior using subliminal messaging, you may not be aware of the danger you are in. The issue with subliminal persuasion is you never know how potent it may be. Some methods of subliminal persuasion can impact our stimuli via eyesight, smell, touch, sound, and taste.

The methods of persuasion via the use of subliminal messages are essentially three-fold. The first is the building of a relationship to make the potential recipient of the subliminal message feel comfortable and get them to open up. This can be accomplished via observing the recipient over an extended period to understand their core moods and states of being. The next is via convincing and powerful discussion, which will connect the recipient to the evocations being induced by the advertiser.

Correct words or whatever forms of media are being used will help the persuader come across as convincing without being conniving or a liar, which in turn helps persuade the recipient they are placing their trust in the right individual.

Finally, we have suggestive power. This is the association of useful components to discussions and interactions. It helps the recipient to open up to desirable ways of thinking. The persuader has to have a central or dominant idea that will appeal to the recipient's subconscious mind and help them come to terms with what the persuader is trying to achieve.

Not all forms of subliminal persuasion are bad. Creating self-help podcasts for weight loss, raising self-esteem, enhancing memory, quitting smoking, and more has become a multi-billion dollar industry. These are all subliminal persuasion tactics that, while benefiting the persuaders, also cause well-being and upliftment among the ones being persuaded. The outcomes of these recordings have not been conclusively studied, although individuals perceive changes, which may just be a placebo effect —but aren't necessarily harmful.

Covert Persuasion

As with any other form involving the art of influencing anybody other than yourself, the categorization of covert persuasion as "good" or "bad" is largely subjective and dependent on what ends you intend it to serve. Every day, hundreds of thousands of words are written about the mysterious workings of the human brain.

We all have different opinions and some of our fiercest debates are about how we think, and how these thinking patterns can be changed or remolded. What we can agree on is this—if we want to persuade someone, *their minds must necessarily align with ours, if not in its entirety, then at least for the major part.* To do this, we have to understand what motivates and drives the other person.

When we have that knowledge, we can position our techniques of influence in a way that those being influenced accept what we say or suggest with little or no resistance. They should think we are on the same terms as them and have their best interests in mind, which necessarily means if they comply with our requests, they choose to gain.

The word covert means something that is hidden or secretive. The word persuasion means the act of making someone do something, whether by reasoning, entreaty, or debate. It also means to win someone over to act upon something, either by inducing or reasoning with them. Further, it can mean making someone believe in something. So, when something is covert, it is not likely to exist in plain sight. It will be concealed from our naked view.

One of the most unsettling aspects of covert persuasion is the fact that all the techniques used are entirely moral. Because of this, it is considered to be one of the most effective methods of persuasion. The techniques of covert persuasion are honest, despite the fact that others may see them as crafty and deceitful. They are considered sinister and ominous due to the fact that no one would ever suspect your motives, which will seem inherently unobtrusive. However, the tactics will be of help to you in convincing other people to make the choices that you want them to make.

Within covert persuasion, one of the most important goals is to successfully convince your clientele, audience, etc., without drawing attention to the fact that they are being swayed. The greatest approach to sway your audience is to master the art of persuasion via the power of language. Rhetoric is a skill that takes use of this human tendency to be swayed by persuasive speech.

In part, the success of covert persuasion depends on the persuader being able to change the client's or customer's mind without them being aware of what changes are happening within themselves. The mere act of achieving this requires the persuader to possess immense faith in their vocabulary prowess because a sure-shot way to persuade anyone is through the power of the right words, spoken at the right time and under the right circumstances.

An enterprising real estate agent is unlikely to make a huge commission trying to sell a house at someone's funeral. Yet, if they go to a funeral with the sole intent of getting information on new or soon-to-be-empty lots, with the right words, they may chance upon all the information they wish to gain.

The Car Crash Study

During the 1970s, Elizabeth Loftus, a leading memory researcher at the time, conducted an experiment that would, later on, be known as the car crash study. She was concerned with how the flow of information after a particular incident's occurrence could potentially affect how the eyewitnesses recounted the event.

Her primary focus during the experiment was to study the influence of misleading information of both a visual and verbal nature on eyewitness testimony. Regarding the verbal aspect, she sought to study how the wording of questions could influence or change eyewitness perceptions.

Loftus's findings were indicative of memory for any kind of event that has been witnessed can, against all odds, be highly flexible and subjected to change depending on manipulation. If someone becomes exposed to new kinds of information or evidence in the interval spanning the distance between the time they witnessed the event, and the time they recalled it, these new kinds of information can heavily influence the amount as well as the substance of what they recall. Original memory, it was found in the course of the Car Crash Study, could be changed, modified, or supplemented.

Along with another psychologist, John Palmer, Loftus engaged in a classic psychology study in 1974, later known as *Reconstruction of Automobile Destruction,* the hypothesis being the language used in eyewitness testimonies could influence and alter memory. They aimed to prove leading questions could change and distort testimony accounts of eyewitnesses and have confabulating effects.

The account provided by eyewitnesses, according to their study, could be distorted by cues supplied in the questions asked. For testing their hypothesis, Loftus and Palmer asked a group of participants to give an estimate regarding the speed of the motor vehicle through different forms of queries.

Estimating vehicle speeds is not generally held as common knowledge, which makes the answers very open to guesswork and interpretation. If you asked me something about a random vehicle's speed all of a sudden, you can bet I'll be taking wild guesses in the dark. This means, *I become very open to suggestions and being convinced since I have no idea whether I'm correct, anyway.*

For Loftus and Palmer, forty-five American students made up the sample for their experiment. They planned the setting as a laboratory experiment with five conditions. Only one of each of the five conditions was experienced by each of the participants.

Seven films involving traffic accidents, ranging from five to thirty seconds in duration, were presented in a random sequence to the members of each group. After the participants had finished watching the films, they were asked to recount all that had happened as if they were eyewitnesses to the accidents which had occurred. Then, they were asked specific questions. One of these questions was on the lines of how fast the cars were moving when they collided, smashed, bumped, hit, or came into contact with each other.

The speeds estimated by the eyewitnesses were all impacted by the verbs used to voice the questions. The verbs carried the weight of information regarding the speed and therefore systematically influenced the memories of the participants as to the accidents. So, participants who were asked questions with the verb "smashed" felt the cars were moving faster than the participants who were asked the same questions, except with the verb "hit" instead of "smashed."

As a matter of fact, the participants who posited questions using the verb "smashed" reported the highest speed estimates of the cars involved in the accidents (at 40.8 mph). They were followed by those participants who received questions using the verb "collided", and who thought the cars were moving at 39.3 mph. Then followed the participants who answered the same questions, except the verb used was "bumped." The group which answered next was asked the question using the verb "hit," and those who thought the cars were going at the lowest speed were asked the same questions using the verb "hit."

The results of the experiment proved the verb had a lasting impression on the speed at which the car was traveling and therefore led to alterations in participant perceptions. Eyewitness testimonies, therefore, could be altered and biased by the questions posed after the occurrence of a crime. There are several reasons why this may occur.

The first cause is the interplay of response and bias factors. The misleading information provided may have influenced participant answers without causing a false memory of the event that happened. So, the participant's memory may be just fine, but the power of the word is such that their answers become manipulated.

The entire representation of the participants' memory may have altered. The use of the critical verb, in this instance, changes the participants' entire perception of the accident that occurred. These critical words can lead to entire differences in perceptions regarding what actually happened, and the participants' memory and recollection of it. This manipulated perception is stored in the participants' memory and becomes the core of what they eventually believe. It may be entirely unrelated to the actual course of events.

If the second explanation is the more relevant to the truth, we can surmise the minds of the participants would "remember" other details which may be completely irrelevant to the real-life incidents that have occurred. To test this, Loftus and Palmer conducted another experiment. In this experiment, a hundred and fifty students were shown a one-minute long film featuring a car driving through the countryside. This clip was followed by four seconds of visuals involving multiple traffic accidents.

After the visuals ended, all students were questioned about what they had just viewed. The independent variable lay in the type of question that was being asked. For fifty students, the question was manipulated to ask them how fast the cars were going when they hit each other.

Another fifty were asked how fast the cars were going when they smashed with each other. The final fifty were not asked any questions at all and formed the control group of the experiment. A week later, the dependent variable was measured. Without being allowed to see the film again, all participants were asked ten questions. A critical one was placed at random on the list. This asked whether the participants noticed any broken glass when they had last viewed the visuals a week back. They were told to answer with a "yes" or a "no." The original film had no broken glass involved.

It was found participants who were asked how fast cars were going when they "smashed" with one another were the likeliest to report the visuals involving broken glass. The results of this second half of the experiment proved memory could be distorted by the questioning techniques used. The information collected after a particular event could interfere or merge with the original memory of the event and result in a reconstructive memory or a completely inaccurate recall.

The findings from experiment two show that this impact is not merely due to a response bias since leading questions really affected the recollection a respondent had for the incident. The insertion of erroneous elements into a recollection of an event is alluded to as confabulation. This has serious ramifications for the queries used in police questioning of eyewitnesses. If used unscrupulously, it can absolutely manipulate eyewitness accounts of crimes that have actually happened, which means that innocent people can end up being blamed for things they did not do.

Turning A No Into A Yes

Now that we've spent a good amount of time looking at what kinds of persuasion we need to be wary of, let me take you through a form of persuasion that may be important to you, especially if you work in a profession like sales. To prove my point, let us delve into a particular case study involving Colleen Szot. Colleen Szot was among the most well-known writers belonging to the paid programming industry.

There is a good reason behind Szot's overarching popularity in the programming industry. Not only has she penned well-known infomercials which have propelled sales for famous exercise machines like the NordicTrack, but she has also constructed a program that went on to shatter twenty years' worth of sales records for a home-shopping platform. Szot's programs contain many elements common to many infomercials. She relies on flashy taglines, posits an imaginary audience that is always extraordinarily enthusiastic, and also leans on celebrity endorsements.

What made all the difference for Szot was changing three words in a standard infomercial line, which resulted in a proliferation of people purchasing her product. These three words made it clear to potential customers that ordering the product could involve a hassle, but they should stick around nonetheless *because the product would be worth it.*

In the world of sales, a familiar call-to-action line that all of us have heard at one point in time or the other goes *"Operators are waiting, please call now."* Szot changed this line to *"if operators are busy, please call again."* The change seemed pretty insignificant on the face of it. It kind of tells the customers (or potential customers) they may have to waste time and patience dialing and redialing the number until a sales representative finally answers. This also feels counterproductive, right? Well, wrong.

Social proof is a very strong thing. When people aren't certain about what course of action to follow, they begin looking to others for guidance. So, if someone has no clue how to proceed with something, they will probably look outside them for guidance on how to act or make decisions.

With the first line, which goes "operators are waiting, please call now," the image is, well, self-explanatory. It suggests the operators are nothing but a bunch of bored people who have nothing better to do apart from waiting for potential customers to call and lift them out of their state of ennui. There is no sense of urgency, and this also means when potential customers keep hearing this line on repeat, they end up thinking their time will be wasted, because, who wants advice or information from someone with too much time on their hands?

It's the age where value has become attached to how busy people are. The more free time you show you have to the world, the more they will think you to either be jobless or someone who thrives off of making mischief and irritating others. I cannot tell you how many times I've cut a call simply because I got annoyed with the representative calling me during a rush office hour.

The first thought in my mind was "have they nothing better to do?" Which is, in retrospect, illogical because *calling me is part of their job.* But we don't stop to think that way. And this philosophy is exactly what Szot understood.

So, consider how things change when the line becomes "if operators are busy, please call again." My immediate mental image is, "Wow, the product must be really popular. That's why so many people are calling to inquire about it." I begin to picture operators moving from call to call without getting time to breathe. I think there are thousands of people just like me, and they believe in the product being sold, which is why this product must be amazing for me too. This tactic has been utilized by marketers for a long time to pique the curiosity of potential customers.

Classical findings in social psychology show the power of social proof for influencing the actions of other people. Stanley Milgram and his colleagues conducted an experiment where an assistant of the researchers stopped to gaze at the sky in the middle of a busy sidewalk in New York City. They did this for a minute. Most people walked around the assistant without bothering to see what he was looking at. But, when the researchers added numbers to make four assistants who did the same thing, four times as many passersby stopped to join them in seeing what they were so busy viewing. In other words, we become influenced by a particular message even more if we are led to believe that there are multiple people out there who believe in the power of this message.

However, if you expect others to own up to this, you are likely headed for failure. If you gather a bunch of people and give them the "if Jack jumps off the cliff, will you follow suit" talk, they will brush Jack off as an anomaly.

What I mean is, that people are very unlikely to admit their behaviors, thoughts, and actions are subject to manipulation and persuasion based on the actions, thoughts, and behaviors of a bunch of other people out there. The point is, that they may not be aware of this discrepancy themselves. People can be remarkably unaware of the various complicated nuances which affect and influence their overall behavior.

The need to fit in is so ingrained in us that we don't even realize how it affects our actions. An experiment by Goldstein and his colleagues in 2008 involved people who work in the business of making tiny cards with encouraging words left in hotel rooms, exhorting their guests to reuse towels. Rather than considering what motivates the larger crowd, these employees made these cards based on the question of things that would constitute the core of their own motivational pursuits.

The problem with doing this is that the employees fail to recognize *their own motivations are the result of influences garnered from the thinking patterns of the outside world.* Consequently, they concentrated on how well the towel reuse scheme would contribute to the conservation of the environment, a motivation that seemed to be the most pertinent to the positive goal, at least on the surface.

The hotel experiment began by acknowledging a fact. Whether unconsciously, subconsciously, or through conscious practice, a majority of hotel guests who found "towel reuse" signs reused towels at one point or the other during their stay.

The researchers wondered what would happen if they simply informed the guests they were doing this. Would this new information influence how they participated in conserving the environment? If yes, would this kind of participation be more, and different from the kinds of persuasion achieved in other, more basic appeals for environmental conservation? The researchers elicited the help of a hotel manager and made two signs to be kept in the hotel rooms.

The first sign contained a basic message geared towards doing your part in conserving the environment. This message is pretty commonly used throughout the hotel industry. It requested the guests to help in saving the environment by showing their respect for nature and all life forms. To do this, all they'd have to do was participate in the towel reuse program.

The tourists were notified on a second sign that the majority of hotel guests reused their towels at least once while they were staying there. The act of letting individuals know that others who are similar to them have done something that society would approve of is an example of a form of persuasion that is known as the social proof appeal method. The hotel rooms were allocated these placards at random. The hotel's room attendants volunteered to collect the data for the researchers.

On the very first day of servicing a guest's room, the attendants recorded if the guest had chosen to reuse a minimum of one towel. The guests who learned the majority of other guests were reusing their towels through the social proof appeal set of messages were shown to have a 26% more likelihood of reusing the towels compared to those who received the basic message asking them to reuse towels for conserving the environment.

That was a 26% increase in participation rates relative to relevant industry standards, achieved simply by virtue of using a few words on signs to tell people what others were doing and encourage them to follow suit.

What are the other things to consider? When promoting your best-selling items, don't forget to invite delighted customers and clients to provide testimonials. It's also critical to include client testimonials when making presentations to new prospective customers who may be skeptical about the value your company can deliver.

Or, even better, you can create a scenario in which your existing customers may speak directly to potential customers about how happy they are with your company and the services you offer. This may be done by inviting both existing and new clients to a brunch or educational event and arranging seats so they can comfortably mix. Talking about the positive aspects of working with your company will be a natural topic of conversation for them here.

Of course, you will not elicit positive responses if you shape the messages in a random or offensive manner. Yes, people do follow others when it comes to being influenced, but they do not like to be told they are being a part of a crowd or a rat race.

If the message had read something on the lines of "other people are reusing towels, so you better do it too," the guests would have likely perceived it as a threat instead of a gentle, encouraging message teaching them how others were doing their part in achieving something great and therefore receiving praise and appreciation for their thoughtful actions.

You see, people choose to go the majority way because they understand this is the route to maximum social acceptance. When they learn a number of people are doing something, they believe if they engage in the same thing, they'll likely reap rewards like social recognition and greater acceptance.

When trying to convince people to follow through on a preferred course of action, keep in mind the actual power of social evidence. Not only is social proof useful in shaping public policy, but it may have a significant influence on your professional life as well.

Have you heard of optional attachments? Let me share what it is with an example. Someone has the option of purchasing one of two pups. They would like any puppy as a pet, and each one is unique. They consider which puppy they might imagine themselves keeping, and regardless of which one they chose, they are concerned that the other pup will be the better of the two. Wouldn't they be pleased with their decision? You'd think they'd be pleased, relieved, or even content with their choice. Nonetheless, they are unhappy. They begin to second-guess their judgment.

When people are given too much time to consider their alternatives, they tend to believe that whatever they chose will cost them something because they are not choosing the other option. The primary issue is the option they are presented with. When the individual realizes they must forego the alternative choice, they experience disappointment and loss. According to a persuasion study, it makes little difference whether the individual has directly experienced both possibilities or is only imagining one. Whatever choice people choose, the alternative seems more appealing because they cannot have it.

After completing my undergraduate degree, I wanted to study a bit more. I applied to a number of colleges and got through to two of those I had dreamed of going to the most. Now, I was faced with a conundrum—which made more sense to me? I thought and thought and ultimately chose the one which was closer to my hometown. I was meant to feel happier with the choice I made, but I would carry a lifetime of regret over not choosing the other college, although I was certain I would have felt the same way if I chose the other one instead of the one I went to. In short, it is human nature to feel the grass is greener on the other side.

According to the persuasion study, it makes little difference whether the individual has directly experienced both possibilities or is only imagining one. Whatever choice people choose, the alternative seems more appealing because they cannot have it.

Skilled persuaders know and understand this, and they can use it to make it seem as if those being persuaded will be getting the best of both worlds. They know how to create a sense of urgency and the fear of missing out on something great, although it may not be real at all.

Consider a website that is selling "limited edition candy, only 200 pieces available." All of those who get to lay a hand on this candy will feel invariably lucky. While the others who thought they made a wiser choice, by not spending extra cash on silly little trophies end up feeling jealous because they missed out on something that's a limited edition. Lo-and-behold, the company announces a resale with just 50 pieces more. Can you imagine the pandemonium that would ensue on the site?

The techniques which constitute the heart and soul of covert persuasion can be summed up before we move on.

A covert persuader begins by identifying the source or the problem they want to change. This problem can be anything.

Someone may no longer be serving their interest in a certain regard. An advertising campaign may no longer be as successful. A relationship may have run its course. No matter what the issue is, the point remains that the persuader *is unhappy because of this particular issue and wants to change the trajectory.* They may either want to remove the offending person from their lives by persuading them they are "better off" without their presence, or they may simply influence them to act in a way that will make the persuader happy.

Next, the persuader begins the act of letting the persuaded understand why they are upset about the current state of affairs. This is done in a way that makes the persuaded feel the existent state is bad for them as well and has become a pain point. The moment they begin to, let's hypothetically assume, consider a relationship or a sales strategy or anything that is displeasing to the persuader, as legitimately bad for them as well, one-third of the persuasion job is done.

A clever persuader will always have their way, but also make the persuaded feel that their free will is of utmost importance. So, in the next step, the persuader will ask for solutions to better the state of affairs. They will make the persuaded think and come up with solutions. Once these solutions are presented, the persuader will either nullify them through strong reasoning or incorporate them into their plan of action. Let's look at how this may happen.

Persuader: I feel that this relationship has grown very stale. We don't get any time with our friends or family. We are always with each other. Don't you think your health is getting affected by staying in the house with only one person day in and day out, too? I feel concerned thinking you aren't taking care of yourself. What's your take on this?

Persuaded: I never thought about it like that. I agree. We should spend more time with our family. Would you like me to hold a dinner for everyone?

Persuader: If you spend all of your time in the kitchen, you won't have much time left to spend with your family. Do you not believe that there is anything you might be doing that would allow you to spend more time with them?

Persuaded: That makes sense. What do you think I should do?

Persuader: How about spending a week with them? I could help you book the tickets and you can go have a relaxing time at home. I have a very busy week with work too, so you don't need to worry about me. All I want is for you to get some time with other people you love.

Now, the persuader may be planning any number of things that the persuaded may not be aware of. Their intentions may be absolutely genuine, or they may be planning a trip to a Vegas Casino, for all I care. The point is, that they are allowing their partner to feel like there is free will involved, although they are the ones pulling the strings here.

Here, you also intrinsically know your audience's pain point. You have studied them long enough to understand they miss their friends and family, which means that you are better equipped to get them to make a decision that will feel like it's coming from their heads but is actually coming from yours. You know they will benefit from the decision you are making for them because it is treating a legitimate pain point. So, a clever persuader *will always take time to get to know their audience.*

The last thing you will notice is that nowhere does the persuader say something like, "no" or "you are wrong" or "that doesn't make sense." Instead, they launch a counteroffensive that is as disarming as logical. The thing is, when you say a blatant "no" or disagree openly with your audience's point of view, you put them on the defensive. They become angry and decide they'd rather trip and fall flat in a puddle of mud rather than agree with someone so condescending.

For this reason, you need to be careful with your counterarguments. Whatever they do, they cannot invalidate the people you are trying to persuade.

UNCOVERING DIFFERENT PERSUASION TACTICS

We know how effective persuasion can be if it is used well. Skillful wielders intrinsically know persuasion is a tool that can serve any number of ends, especially if human emotions are concerned. This brings us to the next topic of discussion. When we speak of persuasion, we necessarily refer to a number of tactics common to all methods used to persuade others. Let us take a look at seven of these tactics.

Tactic One: Concealing Your True Intentions

This tactic can be used to both good and bad ends. Let me first explain why it isn't all bad. Back in college, I used to be a very open person. In that, I literally had no tricks up my sleeve. If I wanted something, I let everyone around me know I wanted it. A placement company visited us during the penultimate weeks of our final semester. I had always been interested in the company, so I told my friends I would be sitting down for the interview. I knew I had the grades and the charisma; so with any luck, nothing would stop me from being hired by them.

One of my friends at the time did some research (or so they said) on the company and warned me about them. They told me the company's retention rates were miserably low, and they also had terrible ethics when it came to employee management. Through this and a couple of other words, they convinced me to not sit for the interview because "my talents were better used elsewhere."

I thought I had dodged a bullet. A month later, I went to the company website to just see who they had hired from my university. And guess what? There they were, in a shiny new uniform bearing the company logo. My friend had ousted me and done it like a pro.

I learned something on that day. Most of the time, when we tell many people about our plans, we will never get to fulfill them the way we'd want to. Something or the other keeps going wrong, for good or for bad. On another trajectory from the instance I just shared, you may have made plans to do something special with your friend, but at the last moment, something more urgent has come up.

Because your friend already knows you are supposed to spend time with them, imagine how disappointed they will be. Think about the fact that you may not have told your friend that you would help them out in the future or that you would do something unselfish for them. Consider this option. Someone who is completely unprepared for your kindness will be completely taken aback by any act of consideration that you do for them. This is one of the many advantages of keeping your intentions concealed.

While you can use this tactic to keep yourself safe from manipulators, it can also help you further your own interests. This law is also concerned with thwarting the attempts of your opponents to undermine your goals and ambitions. When your competitors in business, sports, or life know exactly what you plan to achieve, it is much easier for them to sabotage your efforts.

This holds true regardless of the context. However, since you have concealed your objectives, they are unable to predict the acts that you will do next. As a direct consequence of this, you will finally be able to pursue your goals without constantly being under the radar of external expectations.

An effective way to conceal your actual intentions lies in acting in a manner that is unexpected of you under normal circumstances. To keep others guessing about your next move, you could, for instance, support a cause or an event or a person you are usually against. While others are left wondering why you have suddenly changed sides and your mind, you can continue to pursue your goals towards your real agenda. This could become a tactic to confuse your enemies and keep you on the right track in the pursuit of your own ends.

Let us look at evidence of this tactic in history. Otto von Bismarck wanted to destroy Austria for the benefit of securing Prussia's superiority. Prussian politicians and officials were opposed to the idea of a long-drawn-out war, but eventually, after years of resistance, Bismarck was able to secure their approval.

However, when the statespeople finally agreed to the war, Bismarck found the time was inopportune. Austria boasted a military that had far more leverage than Prussia's, was better trained and had immense manpower. Under these circumstances, Prussia's army would never win the battle against Austria, and Bismarck would have to deal with an embarrassing, not to mention devastating, defeat.

Bismarck cleverly met with the King of Austria and convinced him that war was useless. He delivered an impassioned speech on the benefits of long-term peace and why they should forgo the senseless killing caused by wars. So heartfelt was his speech that the Prussian king requested his troops to stand down. Bismarck used this time to prepare his troops.

Over a period, when the Prussian forces had gained enough strength and were prepared to fight a titanic battle, Bismarck went against the very things he had told the Austrian King. He advocated for war, and the Austrian King, taken aback by his sudden change of heart, did not think twice. The war resulted in an insurmountable victory for Bismarck.

In the year 1711, the Duke of Marlborough, who was in command of the English army at the time, planned to invade France and found that a French fort stood in the way of his plans to do so. As a result, the Duke desired to demolish the fort. The purpose of his ruse was to give the impression that he intended to keep and improve the fort by capturing it and garrisoning it with more men.

When the French attacked, he surrendered and let them retake it. After they regained possession of it, they decided to destroy it so that the duke would not be able to use it. After it was destroyed, the duke had little trouble marching into France. This is one of the many benefits of keeping your goals a secret.

Most of us aren't any different from the ruler of Austria or the people guarding the French fort. We tend to go on appearances and on what people tell us. This is one of the important reasons why so much in this world is still governed by the power of first impressions. So many of us form an instantaneous idea of how a person will be based on our first encounter with them.

We ask ourselves the basic essential questions—do they dress well, are they cheerful, is their manner of speaking confident, and so forth. While these impressions are subject to eventual change, they do leave an indelible mark at times. If you want to be in the role of the persuader, you need to use this human tendency to your advantage.

People have a propensity to be "open books" since discussing their emotions and goals is something that comes easily to most. It takes work to keep your mouth in check, to monitor and manage how you speak, and to watch what you say. In addition, they have the belief that individuals may be won over via honesty and transparency.

But being truthful comes with a few significant drawbacks. You will find that honesty feels very subjective when it is far from what people wish to hear. A successful persuader is able to understand and use this concept. It is often more beneficial to tell people what they want to hear than the reality, which may not be as attractive.

If people find your actions predictable, the majority of them will think you are a pushover—someone with no voice or fight in them. They will cease to respect you because, well, *you appear easy. There's nothing challenging about pursuing or understanding your motives.* The more you act out in ways that are "expected" of you, the more people will know how to trick and deceive you.

On the other hand, if you disguise your goals, you have a better chance of gaining and keeping the upper hand. The good news is that it is simple to hide your intentions since it is in people's propensity to believe what they see and hear; the alternative, which is to reject the truth of what you see and hear and to imagine that there is always something else behind it, is too taxing.

You can begin doing this by working on those you want to persuade in secret. Don't let anyone know what your actual intentions are, regardless of how close the people may be to you. If no one can guess what you are working towards, and you end up achieving what you had set your mind to, the achievement may well appear more impressive.

We see this happening around us in our daily lives. That seemingly unassuming coworker who we thought would never get a raise or do anything worthwhile knocks it out of the park by closing a tough deal. The quiet classmate who always seems so boring gets a straight A in their lessons and goes on to join an Ivy League, ultimately becoming the boss of the very people who used to insult them in school. The friend who you always wrote off as unassuming becomes a successful performer. In each and every instance, you will notice there is an element involving covert operation.

Consider another scenario. Let us hypothetically assume you know someone who is very skilled, and only seems to enjoy one big win after the other. There is nothing they can possibly do wrong. You are in absolute awe of how sure they seem of themselves, and like everyone else, you feel they are invincible. That they cannot possibly make any mistakes.

What you do not see is how this person operates within the four walls of their home and office. They probably spend hours honing their skills and craft. They practice every outcome, and mull over every situation. Within every trial run they make, they may encounter ten losses and one win. What matters is that each of these trial runs helps them know what will work, and what will not.

You, at the end of the audience, only see what works, which is just what they intend. You see nothing save the cool, collected person who is a winner at everything while they work, keeping their operations hidden from the public eye.

Therefore, if you provide a decoy or act out your ambitions without letting the entire world know what you are doing, people will mistake the appearance for reality, and they will not notice what you are really doing. When the time comes, everyone recognizes success over a lot of other wonderful traits. Consider this before deciding to let others know all the plans you have for your life.

You could, for instance, be able to deflect attention away from your actual objectives by creating the impression that you are backing a concept or cause that you have in the past openly opposed. Because individuals don't normally change their minds about anything for no good reason, most people will assume you experienced a genuine change of heart. Or, as another option to keep others guessing, you might appear as if you desire something that you aren't genuinely interested in, which can cause your competitors to get confused and make incorrect calculations.

Tactic Two: Outlining

If you're thirsty and someone brings a drink of water in a glass. You notice the glass is only half-full. So, you respond by saying, "The glass is half full." In this sense, an optimist would "outline" the truth of the glass of water. Even more important than the content of your message is how it is delivered to the recipient. It's not a simple task to structure a message. In order to persuade someone to do anything, you must be careful about how you phrase what you're saying.

Frames operate because the human brain is wired to sift and organize data in a world full of distractions. Personal views, societal influences, and other components of an individual's character all impact how individuals see the world around them. To understand how and why individuals arrive at contradictory conclusions and behave differently, think of these screens from the perspective of the context they offer a person.

Tact and a grasp of the human mind are necessary for effective message framing. An effective argument is one that connects with your audience. So, when you tell someone a glass is half-full rather than emphasizing it being half-empty, you try to frame the message to say they are not completely devoid of everything.

Hypothetically, you are letting them know they have it better than many others. Outlining or framing is the process of carefully presenting or describing information in such a manner that the recipient's interpretation of the information presented is influenced.

We may change the way we categorize and link everything in our life by using outlining as a method. Outlining has three core elements. The first is placement, which means choosing the right place, time, and people to communicate with for maximizing impact. The second is approach, which lies in being careful about constructing the manner of presenting an argument.

People will respond far better to positive viewpoints than being told they are stupid and must listen to you. Wherever possible, always show them what they stand to gain from conforming with your point of view. Finally, you always need to have the right words when it comes to changing perspectives.

Consider the headlines of an article. "FBI Specialists Raid Small Christian Gathering of Women and Children," another title for the same article, paints a far different mental image than "FBI Operators Surround Cult Leader's Compound." Even while both headlines may be able to express the events that had taken place, their chosen words have a direct influence on the reader's thoughts, feelings, and reactions.

All government officials and politicians, in general, rely on the use of outlining. Advocates on both sides of the abortion issue, for example, use the terms "pro-choice" and "pro-life" to describe their respective stances. Because "pro" has a more positive tone to construct arguments on, this is a deliberate choice. Emotional words may be used effectively to convince others to perceive or accept your point of view while describing an event, business, or service in this manner.

With the right words, you can craft a message that elicits an emotional response from your audience. A single stimulating word may sometimes make a world of difference.

In other words, framing or outlining gives you the opportunity to come across as persuasive, even if your core message may be something the persuader cannot necessarily relate to. Anything is possible when the words are powerful enough and the circumstances are ripe for their use. Of course, you need to take every factor into account, including what the other person is gaining from heeding your logic.

Our purpose here isn't to hurt the people whose ideas or perspectives we are reframing. Rather, we are trying to direct their thinking in ways that will bear a measure of mutual benefit.

Tactic Three: Reflecting

One may achieve what is sometimes referred to as "the chameleon effect" through reflecting, which is a method in which a person imitates the nonverbal signals and mannerisms of the person they are attempting to persuade. If you act similarly to the person who is listening to you, it may give the impression that you have empathy. Different body motions, such as hand and arm gestures, leaning forward or reclining away, communicating with the eyes or a smile, or different head and shoulder movements, may all be examples of nonverbal communication.

Most of us do this without even realizing it, but now that you are conscious of it, you will consciously notice other people reflecting yet others. It is vital that you copy motions with elegance and care, and that you only allow a few seconds to pass between the time the individual whose behavior you want to influence performs the movements and the time that you imitate those movements yourself.

The tools of reflection are ingrained in psychology wherein psychiatrists and health counselors are often entrusted with the responsibility of reflecting on what their patients say back to them in the attempt to get them to understand some perspectives a little better. Indeed, reflection forms one of the core concepts of Motivational Interviewing, which is a form of counseling entrusting patients with the power to better their own health. Reflection has two core practitioner components.

The first is mirroring, which is a reflecting style that involves pretty much an exact repetition of what is being said by the speaker. The persuader who chooses to employ the technique of mirroring will know that the trick lies in keeping things simple and short. It usually works well enough to simply repeat key words or the last few words spoken by the persuaded.

Mirroring is enough to show them the persuader understands what they are referring to and where they are coming from. This encourages them to keep speaking because they feel they have a receptive audience they can trust. The persuaders know how to strike a balance between not mirroring enough and going overboard. Too much can make it seem as if you are trying to make the speaker's problems all about yourself. Your goal here is to make it seem as if you are the best listener they will ever chance upon, nothing more, nothing less.

Paraphrasing is the tactic of using other words as an accurate reflection of what the speaker has said. The intention of paraphrasis is not just to show the speaker you are listening, but also that you are truly attempting to understand what they are trying to say by putting yourself in their shoes. If the speaker is sensitive, they may have become a victim of the prejudices of stereotypes.

Since most of us are wired to hear only what we expect to hear, the speaker is likely in a place where they are afraid of being misunderstood. It becomes a breath of fresh air when they encounter someone (that is, the persuader) who makes their voice count, and who does not fall into the traps of preconceived notions. In paraphrasing, the persuader will study every word and the consequent emotion behind the word being uttered by the speaker. It is only after this that they will respond.

Their response will not just reflect the speaker's words, *but also their intention and emotion.* For this, it is important to not introduce the persuader's own ideas, questions, or narrative into what the speaker is saying. The persuader's voice has to be non-directive as well as non-judgmental.

The act of asking questions often comes by way of natural human curiosity, which makes abstinence from questioning pretty difficult at times. So, at the onset, reflecting may be very unnatural. The persuader has to stick to their skills and keep practicing until they develop a measure of comfort with this skill.

When the speaker is communicating something, the most immediate aspect to take into consideration is the content of the message. This will bear information, events, actions, and experience, verbalized in a manner that is true to the speaker's nature.

Reflection not only places focus on a situation, it also helps to bring relevant feelings and emotions to the foray. A successful persuader is able to reflect in a manner that will help the speaker accept and own their feelings, and therefore become ready for change. A good listener will be able to pick it up on the speaker's emotions via nonverbal indicators like body language and vocalizations. "How does it make you feel?" is a question that may not be acceptable in various situations. Identifying strong emotions like love and hatred is simple, however nuanced sentiments like affection, guilt, and perplexity are more difficult.

Nonverbal signals like body language and voice tone may help the listener understand the speaker's emotions as well. Listeners must examine the speaker's level of intensity as well as the emotions he or she is expressing.

Reflecting meaning enables the listener to echo the speaker's experiences and affective responses to those experiences. It connects the speaker's words to the speaker's thoughts and feelings. Therefore, reflecting combines both content and feeling to make sense of what a speaker has communicated. Let us understand this via an example.

Speaker: I just cannot understand what my boss wants from me! One minute he asks for one thing, and when I do it, he changes his mind almost instantly! I feel like I am chasing riddles in the dark.

Persuader: That is terrible. Do you feel very confused because of his actions?

The persuader says only two lines here, but these two lines are enough to show the listener they are truly involved in what is being said. This is a huge encouragement to the speaker, and they will probably go on to share the source of unhappiness and conflict within the office.

Here, there is a matter of choice involved. The persuader can either choose to do good and help the speaker vent without taking any other steps. On the other hand, if the persuader works in the same office, they may use the information they've gathered from the speaker and use it against them to rise to higher ranks. So you see, the act of persuasion isn't the thing that is harmful or bad here. It is *the purpose this act is intended to serve that makes it what it is.*

Tactic Four: Highlighting Scarcity

Scarcity refers to a condition where the number of resources available is insufficient in terms of the demand for these resources. When people have access to limited supplies, they behave in some predictable ways. This includes buying in a frenzied manner because of the fear of missing out on something that won't return or come with the "exclusive" or "sale" or "for a limited time only" tags.

So, have you ever purchased something you had no need for simply because you found the item to be on sale? Did you squabble with your brothers or sisters for getting something different from you? When I was a child, our parents got different presents for my siblings and me. They were all lovely gifts, and now that I look back on them, probably with equal commodity value.

However, it always felt as if my siblings were receiving better gifts than me, for the simple reason I couldn't have what they got. I think we have all been in similar situations. The concept of scarcity, whether in full form or unconsciously, was at play in all the above situations.

Scarcity enhances our attention spans to the extent of helping us focus on the one thing staring us in the face alone. So, when we are faced with a remarkable tag like "sale" on an otherwise unremarkable product, our brains tend to blot everything else out and draw our sole focus only to the items on sale. It increases the cognitive processing of relevant information and leads to the building of value perception.

While this perception may not always be valid, it is definitely overwhelming since it appeals to human impulses. It makes us focus on short-term needs over long-term goals and weakens cognitive decision-making abilities.

I will tell you how this works. We see a product on, let's say, an online platform like Flipkart or Amazon. This product has caught our eyes at different times, but we have never felt tempted enough to go ahead and buy it. There may have been any number of reasons for this. Perhaps the product was priced too high. Perhaps we did not find it "useful" or "relevant" enough.

Perhaps we wanted to look for cheaper options or simply wait around for a newer model. Now, suddenly, while scrolling by the platform one day, we find a tag attached to the product. It says that it is in low stock. Panicking, we check the product availability on other sites on the Internet. Everywhere, the item is either in low stock or sold out. We begin thinking if we do not make the purchase immediately, this product will be gone for good. Our decision becomes solely hinged on this one tag, to the extent of making us lose control over our sane thinking capacities. This is the power of highlighting scarcity.

As a result, when something that was previously readily accessible becomes rare, the resulting "threat" to our independence to own it increases our need for it even more.

When we see something that we wish to be less accessible, we feel physically tense. Direct competition exacerbates this problem. Intense emotions and a narrowed concentration might make it difficult to remain calm. When there is a limited supply of a certain opportunity, we see it as more desirable. Human decision-making is heavily influenced by the concept of prospective loss.

The fear of losing something is more powerful than the hope of acquiring something equivalent in importance to one's motivation. More important to us than making money is averting losses. There is a clear correlation between this and FOMO (fear of missing out).

Pamphlets encouraging young women who are at risk of breast cancer to perform self-examinations are more effective if they emphasize the potential harm that could be caused by not doing so (e.g., You could lose so much by failing to spend just five minutes each month carrying out a simple self-examination) rather than the potential benefits (e.g., You can gain a lot through just five minutes of self-examination every month).

A second negative emotion that might impact our purchasing decisions is the fear of feeling guilty afterward. To put it another way, the emotion we get when we contemplate how our lives might be different if we made the incorrect choice.

Decisions have to be made quickly in time-limited offers, which creates urgency in the decision-making process for the user. In reality, you may not know it, but you yourself thrive on the scarcity theory pretty often. If you are anything like me, you would have waited till your semester examinations are literally breathing down your neck and you can palpably feel the hours go by before beginning your syllabus.

This sense of urgency comes from making a scarce commodity out of time, which pushes you to study harder and block out anything else that tries to get your attention.

In the world of digital influence, platforms like Flipkart often have a count-down timer for the start and end period of a discount price for some of their products. The motivation is to compel users to grab the item with a discount price before the end period strikes. This can be even more effective than time-limited scarcity since availability now hinges on supply and popularity. You think if this sale ends, you will miss out on a steal deal.

The companies can either project the sale items to be of limited supply and therefore more desirable. Or, they can take a real-world influence. As an example of the latter, countries like India are constantly experiencing roaring oil prices because of limited supply. On the other hand, oil prices are remarkably cheap in countries like Saudi and Kuwait because of surplus availability.

Amazon does the same thing with digital influence when they make tags like "only 1 left in stock". This highlights the diminishing availability of a product and compels the user to make a quick decision. A product's popularity gives us confidence that it must be intrinsically valuable, so we jump at the chance to buy it.

In 1975, a group of participants in a research study was asked to assess chocolate chip cookies by Worchel, Lee, and Adewole. They divided the cookies evenly between two jars, one containing ten and the other two containing two identical cookies. Although the cookies in both jars were the same, the two-cookie jar cookies earned better marks, even though both jars had the same cookies! This is an example of a real-world influence of highlighting scarcity.

The notion is that if it is rare, there will be a lot of interest in it. For example, a new product advertisement may say: Get one today! They're swiftly selling out! Again, it actually pays to be aware this is a common persuasive method. Consider this thought while you make your purchasing decision. Because this approach instills a sense of urgency in most people, it works best in marketing and sales material.

Tactic Five: Reciprocity

The concept behind reciprocity as a persuasion tactic is pretty simple. Do, and it will be done unto you. When someone assists us, we feel obligated to reciprocate in kind. Overall, if you need someone to do something useful for you, think about doing something unexpectedly nice for them first. Reciprocity is a social norm that molds all human relationships. It happens when the recipient reacts to a particular situation, whether positive or negative, with another related positive or negative action. Salespeople use reciprocity as a tool for generating agreements between stakeholders and teams.

As Cialdini would write, this technique of persuasion is hinged on the principle of *people saying yes to those they owe something to.* You need to give something that will have value to the receiver but will not cost you too much, emotionally or otherwise. If it is of worth to the target who gets it, they are likely to appreciate you and want to keep you around or return the favor. This something should not just be useful to the recipient, it should not cost you too much time or labor either.

This technique is well used in different forms of sales businesses, including the sale of books. You will often notice an email or a handout from an author, giving you access to a free item or resource of value once you have purchased their book. This is called the Lead Magnet, and it is supposed to be a gift to you, which you get for doing the service of buying something from them. In other words, an act of reciprocity.

Do you recall a moment when someone showed kindness to you seemingly out of the blue? This may seem to be an unusual occurrence. Maybe that's why it's so noticeable when it does. We feel thankful when someone helps us in any manner. And when we are appreciative, we are moved to want to help the other person in some way. The rule of reciprocity is what you're sensing when things go wrong.

As a result of our desire to assist others or offer them something, we may use this motivation to help us reach our desired outcomes. It is common for small businesses to give out something for free in order to attract new clients. Most of the time, they are things, but they might also be bits of advice or services.

The software sector is a good example of this. People want to test out new software before they purchase it because they regard it as exciting. There's a chance that they'll love it after a two-week trial period. This is why 40% to 60% of free trials end up being converted into paying memberships. Providing a free trial of a new product tells the firm you can put your faith in them and their goods.

A sales presentation may begin with the representative giving you a handout containing some useful information and statistics that you will need in the course of your life, besides adding an element of context and value to the presentation being delivered.

In other instances of reciprocity, various businesses can offer consultations or complementary reviews via telephone or video conference. Or, there are those "buy one get one free," or "buy products worth so and so value and get two items free" sales taglines that hinge themselves on reciprocal benefit.

An important point to remember about this persuasion tactic is that the persuader has to offer help freely and without expecting anything in return. There is always the risk people will take advantage of this situation, but in most cases, the persuader doesn't need to worry about it.

The free item you have offered should not bear much material or intellectual value—only enough for it to be deemed as something "useful enough." Additionally, the message behind giving the freebie makes you come across as someone who is truly passionate about the service you are providing, which has a powerful echo effect. People tend to share these things with others. They tend to let the larger groups around them know they got something for free and it was useful to them.

Customers get the impression that a firm values them more when the organization demonstrates gratitude toward them. Because of this, we really like it when businesses reward us with "special discounts" for being long-term clients of theirs. It may not be costing them anything—indeed, the discounts offered are all factored into the way they function. It is nothing more than a principle to keep your interest and loyalty hooked so that you remain a long-term customer.

Tactic Six: Timing

Lack of time is a controversial persuasion tactic. It relies on the principle that before you get someone to do something for you; you wait until they have achieved a level of mental exhaustion. For instance, it helps if they have completed a mentally challenging task and are likely to give in to anything you want so long as you leave them to spend some time in peace. The controversy behind this tactic naturally follows since you will be hinging upon using someone's vulnerable state of mind to fulfill your own objectives.

The lack of time method actually relies on the persuaded individual making a decision on their own. So, while your timing plays a role, it is heavily influenced by the choice of the persuaded individual to agree to the demands you are making. For instance, a parent returning home after a long, exhausting day at the office may be likelier to give in to whatever demands their children make because they just want to get it over with.

In general, timing plays a very important role in persuasion. You need to know that your audience is mentally in a place where they are looking for external advice and guidance before reaching out to offer your services to them.

Tactic Seven: Fluid Discourse

A skilled persuader is one who gets away with being a smooth talker. When your sole ability to win others' favor lies in convincing them to listen to what you have to offer, there is no room for jumbled sentences using phrases like "um" or "like" or "uh." Any phrase that gives off a vibe of you being confused about what you are trying to put across impedes your ability to be persuasive.

Essentially, persuasive people tend to be smooth talkers. They know what they want ahead of time, and they also understand their subjects well. When going into any conversation, you can be assured a smooth talker will always come prepared. Going blindly into something is not their style.

While some aspects of interaction will always be left to fate and circumstance, they know that if they have the basics down—such as what their listeners like, their basic characteristics, things they dislike, their general beliefs, and so on, they will be able to turn a conversation in the direction of their choosing.

They also have a clear knowledge of what they want from an interaction and go in with clear goals. Even more, they understand what the other person (that is, the listener) may want from conversing with them.

It is in the nature of smooth talkers to build a personal relationship before getting into the professional nitty gritty. Before going into the specifics of why they are really having the discussion, they will always ask about the person's day or how they are feeling. The reason is not that they care about the person. Rather, they want to wait until the person's guard is down before beginning to talk. More often than not, their true intentions will remain hidden behind a mask as they work the listener's mind into a state where any demand they make will be favorably accepted.

Before getting started on the business relationship, you should have some time to communicate and create a personal connection. People are nicer to people they feel connected with, and the skill of smooth-talking is the ability to bring out the best, warmest, and friendliest qualities in everyone to increase the likelihood that they will assist you. When you immediately start talking business, you run the risk of making a lot of people feel misused, which is the complete antithesis of what a skilled, smooth talker wants to do.

Many persuaders who have achieved success in getting people to act upon their whims know how to get their point across without being pushy or overbearing. This is a skill in itself, and it mandates a lot of practice. Understanding the thin line separating persuading someone from irritating them takes time and an acute awareness of the subject matter.

Before we conclude this chapter, I am going to make an assumption that you need to use the persuasion skill to some end, hopefully positive. I would be living under a rock if I did not know that in this day and age, every single person is trying to persuade someone else to do something. You could be selling a product, asking for a raise, or trying to win a debate. But in all cases, you will notice if you push too hard, the only thing you visibly achieve is annoying others.

Persuasion is a give-and-take situation that allows people to move at their own pace while slowly and gently easing them in the direction of making decisions that will be favorable to the persuader. The first thing you have to do is show the people you are trying to persuade what they need, and why they need you to give it to them. People should be able to clearly understand your or your service's value and relate to it. The more they realize how useful it is for them, the likelier they will be to give you their time of day.

Opposing views are more effective than adhering simply to your own. Ideas and projects seldom come to fruition without flaws. Your audience is aware of this; they are aware of the possible outcomes and various viewpoints. So go head-to-head with them. They're already thinking about these things. Talk about the possible disadvantages and illustrate how you plan to deal with or overcome those issues.

Individuals tend to be convinced if they know you are aware of their reservations. Talk about your opponent's side of the argument, and also do your best to demonstrate why your stance, objective, service, or argument wins in spite of all constraints involved. At the end of the day, people want to know you are giving them something of value. A skilled persuader knows how to make it seem as if they are acting for the benefit of the persuaded, although the actual situation may be very different.

We have discussed how people tend to wield persuasion and manipulation in these few chapters. In the next chapter, we will go into greater detail about what manipulation looks like and how it has helped propel so many businesses to success.

CHAPTER 4
MANIPULATION 101 AND DARK PERSUASION

HAS it ever struck your mind why some people almost always seem to win in life, all the while some others remain in their shadows? The will of nature dictates a clear division between leaders and followers. Most of humankind falls into the latter group. Yes, birth, heritage, demography, and culture always have a weighing factor on who gets an easy thrust into a privileged life, but what of those who have made their name through nothing but sheer effort and clever work? You may think the hard effort is the only reason behind the success of these few people. To an extent, you'd be right. For those who have to climb their way to the top, effort is a precious thing. But it certainly isn't the only variable.

Success is a subjective thing. To you, a measure of success could mean closing a big business deal that 95% of your colleagues have failed to achieve. To someone else, success could mean convincing pretty women to date them in spite of having average looks and a normal income. The point is that the very foundation of this society, and indeed all the living world, is unfair. At every point in your life, you will either be at the receiving end of or confront, the brunt of favoritism and bias.

A survey that asked employees of a business firm what had contributed to their success the most revealed the most important factor across different employees was "getting close to the boss." The boss themselves may have a hundred people trying to get close to them. So, how do the small few succeed, and the rest are swatted away like flies?

The manipulator accepts the reality of the world and calculates methods to turn situations to their advantage. They know they must cultivate a measure of friendship with the people who are instrumental to their own success. A point comes where we have to behave ourselves before the very people we would not want to alienate under normal circumstances.

A manipulator understands that if they do this successfully, their own career (or whatever advantage they are seeking) will stand to benefit. They intrinsically understand that unless they make favoritism work for themselves, it will act against them because someone or the other *will always win the superior's favor, no matter how hard they claim to be unbiased.*

Let us consider people working in the consumer web industry. The entire business is hinged on manipulation. Employees of this industry make products geared to persuade consumers to act in ways benefitting the makers over the consumers. These consumers are often called users, and while this term has been generally considered derogatory, I can assure you many employees of the consumer web industry rely on consumers getting addicted to their products.

Social media is a form of addiction and a dangerous one at that. I had a phase in between when I'd wake up in the wee hours of the morning. Rather than trying to go back to sleep, I'd scroll through social media mindlessly, reading one piece of celebrity gossip or trying to figure out if a prolific web industry could guess my age right through their mindlessly silly yet extremely addictive quizzes.

We may not know how deep in the rocky end we already are, and to think about it, I am not sure I could go even four days without checking my phone for a useless update or a new product or a piece of news that will not benefit me in any plausible way. The experience of manipulation in and of itself is one that has been crafted with the intention of changing behavior patterns.

People always get uncomfortable if they can visualize or clearly understand someone is trying to force them to do something. Usually, manipulation does not fall back on brute force unless that's how the manipulator wants to roll. The techniques often occur on the sly and work on the manipulated individual's minds in the subtlest of ways to induce fear, dependence, and utmost submission towards the manipulator.

So, how can you understand or tangibly grasp when a manipulator is working their subtle charm on you? And out of curiosity, what methods could you apply yourself if you are seeking to persuade someone to choose you over a hundred other competitors? Let us take a look at the different methods manipulators use to achieve their desired ends.

METHOD ONE: THE LONG CON

One of the primary reasons why some individuals have the capacity to resist being persuaded is because they have the impression that the other person is putting pressure on them, which may force them to back off from what they were about to do. They will avoid it as well if they get the impression that the person who is attempting to convince them does not have a good connection with them or that they cannot trust them.

With the Long Con method, the manipulators are able to go over these primary challenges and provide the persuader with precisely what it is that they are looking for. It necessarily implies the involvement of more time and effort on part of the manipulator, but it almost always results in a complete submission on the part of the victim—which is why the Long Con is so successful.

The dark persuader will need to take their time and put in the effort to win their victim's confidence in order to successfully pull off the Long Con. They want to spend some time befriending the victim and ensuring that the target believes and likes them before they proceed with their plan.

This is going to be accomplished by the persuader via the use of strategies such as artificially creating rapport and other methods that will serve to raise the levels of comfort in interactions between a target and their manipulator.

All of this lies in a game of confidence. In a relationship, someone will always be the primary persuader, even if just by an inch. The concept is rooted in basic human psychology. For the manipulator, the Long Con begins with identifying their victim. Who are they? What do they want? How can the manipulator play on the victim's wants and desires and change that in a way that benefits them? The play runs on the creation of a relationship based on rapport and empathy.

In other words, the onset of the Long Con is hinged on a stable emotional foundation. This is essential before any scheme is proposed or before the game is afoot. Once the emotional base is rock-solid, the manipulator understands when the time is ripe for turning to persuasion and logic via a convincing detailed relay of events supported through concrete and believable evidence.

Not only do these events get presented in a manner that makes the victim feel as if they will gain from listening to the manipulator, but the manipulator also comes out of the entire situation with full points, having achieved the very thing they set out to.

As soon as the persuader determines that the victim is mentally prepared appropriately, the persuader is going to begin their efforts to convince the victim of anything. They could begin with some fake attempts at positive persuasion at first. Their victim will be led to make decisions or take actions that will benefit the persuader, rather than the other way around. The person trying to convince others will benefit in two different ways from this. First, the victim becomes accustomed to being persuaded by the one who is doing the convincing. The other thing is that the subject will begin to form a mental link between a favorable result and the persuader.

Once the victim is well inside the manipulator's web, escape becomes more and more difficult until one day, it is practically impossible. We have become far too dependent on them. By the time the victim can make sense of what has happened, they tend to become emotionally and physically attached to an extent that they start *persuading themselves to hang in or keep doing what the manipulator wants them to do.*

Does this sound like the hallmark of an abusive relationship? That's because it is. The manipulator knows the victim's most vulnerable sides and also knows how they can bring these sides out in their naked shape. The victim may end up feeling as if the only way to save the situation is to increase their involvement, and the cycle of abuse goes on and on.

Because the manipulator does not want to be too apparent about what they are doing, the Long Con will take a long time to accomplish. A victim who has just been widowed is an excellent illustration of this. She is particularly susceptible because of her advanced age and the recent nature of her loss.

A man begins to get close to her after her partner's death. There is a good chance that this man is someone she knows through a common friend or is perhaps a member of the same family. After spending a lot of time with her, he shows incredible love and patience, and her guard falls quickly when he is around.

He then begins to engage in the tiny acts of persuasion we previously discussed. He can recommend a better bank account or a better method of reducing monthly expenses. The victim will appreciate the man's efforts and his desire to assist her, so she follows his counsel.

The man then attempts to apply some dark persuasion over a period of time. It is possible that he will attempt to convince her to allow him to invest part of her money. Because of the positive influence that was employed in the past, she agrees. Of course, he's going to try to extract as much as he can out of her as possible.

Depending on the manipulator's competence, she may believe that he was truly trying to assist her, but he lost the money because he had some terrible luck with the investments. You'd be surprised at just how far the dark arts of persuasion can go.

Truly, the mastery of the Long Con is that the con artist may eventually no longer need to do any convincing to make their victims stay or do their bidding. The victims will be too afraid of the things that may happen if they don't. At each step, the manipulator will run the way we think and all the things the victim believes in. As the victim becomes more committed, the manipulator gets more material to work with.

METHOD TWO: GRADUAL DECEPTION

Dark persuasion sometimes seems implausible and ridiculous when described. This evil influence will never come as a huge or unexpected request. You are never going to meet a dark persuader who will put a long hat on your head and claim to work black magic on you. The changes that happen are often far more subtle and extended over time, to the point that when you realize what has happened, it is usually far too late. What is at play here is gradual deception.

Dark persuasion is like a stairwell. Right at the onset of their relationship, a dark triad personality will never convince the target to do something that is horrible or out-of-the-world unusual. Instead, they will instruct the victim to take one step at a time, and only after building a good relationship with them. Having the aim to take one step at a time makes the entire process appear less important. So the victim thinks it is absolutely fine to do one favor. Then the favors keep happening. One after the other, the dark persuader takes and takes until, through the sheer power of graduality, they have acquired everything they set out to.

Gradual deception is a key component in political persuasion. A politician's game, as they say, never ends. Their ability to persuade the masses that the majority of what they do is for the betterment of the people, despite the occasional unpleasant deed here and there, is crucial to the longevity of their effectiveness as leaders. Take the impact of political advertisements, for instance.

Political advertisements have become an inherent part of canvassing, and as a matter of fact, they have been in use since ancient times. While rallies, billboards, door-to-door visitations, and calls are all helpful, nothing sells like a key message delivered in a palatable form. It lets the people know the politician will work long-term towards the things they desire the most—or at least, the majority of them. An important aspect of delivering this message is to ensure people understand the long-term aspect. Big changes cannot happen overnight, and any politician who claims they can change the whole hubris of society in the span of a week or a month will probably fail. The ones who remain in the game are the ones who are able to produce gradual, but noticeable changes, within an extended period.

When does this become dangerous? Well, a dark persuader will use the power of gradual deception to get people to share their deepest, darkest secrets, one by one. This can include instances where the people have done something they now regret, or felt something that wasn't core to their inner being. Since they are subject to gradual persuasion, they share these secrets willingly. The persuader is good at coming across as someone who is a good friend—someone the victim can trust with all of their secrets and their core being.

Then, when the time comes, the persuader knows how to use all the information they have gradually acquired and wield it over the victim's soul. The victim, confounded into submission, now has no way except to comply with whatever is being asked of them.

METHOD THREE: MASKING AND REVERSE PSYCHOLOGY

This method is possibly the most effective tool in the hands of manipulators. Let me explain by virtue of the story of Ninon de Lenclos and the Marquis de Sevigne. Ninon was historically infamous as the most renowned courtesan in the French courts during the 17th century. Coupled with her knowledge on matters of the heart, and over sixty years of experience, it was little wonder that she held an air of mystification, which made young men turn to her for advice.

One such man was the young Marquis, whose reason for heartache lay in failing to seduce a countess because he, while handsome and otherwise desirable, was hopelessly unskilled when it came to romance or seduction.

Ninon instructed the Marquis on many counts. All of them involved an element of masking the Marquis's true intentions to woo the countess. The first instruction was to approach the countess by assuming a manner of distant nonchalance. She could not come to the conclusion the Marquis was fawning after her, because this would take away from the thrill of the chase. The idea was to throw the countess off her scent and think the Marquis wanted nothing more to do with her than be a casual friend. The next step would be to instill jealousy in the mind of the countess. The Marquis was instructed to show up to numerous social events with beautiful women hanging on to his every word. The intent lay beyond simple jealousy—it was also a mask of how desirable the Marquis was in the eyes of society.

Ninon's reasoning for this was a woman who displayed an interest in a man would, to a certain extent, want to see other women interested in him too. It gives a "winning" perspective to things. Not only is it instrumental in raising the value of the potential suitor, but it also gives the notion that the one who wins will win over a hundred beautiful women. Why? Because people always want what they cannot have.

Ninon's next advice was for Marquis to pull out of all events where the countess expected to meet him. He would, instead, show up in places where she was not expecting to run into him. This was to add to the air of mystery which is so core to masking one's true intentions. The countess would not be able to predict the Marquis's next move and would land in a state of confusion. This, in turn, would form the base of a successful attempt at seduction.

Now, Ninon's plan worked remarkably well. Through her clandestine spies, she heard that the countess was responding favorably to all of Marquis's interactions. She was asking questions about him, listening closely to his stories, and in general, far more interested in him. Things were going as they should have.

But then came the rush. The mask fell too soon—and the manipulator was not successful. A few days into this game, the Marquis and the countess were at home, alone. He fell prey to the dangerous whim of impulse and decided to go back on everything Ninon had taught him. So, he took the countess's hand in his own and professed his undying love for her.

That did it. The countess's spell was broken, and she felt visible confusion. She excused herself from the room and, for the rest of the evening, avoided all contact with him. The next couple of times he visited the countess, she excused herself by saying she was not at home. When they ran into each other again, there was only awkwardness and confusion.

What led to this occurrence? Ninon had a fundamental understanding that, while men and women are different in many ways, they experience the same feelings with regard to being seduced. Even if they are aware that they are being led into a bait at one point, many of them like being led on since they are aware that they are venturing into unexplored terrain.

In other words, the thrill lies in the newness of it. There is something exciting about stepping into the unknown, about constantly wondering what the seducer's next step will be. When all of that is suddenly taken away and replaced by a forlorn, hapless lover, the chase is cut prematurely short. This ends the journey the seduced individual was reveling in, and therefore the whole plot is reduced to nothing.

The mere act of seduction relies heavily on implications—riddles in the dark if you will. The seducer can never announce their true intentions by way of plain speech. The key lies in throwing the targets off your scent by looking for and investing in decoys.

When the target displays favorable symptoms like jealousy or the desire to be exclusive with the seducer, then the iron is hot enough to strike. Such patterns cause more than confusion, they also excite the mind of the target and make them consider themselves more desirable.

Today, the act of masking one's true intentions has been relegated to the background of being labeled as playing frivolous games with people's minds. Done right, it can still assist in winning favors. The essence of this method lies in exciting the target's emotions and keeping them guessing about what will come next.

The countess, for instance, may well have sensed the Marquis was playing a game with her. However, since she did not know where things were going, she was likewise intrigued to keep playing along. The moment this changed, and the Marquis seemed like a young boy lost in love, she hastened to exit the scene.

So, deception remains the best strategy when it comes to masking true intentions. Deceptions do need a screen of smoke which will distract the attention of people from what your real purpose or intent may be. A bland poker face is often considered the best smoke screen. It enables the manipulator to hide their intentions behind a nonchalant, neutral demeanor. The premise? *If you lead the fool through the familiar path enough times, they won't catch on when you lead them into the spider's web.*

The 1920s in Ethiopia was dominated by the rule of warlords. A young noble, Haile Selassie, was ousting all warlords to claim himself as the ruler supreme. He compelled warlords to come to Addis Ababa to recognize him as their one and only leader. While most complied, one warlord, Dejazmach Balcha of Sidamo, did not. He considered Selassie to be weak and unworthy.

Selassie insisted Balcha show up until he brought 10,000 men along with him. Balcha stationed these forces three miles from Addis Ababa and called upon the king to come out and visit him on the field. Selassie reversed tactics and sent missionaries to request Balcha's presence at a banquet. Balcha knew earlier kings had used this as a ruse of entrapment. So he agreed to attend the banquet, but only if he could bring six hundred of his ablest soldiers along, all armed and ready to defend him.

Selassie responded with the utmost respect and granted the request. A large banquet was held where Balcha's name was sung and he was offered the best drinks in all the land. Selassie treated Balcha as if he really needed him. But Balcha refused to play along. He did not drink and refused to allow his men to drink as well. He instructed his army that if he did not return by nightfall; the army had orders to attack Addis Ababa.

Selassie acted as if Balcha intimidated him, and he wanted to give him all the power. Later that night, convinced of his superiority, Balcha returned to his camp in a celebratory mood. The moment he reached the site, he could tell something was wrong. His army was gone, replaced by only smoke and fires. A witness reported a large army, under Selassie's command, had visited Balcha's camp. Their intention was not to fight. They surrounded the army and bought each weapon from them. In a few hours, the entire army was disarmed, and they had scattered in all directions.

Balcha found himself walking on a tightrope destined to break. If he marched to the south, the soldiers who had disbanded his army would seize him. If he marched to the capital, Selassie would destroy him. Selassie had cleverly predicted all of his moves, and by masking his own intentions, checkmated him. Balcha could do nothing else but repent for his sins and surrender. He went on to join a monastery.

Here, the manipulator (Selassie) played on Balcha's tendency to be suspicious. Balcha was right to consider the banquet to be a trap. But through the guile of his actions, he made Balcha feel as if Balcha controlled everything. This was an impenetrable smoke screen concealing everything happening just a few miles away.

So, people who are wary or paranoid are the likeliest to be deceived first. If you can win their trust in any area at all, the smoke screen becomes easy to build. A helpful gesture or an honest recounting is often enough to convince them they are too powerful for you to fool around with them. Here, the act of masking your intentions lies in you, making them feel as if they control the world, and you are just living in their shadows—which is just what Selassie did.

It isn't that these people who are so skilled in masking and deception are magicians who weave impossibly believable lies. The finest of them undoubtedly seem unremarkable and uncomplicated, and they are so unassuming that you would never guess that someone who appears to be so average could be capable of coming up with ideas that are so out of the ordinary.

The best deceivers know to keep their words and actions simple. They do not want undue attention on themselves. Rather, their ambitions lie in making the targets feel like they are the real stars while they work their charms in the background. The simplest of actions—a smile, a frown, or an unreadable blank expression—could hide the most sinister of intentions.

Former United States Secretary of State, Henry Kissinger, would bear a characteristically intoned voice and a blank look while reciting boring details over and again. His opponents would be so bored their eyes would glaze over, when suddenly, he would attack them with a list of bold terms. This would often make him the most intimidating statesperson in the room.

Another smoke screen is through gestures that are, on face value, seemingly very noble. People want to take these gestures as genuine without questioning any hidden motives.

Sincerity and honesty are two concepts that are often confused by people. Be aware that their initial inclination is to accept what they see, so don't be surprised if they don't question you and see through your ruse. It's hard to discount your remarks if you really believe them. Always keep in mind that the most successful swindlers will go to great lengths to hide their true nature. They put on a good front in one area while hiding their true colors in another. Sincerity is nothing more than a masquerade that they have perfected over the years.

To an extent, this is like preparing for a long and difficult battle. You will not meet a general skilled in their craft who announces what attack plans they have on their enemy. The core concept lies in hiding progress. If you do not disclose the make of your designs till the time they cannot kindle any opposition, you will not win the game of persuasion.

The notion is to ensure victory even before the war has been declared. However, like any other tactic of deception, maintaining an image is essential. No manipulative tactic will succeed if you have earned the reputation of being a deceiver. Perhaps this is why the most skilled of manipulators will always rely on a number of tactics, rather than a singular one when it comes to winning over people.

METHOD FOUR: LEADING QUESTIONS

Leading questions are one of the subtler tactics used to manipulate people's wills. A manipulator skilled in the art of asking leading questions knows what to question in a manner that will only earn the responses they desire from their targets. While the target feels "seen" and thinks the manipulator is being thoughtful for asking such insightful questions. In reality, these questions do nothing for them except make them spill all the information the manipulator wants to gather from them.

A leading question is a kind of query that will push respondents to answer in a particular premeditated manner, based on the manner in which the questions had been initially framed. More often than not, these questions contain information that the manipulator simply wants to verify rather than get an unbiased or true answer to what they are asking. These come with a form of bias that is traditionally always in the favor of the manipulator.

Questions that are designed to foster bias in respondents are called leading questions, and the responses to these questions are controlled to conform to the goals of the manipulator. The questions include certain degrees of speculation and assumption in their wording. These are the kinds of questions that are often posed in order to get a better understanding of the repercussions of a scenario, rather than with any single respondent's perspective in mind. When it comes to receiving feedback, they have a tendency to be somewhat aggressive.

Verbal persuasion may be quite powerful when it is used in thoughtful and calibrated ways to achieve one's goals, as you may have experienced in the past when dealing with a professional salesperson. Questions designed to guide the conversation are one of the most effective strategies that can be employed vocally. These leading questions are going to be any inquiries that are meant to elicit a certain reaction from the victim. The victim is going to be led in a certain direction by the questions.

The person trying to convince the target may pose a question to them along the lines of, "how terrible do you believe those individuals are?" The answer to this question is likely to give the impression that the individuals the persuader is inquiring about are unequivocally dishonest to some degree. They may have asked a question that didn't lead to any particular answer, such as, "how do you feel about those people?" but instead, they chose to use words that will categorically lead to the target responding with some information giving away how terrible the people of interest in the question are.

METHOD FIVE: THE LAW OF STATE TRANSFERENCE

Have you ever been part of a discussion where you suddenly felt as if your very mood is mirroring the mood of the other person? I often find that, particularly when I am in the middle of a conversation where the other person is predominantly sad or grieving, at one point in time, I become the same way. This is the magic of the law of state transference. In other words, in this technique of manipulation, the deceiver will make the target feel the same way as them and then work on their mind in an attempt to manipulate them.

The law of state transference begins in seemingly innocuous ways. The manipulator starts by matching their mental state to the mental state of the recipient. In a conversation, if the target is bothered by something and this reflects on their mood, the manipulator will make it seem as if they completely understand how the target is feeling. They will match the target's mood and gestures to theirs until the target starts feeling that this is a human being who truly understands the predicament of their situation.

The transference technique involves the use of various words, images, and illustrations, all shared in a certain manner that will benefit the manipulator. The manipulator's principal goal here is to earn the target's trust and confidence. Then, the manipulator will test the waters with small tactics like speeding up their words or the pace at which they are talking to see if the target follows suit. The target, now enthralled by how similar the manipulator's mind is to their own, begins to follow suit. Soon, the manipulator gets the target to the exact state of mind where they need them to be.

METHOD SIX: FEAR, THEN RELIEF

The uniqueness of the "fear, then relief" technique lies in building an environment of terror where people are bound to look for a solution—any attempt to get out of a seemingly messy situation. When the targets begin seeking solutions, the manipulator uses the opportunity to guide them in the direction of the manipulator's choosing. The manipulator invokes fear by holding up some points or eliciting those needs without which the target will find themselves rendered helpless. Then, they offer relief if the target will comply with what they request.

While using the "fear, then relief" technique, it is important that the manipulator doesn't come across as overly aggressive. The point is not to instill so much fear that the targets either end up running away or become more focused on defending themselves. Here is a simple example.

In an office scenario, let us consider two colleagues who are working under the same boss. One day, colleague A tells colleague B, "the boss came around at lunch and saw you weren't at your desk. Someone may have told him you went home for an hour. But don't worry. I told him you were in a meeting to discuss ideas. Could you cover for me tonight? I want to leave before the night shift." Here, the manipulative colleague is creating a situation of discomfort, or fear, in the target colleague by telling them the boss was enquiring after them. They are also offering the solution, in return for a little favor—which will probably be granted because of how relieved the target colleague will feel about the manipulative colleague "saving" him from his "fear situation" and giving him relief.

The cycle of fear and relief is a commonly used interrogation technique since it is too exhausting for potential offenders to keep up with the constant verbal battering. Whenever a criminal thinks they are being uplifted from a potentially difficult situation, they feel a sense of relief. Then, the interrogation turns and lands them in another fear-invoking situation. This game of cat-and-mouse continues until the victim cannot take it any longer—especially if they are relatively vulnerable and unused to hostile prison settings.

In 2010, Nolan's Cheddar Cheese campaign took the world of advertising by storm. It even earned the Best Advert of the year. Consumers could see a mouse moving around a trap. The immediate response was a deep sense of fear that made them feel remorse and horror at the supposed fate of the doomed mouse. This horror would peak at a point that showed the mouse getting trapped within the mouse trap. Then, the relief would come flooding when the consumers would see the mouse, instead of dying in the trap, was using it as a weighing machine!

This is a prime example of the "fear, then relief" paradigm where the viewer, after experiencing a prolonged bout of fear, is glad for any iota of relief coming their way. The fear rose from the misguided notion of the mouse having perished, and the relief they get from finding out this is not true makes them more compliant with what follows next. In a checkmate move, the ad goes on to recommend the cheese and asks the consumers to purchase it.

The seesaw of emotions is bound to tap into the mindlessness that follows once people experience an adrenaline rush from seeing something considerably harrowing. The viewer is disoriented by the rapid fluctuation in their emotions and less likely to consider the pros and cons of any request—meaning they will comply far more easily.

In 1998, Dolinski was the first person to look into the use of the "fear, then relief" paradigm. He performed a series of experiments to test the notion. Individuals were told to jaywalk on a busy street. A concealed person would blow a whistle sounding like a police warning. This was to incite fear inside the individual. Once they realized there was no policeman involved, they experienced relief. The control group involved two individuals, of whom one had jaywalked without hearing the warning whistle, and one had not jaywalked at all.

Afterward, the individuals were told to complete a questionnaire, which was the act of testing compliance. It was seen that those who heard the policeman's whistle and experienced fear and relief were more prone to comply with the request to complete the questionnaire.

If you think about it, there is a very logical method behind the functionality of this principle. Imagine someone comes to you and tells you that something you have been afraid of happening the most has actually happened, but wait, they have been able to help by either shielding you from its effects or reducing the damage. You would feel a natural thankfulness towards this person and a desire to give them what they ask for.

In that heated moment where your building dread gives way to overwhelming relief, you may not stop to question how this person knew about your worst fear, or what they actually did to stall or reduce the impact of this fear being translated to reality. The "fear, then relief" technique relies entirely on the impulsive nature of human beings—but perhaps this is just the biggest reason why it is so successful as a manipulation technique.

All of us want solutions to our problems. When someone comes along with a legitimate promise of delivering these solutions, it isn't surprising that we'd get enormously swayed and be poised to give them the world.

METHOD SEVEN: THE MIRROR TECHNIQUE

Mirroring, or imitation is among the commonest methods used by narcissists and other members of the dark triad. But, it is not always a bad thing. People often imitate the actions and speech tones of others in an attempt to connect with them, demonstrate their liking for them, pull them closer, be of service to them, or gain knowledge from them. For example, when a salesperson cares about their clients and wants to assist them in resolving their issues, their conduct may resemble that of the consumers.

Others use mirroring as a deceptive strategy to further their own nefarious or harmful ends. One way to boost social standing or align people with one's goals is via Machiavellian qualities. It's possible that an unscrupulous salesperson may use mirroring to make consumers like and trust him or her, even if it's bad for the client. Individuals with psychopathic tendencies lack empathy, thus they will imitate the emotions of others in order to look trustworthy.

When a narcissist discovers something in the custody of another person they want but does not have, they are likely to experience intense anger and make an effort to imitate it. For example, let's imagine you're an eloquent speaker. Both your diction and your manner of speech are impressive. The narcissist will often make an effort to mimic these behaviors.

The process of mirroring begins at the very onset of a relationship. Know that a narcissist is unlikely to enter a relationship on a whim or fancy. They will have a specific agenda in mind, and it is for the purpose of fueling this agenda that they will single out the people they form bonds with.

To begin the process of bond formation, they will analyze their subject, sometimes for days to months at an end. They will make a note of the essentials of your nature, how you behave around others, your basic likes and dislikes, and everything you look for in relationships. Based on the information they gather, they will plan out their next steps.

If you are someone seeking an adventurous relationship, they will give you more thrill and excitement than you could have deemed possible. If you appreciate clarity and honesty in relationships, you will find them to be the most genuine people in the room. They mimic all you have ever wanted to be and desired, and they mirror the finest version of yourself and all of your goals back at you. In other words, they fulfill your wildest dreams. In the process, you begin to think, "at last, here is a person who epitomizes every single thing I have ever searched for."

The dark triad personality will not stop at merely imitating the things you desire. They will also pick up traits that are inherent to you by means such as copying your physical appearance. For instance, they may imitate the way you speak or style your hair, the way you wear your makeup, or how you dress, right down to tiny mannerisms that are unique to your being. This is even more true of same-sex friendships and romantic liaisons. The friend or partner steals your entire identity but does all of it in small, subtle steps. In the end, it will feel as if you, and not them, are the copycat.

Let us say that you have a great sense of humor. People talk about how witty and entertaining you are, and how your sense of humor is one of a kind. The narcissist continues to replicate your behavior. They attempt to laugh and goof around in the same manner that you do. You may not know this, but behind your back, they may be repeating the jokes you told them to other people to earn their appreciation.

Or, since you are such a kind and generous person, people look up to you and respect you for it. Even if the narcissist doesn't really feel the need to assist other people, they might get incredibly envious of the acclaim you're receiving for being such a caring and compassionate person. Therefore, in an effort to get approval, they strive to imitate the generosity that you have shown.

In the effort to earn your trust and vulnerability, the dark triad personality can also mirror the things you like to do. If you enjoy going golfing, you will find they are absolutely crazy about the sport. If you like a particular song, they will give you the entire background histories of the artists behind it. It may feel like it is absolutely fine to have common interests, but with time, you will come to realize that nothing feels like it is "yours" anymore. Everything you like is being copied and absorbed by them.

Slowly, they also begin reflecting on the things *they like* and want you to emulate. And so, this becomes an ascent into state transference.

The mirroring technique also enables dark triad personalities to reflect character and principles that aren't their own but copied from the people they are manipulating. So, if you are someone upfront and honest, they begin behaving the same way. You look at them and feel fortunate to have come across such a match— someone who has such admirable values. In reality, the values you are observing in them are *actually yours*. The dark triad personalities, particularly the narcissists, are excellent when it comes to making *every single thing about themselves*. While you keep admiring their qualities and forgetting who you are in the process, they revel in the prospect of stealing your identity, piece by piece.

METHOD EIGHT: THE GUILT APPROACH

Oh, the intention behind the use of the guilt trip. It can make us feel terrible for one small mistake. For instance, when we feel guilty for having eaten too much, treating someone more harshly than they deserved, or disregarding something that demanded our attention, we are constantly guilty of doing this to ourselves. We do it all the time. Even when we do it to ourselves, guilt trips have the power to destroy our sanity—so imagine how it will feel if another voice is constantly badgering you to the extent of making you feel absolutely terrible about every aspect of your existence?

A guilt trip works by making other people (the targets) feel guilt or a deep sense of unavoidable responsibility in terms of either acting in a specific way that will be conducive to the manipulator or altering their behavior entirely. Guilt can be a very powerful motivator and it can work on human emotions the way pungent garlic works in curries and soups—in other words, once it settles in, it runs the risk of overpowering all other emotions and thoughts.

Manipulators know how to use guilt as a tool to alter the manner in which people think, feel, and act. On occasion, this may involve leaning on an aspect or action the target already feels guilty about. In other instances, manipulators may invoke feelings of responsibility or guilt even though it is completely unjustified, simply because it serves a particular end.

If someone has ever made you feel terrible about something, and on further introspection, later on, you found that you should not have been victimized this way; you have likely been subjected to a guilt trip. Dark triad personalities use bad feelings to get you to comply with their requests or do favors for them by making you feel as if you need to do these things to earn redemption.

The issue is, that it's possible that even you have used guilt to coerce other people into doing things in the past. Guilt tripping can be as intentional as it is unintentional. Let me explain the unintentional variant. In the following scenario, we have a little girl—let us call her Maria. Maria's mother has promised her that if she does well in the year-end examinations, they will go on an enjoyable trip to Disneyland. Now, Maria has been dreaming of this visit all year long. It is justified since it is a promise that has been made to her. So, she studies very hard and passes all papers —even the ones she detests—with elan. Her teachers are pleased, and she goes to her mother, sure that the Disneyland trip is bound to happen now.

Unknown to her, over the last few months, her family has been experiencing terrible financial turmoil. Her father has lost his high-profile employment. Her mother is working 24/7 to make basic ends meet. She sees that her mother seems busier than usual, but to her, since her mother has always loved working, nothing is out of place. With her results in her hand, she goes to her mother and asks that she keep her promise.

Her mother is overjoyed, but she is aware that she cannot take a vacation to Disneyland right now due to financial constraints. Instead, she buys her a lovely bar of chocolate and promises they will go somewhere in a few months. However, Maria is not going to take that lying down. She kicks up a ruckus about how her mother promised her they would go to Disneyland, and how she has worked so hard so that she could go on this trip. She cries and wails until her mother feels compelled to borrow money from her parents so that they can go on the trip. Why? Because the guilt trip, while unintentional, is too much to cope with.

Guilt tripping as a behavior can be easy to spot at times, but occasionally, it can be so subtle that you wouldn't be able to tell you are being manipulated into doing something until it is far too late. You feel, "it's okay, let me try my best to sort this out," because at that moment, the feeling of shame or sadness is too much, and you would rather use your resources (although they may be scant) to repair the damage rather than stay in this dark place. Consider the following statements:

> *"If I would not have helped you, you would never have gotten into college! I am not saying you need to do the same, but would you consider helping me out?"*

> *"I have given you so much love and done so much for you! I know you have tried hard in this relationship, but do you think you have done as much as me?"*

> *"I am working all the time while you keep visiting your friends and spending time outside the home. Don't you think I deserve this?"*

> *"If you won't come over, I won't invite anyone else. What good will it be if you aren't there?"*

These are all examples where guilt tripping is the key factor. These trips can involve others making comments proving you have not done as much work as them. Or it may involve mistakes you have made in the past or choices you would not make in the present circumstances. Suddenly, you feel as if they are constantly referring to who you were in the past to either make you feel terrible or to get things done. Or they can remind you of favors performed in the past.

They can also act angry and give you a long "silent treatment" until you feel you must ask what is going on and why they are treating you so coldly. Or, they could use their body language, vocal intonations, and facial expressions to make you feel guilty about doing something. The most obvious is when they say things like, "you owe me," make sarcastic comments on your progress or efforts and engage in passive-aggressive tactics.

A person may be persuaded to take part in an activity that the manipulator wants if the latter uses the tactic of playing on their sense of guilt. By portraying oneself as someone who has been wounded as a result of the conduct that the other person is expected to feel guilty about, an individual may be able to elicit compassion and quick responses.

There are many outcomes that might result from trying to alter someone's conduct by appealing to their sense of guilt. Whether the use of guilt is deliberate or unintentional, it has the effect of stifling good communication and interactions with other people.

While guilt trips are common in all forms of indirect communications and interpersonal relationships, they are more likely to occur in partnerships involving close emotional connections. This includes romantic, familial, parental relationships, and friendships. Guilt trips may not always be with the sole intention of manipulating the target. Of course, sometimes, the primary goal is to manipulate someone into doing something that is either extraordinarily difficult, given their circumstances, or something they would not normally do. In other instances, manipulators use guilt trips to avoid getting into trouble. It helps them to get away without needing to engage in direct conflict.

A manipulator may be able to guilt others into doing what they want, but it comes at a price. If the other person thinks they are being controlled, it might lead them to lose faith in the relationship. Guilt trips may damage relationships by instilling anger that lingers for a long time. Accompanied by sentiments of bitterness from being influenced by guilt, guilt-trippers experience unpleasant emotions.

It's possible that a single instance of someone using guilt as a tool to influence your conduct won't have a significant effect on the connection between you and that person. When guilt trips are used too often, they might leave lasting feelings of resentment. There are a number of acute and unpleasant feelings and symptoms that might arise when someone experiences guilt.

Developing a guilt complex, or the notion that you have (or will) done something wrong, may also be a result of this covert manipulation. Guilt may morph into humiliation if left unchecked. Because of shame, the victim may retreat from social situations and isolate themselves, which may be just what the manipulator wants from them. The lonelier they are, the easier they will be to target and brainwash.

METHOD NINE: PLAYING VICTIM

Well, this one is a bit of a doozy. On the one hand, I could say that many of us have, at some point in our lives, blamed others for our mistakes. For instance, how many of us have blamed our siblings when we were the ones responsible for breaking an expensive artifact or licking icing off a cake meant to be unveiled at a party?

How many of us have tried to shirk off blame by putting the onus on someone else's shoulders? If we stopped to think about it, we would be surprised at just how many times we have laid the guilt on other people without even understanding what we were doing.

Manipulators, especially narcissistic personalities, refuse to take responsibility for any situation or circumstance of their making. They try to point the finger (most often successfully) at others and make them feel guilty. On other occasions, they will blandly ignore the role they have in creating and perpetuating a pressing issue. The victim mentality rests on making the targets believe that whatever bad is happening to the manipulator results from the wrongdoings of other people.

There is no instance where they would stop to consider their own role in the process. Everyone is at fault, and they are the good people, the sufferers left to endure the misery inflicted upon them by the world at large.

When the manipulator is portraying themselves as a victim, they are not going to look at themselves as victimized. They merely want the targets to see them as injured, hurt, or suffering in a manner that will surely draw their sympathy and cloud their judgment of who the real sufferer is. The manipulator builds an impression around the target that becomes so pervasive the target cannot see through the smokescreen to identify that they are the actual ones becoming victimized.

A dark triad personality knows full well that most individuals will hate to see others suffer—or be the primary causes behind someone else's suffering. This is why playing the role of the victim becomes an effective manipulation tactic.

I will illustrate this here. A long time back, I had a friend. They were otherwise well-placed in life, but whenever anything remotely positive would happen to me, she would portray an image of sadness and grief until I would lose all joy of being in the moment and be forced to ask her what was wrong. On asking this, she would inevitably make up some story or other to point to how she was missing out in life because of her family troubles and how "no one" seemed to understand.

This went on and on until one day, I realized I was giving up on all of my feelings of happiness because I did not want her to be hurt in the process. In my mind, the constant drumming noise kept saying, "Oh, look at the poor thing. She's suffered so much. I don't need these trivialities when someone else is facing so many difficulties." This is what bearing a victim mentality and using it to influence others can do—and it is a more innocent variant. Done cleverly, this mentality can be used to earn anything the manipulator wants.

People who have been through very harrowing experiences and who, because of the psychological damage caused by those experiences, cannot break free from the cycle of self-victimization are not to be confused as manipulators. These individuals do not purposefully seek to exert any kind of influence on anybody else. They have been exposed to such a traumatic experience that it has caused them to suffer from PTSD or another mental disease. As a result of this, individuals are unable to extricate themselves from this situation without the help of a psychologist.

The inability of a person to accept any responsibility for their own acts or ideas is one of the telltale symptoms that the person views themselves as a victim rather than an active participant in their own life. Their lives, and particularly their thoughts, have not moved forward from the tragedy since it occurred.

Long after the incident has passed, the anger that they felt because of it is still very much present. They have the misconception that it is hard for them to govern their own life. Because of this, the true victim often feels helpless in their own life, which makes them more susceptible to manipulation. They have a difficult time putting their faith in others.

Former victims of abusive partners who are now resolute in avoiding being victimized again have gained the ability to enfranchise themselves by learning to see through the many manipulation tactics, particularly the playing the victim card. This has enabled them to take back control of their lives. In order for them to cease becoming victims, they first need to have a more solid understanding of the differences between a victim and a person who victimizes others.

Their lives are forever altered once they gain the ability to differentiate between a defense and an offense (in all of its various covert forms), become keenly aware of the differences between cold-blooded manipulators and those who are victims of repeated emotional or physical abuse, and give up outdated, worn-out, and erroneous interpretations about why individuals do the things that they do.

METHOD TEN: BUT, I LOVE YOU!

The "I love you" manipulation tactic goes hand in hand with "if you actually love me." They are common ways to manipulate people engaged in very close relationships with each other. Because of the nature of the relationship itself, it becomes very hard to understand whether you are being manipulated. The key signal to look out for is whether the terms of endearment are being used by the manipulator to get what they want. Healthy relationships are never a one-way street where one person is getting all the favors and the other person is going on giving them.

Rather, it is a constant conversation about finding the middle ground in close cooperation with each other. In any stable relationship, you know your partner well enough to not have to manipulate or bribe them to get what you want. Simple, clear conversations about setting priorities and boundaries should be enough under most circumstances.

Manipulative partners will look for the tiniest of flaws and cracks and amplify these to make it seem as if your life will fall apart unless and until you give them what they want from you. Without complying with their request, they will come across as complicated and difficult to make sense of.

Examining all the little flaws that you and your partner have is another method for determining whether or not you are in a relationship that is manipulative. They could magnify simple things like not putting dirty laundry in the hamper or never placing dirty dishes in the sink to a place where you feel like a criminal for not helping them out.

There are little details about the individuals we spend the most time with that get on everyone's nerves at some point or another. In order to have a good relationship, it is important to talk about these things and also to be able to laugh at the silly things that happen.

A relationship that is characterized by manipulation is often typified by nitpicking. The manipulator will make sure that every action you do is disclosed in a way that is critical of you, causing you to feel awkward and self-conscious. This is a method for exerting control. If you find yourself in a situation where you are forced to listen to phrases, such as "I love you so much," "Don't you have a heart," or "But I was so sure you loved me," there is a significant probability that you are being manipulated.

It is not always a "this is over" situation all the time. It's possible that they just want something but are too frightened to ask for it, but in any case, you should address the issue as soon as possible.

A surefire way of knowing you are in a manipulative relationship is by watching whether your partner is constantly convincing you to do things that you don't want to do. In a normal relationship, you would never have to do certain things you hate doing simply because you are afraid of earning your partner's disapproval.

In a manipulative relationship, your partner will constantly push you to do things by claiming to love you. At other times, they will switch up the tactics and say things like "you are too good for me, maybe I don't deserve you. Do you think we should end this?" to confuse and frighten you into thinking if you do not comply with their requests, they will leave.

You will also notice the "I love yous" become increasingly prolific when the manipulative partner wants something from you. It could be they want to go for a night out with their friends. It could be they want an intimate favor when you aren't in the mood or it could be something else entirely. In any case, you will feel as if the only thing that matters is them getting their dues fulfilled.

Then, if you need them to prioritize you for something, it goes south. They are never there, and if you ask why they are so unavailable, they will tell you they love you, but you are overreacting. At each point, you will feel as if you are constantly making mistakes. The mere notion that your partner should be around to listen to you will feel like a distant dream—something that only happens in books or films.

The manipulators who use endearment terms for getting their desires fulfilled will always shame and blame their partners for having an independent voice and lifestyle. While ideal romantic views often ascertain that long-term partnerships are based on two people becoming one, I find this concept a tad redundant.

Rather than becoming one, a healthy partnership is one where two independent individuals are allowed to have and pursue their own dreams within the purview of keeping their partners in the loop and taking their situation into consideration. Yes, compromises will always be a part of long-term relationships. But guilt or shame or being forced to live a certain kind of life should definitely not play a determining role.

So now, you know the major methods used by most manipulators when they want to get something from you. Understand that sometimes manipulation can be so entrenched it becomes physically impossible to keep away from it. You may have done it yourself, or you may have been a victim. In most cases, it is possible to take your stand and defend yourself from repeated instances of abuse. For that, the most fundamental knowledge lies in understanding your vulnerabilities, and how others may exploit these vulnerabilities to get what they want.

We will move into a discussion about weapons of influence. There are certain tactics out there that convince people to respond and act according to the whims of a select few. Attorneys, salespeople, and public speakers are among the influencers who wield these tactics to win over and hold attention. But, more on this in the next chapter.

CHAPTER 5
OPERATION MIND CONTROL

GIVEN the apparent bad rap that manipulation usually faces, no one would willingly like to be at the receiving end of behaviors they can visualize as obviously manipulative—like name-calling, bullying, aggression, and so on. However, more insidious and seductive forms of manipulation are so deeply entrenched within professional operatives that the game of business has basically become an art in "who can manipulate in the most convincing way." Leaders who shirk manipulativeness on grounds of authenticity can end up limiting their effectiveness in a world where so much is given to the power of appearances.

The question, for many, has become not about "if" they should manipulate, but rather, "to what end" they are using the manipulation. Whether we choose to accept it or not, manipulation can be a very powerful tool to get people to act in their best interests. For example, New York, as a state, runs several manipulative anti-smoking public service announcements. These adverts depict the sufferings that result from smoking to, sometimes, a vividly disturbing extent. Where I grew up, in every film hall before the real screening would begin, several advertisements and cautionary montages would play on the big screen.

One of them was about the dangers of smoking. There is something so visually horrid about seeing the impact of smoke-induced lung damage magnified on such big screens. It would, in my mind, certainly thwart impressionable people from taking up the habit.

As another instance, consider those effective anti-littering music videos made by school children, which send messages requesting people to be good adults and save the world for future generations. Other well-meaning adverts use personalization and story-telling to highlight instances where a father has not been able to return home to his waiting children because of drunk driving.

Each of these instances encapsulates an aspect of manipulation—but who in their right mind (save for someone who actually wants to harm themselves and others around them) would object to them?

Now that we have discussed so much about manipulation, what do you see it as? Does it always have to be intentional and sinister, or is it also the simple use of human emotions to elicit certain approved responses? And if it is the latter, who can rightly claim to have never used manipulation to certain ends?

As human beings, we often remember concepts and ideas far better when they become attached to our emotional experiences. So, manipulators who are actually concerned about both themselves and the people around them will use manipulative tactics in an attempt to drive something home.

Consider the film, Dead Poets Society. I know this film has a special place in the hearts of multitudes. But if you stop to think for a moment, Keating isn't without his manipulative influences—whether for good or bad. He tells his students they will learn to think for themselves after insisting that they rip out the introductory pages of their poetry textbooks. What was the reason behind asking them to do this? Simply that Keating did not agree with what was written in the concerned books. That itself is somewhat contradictory to the premise of learning to think for yourself.

A person who claims to be an unprejudiced thinker must necessarily consider conflicting perspectives before arriving at any judgment. Here, the students don't get an opportunity to do that. In fact, the power and magnetism behind Keating's words and his style of speaking are so profound that almost all of them unanimously agree with him—*without stopping to question, "why do I not get to read the damned introduction and form my own opinion?"*

In other words, Keating used manipulation to convince his students that his opinion on them "making their own judgments" was primary, and much more important than what they would read in the textbooks. Perhaps that was true. But the children did not get to judge that.

Business administration students are among the most manipulated of all learners. Expensive business schools churn out a steady, heavy-handed diet of case studies claiming to be adapted from real-life scenarios. The narratives within these studies entice emotional conversations which manipulate the students to form a way of thinking and speaking that will help sell products and gain more customers for the companies they work for.

This is pretty much ingrained into them, and they proudly perpetuate this philosophy all throughout their professional and personal life. The mere thrum of this goes "sell, sell, sell." No successful sale can go through without a floral word here or there. "Authentic handloom," "60-day money-back guarantee," "millions of happy customers," "real silver and gold embroidery," "designer label—" how many of us stop to wonder why these expensive labels we spend on come with tiny disclaimers that go on to say products have been made in China or sourced from third-world countries? Not too many, right? That's what business manipulation does.

In 2020, the New York Times came up with a riveting article. Schultz, Payton, and Jay, the reporters for the piece, highlighted the making of designer garments by Indian artisans on top of staircases sprinkled with sequins and dirt. These hapless artisans poured in hours and worked with needles and their bare hands to make clothing for the world's most powerful brands.

They worked without health benefits within a suffocating factory ensconced by caged windows, lacking access to basic safety facilities like an emergency exit. The workers earned a few dollars daily for international clients' subcontracted orders. Some had no choice but to make their beds on the floors at night. Because—that's okay so long as the things high-profile people wear come with brand names attached, right? So, who were the parent companies?

Before you say "must be fast fashion brands," wait. Dior and Saint Lauren owned the garments, among other big names in the fashion industry.

The most expensive runways in dream cities like Milan and Paris employ thousands of people from the developing world without caring about their primary living conditions. Ateliers and export houses in big Indian cities like Mumbai become the intermediaries between these brands and the highly skilled and extremely underpaid artisans who not only design parts of the clothes but sometimes, the entire garment up until the finishing touches. To this extent—Jennifer Lopez's stunning Versace gown of 2019 was embroidered by Indian artisans.

Stop for a minute to consider how many of us truly look into these hidden facts. The love we have for brands can be so overpowering —in part because of how their end products look and the marketing gimmicks they follow—that we often forget to consider whether our minds are being controlled and we are being "made" to think a certain way.

And well, who can blame industries for resorting to these textbook traits for holding onto your attention? Leaders who forgo manipulation default to fact-based decision-making. There is nothing wrong with this, indeed, facts serve as essential components to all decisions, but they cannot form the main character, especially when the audiences are seeking some form of an emotional connection to the products or the companies in which they invest their time and resources.

In the real world, many politicians and people, in general, have to come to solutions without having access to the necessary facts. In fact, there are problems that you cannot possibly solve with facts alone. These include issues like environmental problems, poverty, and social and economic inequality. Leaders who swear by ethics can sometimes become so afraid of persuading people around them to undertake actions that they end up failing the very people who are looking up to them for a solution—for, as it happens, a way to act.

Mind control techniques like using metaphors, storytelling, analogies, and emotional appeals are all employable for worthy ends. In the same breath, they can also be used for dishonorable ends, like getting people to cheat, engage in fraud practices, lie, or steal.

A leader is essentially a human being who can make others feel worthy of themselves. But there is so much more to that. How many of you have watched the series "The Dropout?" This is inspired by the very real story of Elizabeth Holmes, a seemingly sweet and brilliant Stanford dropout who went to great ends to manipulate her investors and employees even after it became clear that the technological foundation of her blood-testing apparatus and company, Theranos, was bogus. But what if this isn't the case each time?

In every situation, a leader has to be able to think on their feet to come up with solutions. Investments are tricky, and people will never budge toward something they cannot be made to believe in. Trust and honor are all lofty words and come with great intent, yet, without mind control and influence, no business would be what it is today.

Storytelling is one of the most recognized ways to control the minds of audiences. It is an effective motivator in driving points home, and perhaps a key reason why so many tales of morals always begin with a story before coming to the actual moral.

When you use a protagonist as the focal point for teaching an important lesson, you are effectively creating a situation in the minds of your audiences as to what may really happen if they were placed in similar circumstances. In many instances, these stories are very relatable, which means audiences already have been through or have thought about the situations being described.

Therefore, it will have an even stronger impact on them if you tell them a tale that they are already quite acquainted with. Take the success of Airbnb. One of the co-founders, Brian Chesky, heavily relies on his skill of storytelling to recount his childhood experiences of travel and his relationship with his family to illustrate the core philosophies behind his company.

Another effective technique for mind control is imparting a vision. Something so seemingly short and simple can have the end of getting entire nations to conform—and it is nothing more than appealing to the cognition and emotional vulnerabilities of the audience. It describes an end that is extremely desirable and gives the means to get to that end. Now, you could use a vision for honorable means, or you could be, well, a contemporary rendition of Hitler. That's how dangerously efficient they can be.

The key that separates a vision that is too viscerally complicated and makes employees and audiences go, "I don't understand what I'm working for," from a highly emotionally charged one that makes them jump and scream their loyalty lies in what I'd say is the core concept of mind control. *To successfully control the minds of your audience, you have to know what drives their minds in the first place.* A highly believable and endorsable vision will use manipulative concepts and words of an emotional nature to excite people into action.

Now, this is where I will attach a tiny reminder. Leaders that are benevolently manipulative want their teams to know how well they are advancing toward their goals. This necessitates a level of honesty that cannot be compromised. In the absence of this trust, people will not believe that the mothership is operating in their long-term interest. Everyone knows that obstacles must be overcome in order to achieve emotionally compelling visions.

So yes, mind control is very effective for both good and bad reasons. It can make or break the success of companies and enterprises. But after a time, reaching the end vision will require your honest input and hard work. The most successful leaders know how to marry mind control, honesty, and work into one invincible whole.

THE WEAPONS OF INFLUENCE

Not too many of us know this, but we are all in the constant process of making decisions depending on the stimuli we receive from the external world. In the same way, the external world is constantly influenced by the decisions we make. Our words, thoughts, and actions leave their imprints on other people all the time.

One of the most famous books on the topic of influence is the work of author Robert Cialdini. In his work *"Influence: The Psychology of Persuasion,"* he essentially prepares a guidebook that is still considered one of the most important things a marketer will ever read.

In this 1984 marvel, Cialdini highlights six markers that constitute the weapons of influence. These are reciprocation, consistency and commitment, social proof, liking, authority, and scarcity. Successful marketing, especially referral marketing, is hinged on comprehending and channeling all of these tools in a way that convinces audiences to take action.

The first principle, or reciprocation, is based on the notion that we will give back to others the kind of behavior which they have meted out to us. This is basic human nature. We like to return favors, almost as much as we like the odd turn of kindness. In 1974, the sociologist Philip Kunz sent six hundred Christmas cards out to people he did not know.

Although all the people who received the cards were strangers, he received more than two hundred thank-you cards in return. People should have stopped to think before responding to a stranger, but the rule of reciprocation mandates that there is a "give and take" mechanism operating at the level of the human subconscious, which often influences the way we act.

The second tool is commitment and consistency. When using these tools to establish control over your audience's minds, you want to ensure that how you behave externally reflects who you are and what you feel *within*. When people make decisions or commit to something, they *want* to be able to justify it. So, people will always look up to a leader who can prove they are worth their mettle.

Perhaps not all the promises they make will be doable. But if at least four out of ten difficult promises are met, the people will at least know that the leader is trying their best to stick to the commitments and philosophies they spewed at the onset.

The third tool is social proof. Human beings are notorious for taking cues from the environment surrounding them. Have you ever been part of a social interaction where you had no clue what was being said, but because others laughed, you felt compelled to chuckle too? Don't feel bad—all of us have been there. I revert to the experiment I shared earlier in the book, where a group of bystanders looking up to the sky elicited so many similar responses from complete strangers.

This arises from our curiosity and a mutual desire to understand each other. When stuck with strangers for far too long, one of us will probably start a conversation to dispel the tension in the room or to simply know different contexts. Social proof can be used as a way of mind control to get people's attention fixated on something specific.

Tool number four is "liking." Cialdini highlights the importance of this tool by referring to Tupperware parties—social hangouts organized by a sales rep to get friends and neighbors to come together for sharing, discussing, and endorsing Tupperware products. The logic is people will be more inclined to purchase products that get endorsed by people they know and like. Very often, we buy something simply because our friend says good things about it.

On social media, we routinely follow beauty and health influencers who highlight the products they love and ask us to use their discounts when buying these products. Maybe we don't need another foundation, face mask, or skirt that promises to twirl as we run. But since we like the influencer and their way of speaking so much, we go ahead and make that purchase, anyway.

The next tool highlights the importance of authority. The end necessity for selling your product is building an environment of trust. We begin learning how to follow our elders at a very early age. First and foremost, our parents (and by extension all adults), followed by our instructors, law enforcement officers, and so on. At some point, it will default to anybody who has the appearance of being superior to us, in some way or another.

We categorize the people in the world into those who are deserving of our obedience and allegiance and those who are below us on the social hierarchy (and who should obey us). The use of authority bias in personalized advertising for the purpose of influencing attitudes is especially prevalent in the contemporary world. Political leaders and other people of authority are also employed in ad campaigns to boost the impact of the advertisement. So, if a loved celebrity is endorsing a skincare brand, it must be the most effective one out there.

We all have a desire for a sense of personal control, which can be satisfied in one of two ways: either we can take charge of the situation ourselves, or we may place our faith in another individual to handle things on our behalf. When one party cedes control to another, there is an unspoken understanding of reciprocity that takes place in both directions.

A concealed threat of using force leads us to cede power in a coercive sense. On the other hand, authority figures in relationships guarantee the advantages of love in the nurturing sense. In each case, the promise of an upcoming action is what ultimately wins over a person's compliance.

The marketing strategy of authority bias is utilized with the goal of increasing the validity of statements made about a commodity in order to promote sales. One common example of this can be seen in advertising, where toothpaste brands advertise the authenticity of their claims by showing people in lab coats in their commercials. As a result, consumers have a higher level of trust in the product and are more likely to purchase the product.

The final tool is one we have already discussed, so I will just touch upon it. The scarcity principle compels us to desire things that are not as easily available—at least to our apparent understanding. Marketing gimmicks like sales, or limited editions of products, are all ploys to provoke interest in items that we would never consider.

This principle is also one of the reasons why age-old fan favorites continue to hold a place in our hearts. We would still buy wands or visit places where the entire decor is inspired by the work of the original creator because "it is so limited or licensed or valuable." The licensed product may itself be a bunch of plastic— but that's the thing about influence. It controls the mind to see *the only things the people at the helm want you to see.*

THE POWER OF NLP

You may be thinking, "Now, what the heck is NLP?" Broadly known as neuro-linguistic programming, NLP is a combination of various cues (physical and verbal) that compel you to react to particular situations, act, think or feel a particular way. It has a number of positives, but it is definitely among the more sinister ways to completely control the minds of those around you. Skilled manipulators can use NLP via vague language and mannerisms to confuse and disorient a target so that they end up doing something they would not otherwise consider.

In a way, it works like hypnotism, but since it is not as widely popular or known, it remains slightly more dangerous. From a young age, we are taught to be wary of things that happen in the dark. NLP can end up being just one of these things.

Neuro-linguistic programming's emergence occurred in the 1970s as a way to reprogram the mind so that people could sort out their personal problems and inhibitions.

So, if a person drank too much or hated working out, or procrastinated excessively, NLP's target was to reprogram the brain to think and act better. Its origins can be traced to the work of John Grinder and Richard Bandler, two college students who had a shared liking of hypnosis, computer technology, and neuroscience.

What began as a desire to explore the fascinating connections between how people think and how they communicate and act would one day become the very means of controlling and convincing people to change the rubric of their thought patterns. Grinder and Bandler developed the theory as a retaliation to the psychotherapy process of trauma exploration, which they found cruel. With the emergence of the Human Potential Movement at the end of the 1970s, the two of them began marketing NLP as a way for people to improve business marketing practices.

The starting point of NLP is that while not everything in your life may be subjected to your control, you can always control the happenings occurring inside the head. The thoughts, feelings, and emotions are not things you have, rather, they are things that you *do*. They can arise from complicated origins—for instance, a person who has been in abusive relationships for years may think and process emotions from a person who has not because their method of "doing" the processing has happened differently.

The benign intent of NLP was to show people how to take control of these influences. It involved the use of techniques like visualization to change the way one would think and feel about previous experiences, fears, and traumatic encounters.

While the notion that we can delve into our minds and heal our destructive thinking patterns via NLP is remarkably uplifting, not everything about this technique is as straightforward. Today, NLP involves a range of cues used by sales associates, business executives, pickup artists, and conmen for different ends—some good, some bad.

In the end, neuro-linguistic programming (NLP) is among the most powerful techniques to change the mind of another person. You will be able to heavily influence what someone will do, what they will say, or what they will put up with, and you can do this by learning to access their minds and priming them to do what you want.

You will have the ability to implant ideas into their heads, making them seem so natural and seamless that it is as if they were always meant to be there. If you are aware of what you are doing and have the necessary skills, you will be able to coerce other people into doing almost whatever you want them to do.

In other words, this is a very potent kind of influence. You can calm someone's nerves or induce terror in them so that you may have more control over them. You may use it to relieve someone else's tension or to make them feel completely helpless.

Effectively, NLP can be as potent as hypnosis since the manipulator works gently and in covert ways to lull their target into a complete state of compliance. When the target is where the manipulator wants them to be, they can effectively instill their own desires and wants in the minds of the target and, therefore, influence their behavior.

The manipulator can ensure the other person thinks, feels, and experiences emotions the way they want them to, all by virtue of tapping into the target's mind. The only thing they need to do well is to induce a state of mind in the target where they have nothing but trust and dependence on the manipulator.

When someone trusts or depends on you, they are unlikely to have their guards up. This is why building rapport is a critical component of NLP, and a manipulator who wants to establish mind control via this method will always take their sweet time to develop a relationship of trust and confidence, irrespective of how long it may take. Let us now look at the various tools indigenous to NLP.

Mirroring

We already know how effective mirroring is. What makes it so useful for NLP? When a manipulator learns to mirror someone, they are essentially taking time to build a solid sense of rapport with them. Under usual circumstances, mirroring can often be translated to the unconscious ways in which we emulate the acts of those around us.

For instance, think of how we begin laughing when someone around us giggles about a mundane joke. Sometimes, it is the very person's laugh that sets off the tickling bone in us, and before we know it, we begin giggling too. When someone yawns, their friends or family present on the scene may yawn as well.

When we spend time with people close to us, many things follow an unconscious synchronization pattern—including the food we eat, how we dress, what we watch, right down to how we walk and talk.

When we mirror someone else, it is usually because we really like and trust the person. A social rapport is in place, and we cherish this relationship and the other human being. If you are mirroring someone around you unconsciously, it is likely because you appreciate them. But this can take time when it happens naturally —unless you have an instant connection.

Dark manipulators, on the other hand, will do this from the get-go, through tiny little steps that sometimes feel so natural. They will follow you and watch all the moves you make before establishing contact. Once you do get to know them, you will be surprised at how similar they seem to you. This will make the process of building a rapport easier, and in a few weeks to some months, they will feel like an inseparable part of your life.

Narcissist mirroring can be so manipulative you get fooled into loving them. They put on a perfect mask to mirror everything you dream and desire so that you feel like you are experiencing a fantasy coming true. There will be something so strong and you will be a sucker for the hold they have on you. Everything will feel right.

But narcissists don't process empathy the way we do. True, they share the basic emotions we all have, which means that they do experience hunger or thirst or the need for shelter. But they are not given higher emotions.

For instance, most of us will be able to temper our spells of anger with logic, but narcissists will not know what to do when one of their fits of ego-centered rage strikes, except blame all of their shortcomings on you.

The first step is to establish a rapport with the other party. This necessitates an acknowledgment on both ends, which may be done by ensuring that the manipulator is looking at the target and establishing eye contact. They pay attention to the other person's tiny hints and attempt to match their breathing patterns. They will nod frequently to show they are paying thorough attention to what is being said and their agreement with it. At this point, the relationship should be developing naturally.

Next, they will look for verbal cues. In the beginning, it may be easier to copy their body language rather than their verbal patterns. The other person's tempo and excitement are mirrored by the manipulator. Locating the punctuator is the final step in building that mirrored link.

We all own a signature facial expression that we use when we wish to draw attention to something. When you want to accentuate something, you may use gestures like pumping your fist or tilting your head and smiling. Observing the other person's body language and inclinations is the only way to discover the target's overall style, and this is something the manipulator will take the time to do.

Once the manipulator has figured out the punctuator, they will use it as soon as the target's cues prove favorable. If the target is about to smile at them, they will do it first. The target may not realize this, and will likely continue smiling and engaging with you. They will feel an instant connection to the manipulator without knowing what is responsible for this magnetic attraction.

The next step lies in testing the connection. The manipulator now begins to do some actions with their hands or face. The idea is to see if the target will follow suit. When the target begins to mirror the manipulator's facial movements and gestures, the manipulator begins using their words to influence them.

In most cases, narcissists will choose people they need for some purpose or the other. They are insecure inside, so if you are someone with money, status, good looks, compassion, or influence, they will latch on to you like a leech to skin.

Let's say you have an apartment they can move into, or you have money in your account, or people look up to you as someone trustworthy. They will use you to get to your resources. That is the only thing driving them, for without what you have and what you can do for them, you do not matter to narcissists.

For example, once the process of mirroring is at the full helm, they will ask you to lend them some money. They will say they have all the money in their account and then some, but it is "locked" or "inaccessible" due to some reason. You, having fallen prey to their seductive allure, have resorted to thinking in accordance with typical NLP responses like "they could never possibly ask for money unless something is really wrong." So, you end up giving and giving until one day, you find there is no one left to lean on other than the very person who has taken everything from you.

Anchoring

A steady form of mind control, anchoring is a technique ideal for advanced manipulators who have already passed the stage of mirroring. Through the process of anchoring, they are able to set the target up to have a definite, predictable reaction to a specific stimulus. It may be that they want the target to change their approach to something, or to do something in response to how they feel as a result of the mood invoked by the manipulator's induced stimulus. The manipulator can use this tactic to get the target to do something specific for them.

Say, for instance, two parents decide to give their daughter an allowance amounting to five dollars each week. They sit her down and explain all the chores she has to do so that she can earn this stipend. Before they can get down to discussing her responsibilities, she interrupts them and demands ten dollars a week instead of five. They argue that it is too much and instead settle on seven dollars.

Hours later, they realize that by introducing an innocent ten-dollar reference point, their daughter had subconsciously anchored their decision to increase her weekly stipend. Even though they had $5 in mind, when she insisted on making it $10, they promptly adjusted the amount to $7 so that it became *closer to the goal she had in mind instead of being what they wanted.* This, in summation, is the anchoring effect.

When a person is relying too heavily on a piece of information offered during the process of decision-making, a cognitive bias is likely to occur. This bias, otherwise known as the anchoring effect, becomes a tool in the hands of manipulators to get their targets to make decisions in close alignment with the things they actually want from them.

Amos Tversky and Daniel Kahneman, two psychologists, first noted the prevalence of this effect in 1974. They came to the conclusion that individuals construct estimates by first coming up with an initial value, which is then modified to produce the final response. In almost all situations, this answer is closer to what the negotiator wants than the original decision of the potential user or target of the negotiator.

In certain instances, anchors manipulate their targets by making easy reference points they feel compelled to follow. Such as a sign at a yard sale or a resale of properties that goes "$200 or best offer," or "$200 or near value," provides a starting point from which negotiations can happen. The target is bound to feel that even if they can reduce the price slightly, it should not go below $120-$175, or they may risk losing the product to the hands of a more willing customer.

A skilled manipulator will exploit the anchoring effect to the extent that they can do nothing but go ahead with the choices and decisions served to them forcibly. Manipulators will employ the anchoring effect very subtly, all the while keeping their targets blind to the play of deception happening below the surface.

One of the anchoring techniques an abuser can use is the irrational baseline. Let us say a seller shows us an edition of a book and says the price is $200. We would balk at the price, irrespective of how pretty the book looks. On the other hand, if the same seller is a clever manipulator, they will first show us an edition worth $400, and then say they can sell it to you for $200.

This sounds far more interesting and is a prospect you would consider, right? The $400 price was the irrational baseline, where the manipulative seller labeled the price at a level costlier than what it actually was. You make the purchase and walk away happily, thinking you have made a steal. Only they know the truth of what has transpired. This strategy can work beyond simple dealings where money is involved.

A supervisor at your place of work may make you spend sixty hours in the office each week. If you do a great job on the other days, he will say that you can leave for home at 5 pm on Friday. The irrational baseline of needing to put in more than ten hours every other day makes it feel like a huge relief to get off early on Friday, and you feel that your boss is the best ever for allowing you this luxury.

Similarly, let us say you have been arguing with your spouse about how much housework you have to do. They finally agree to help you out, but not before they make a statement. "Sam helps around the house only four hours a week. And Bob and Henry do about two each week. I don't think Adam's wife lets him do anything around the house at all!" You originally wanted your partner to at least give seven hours to help you with chores, but this feels very unreasonable now because of the anchor he has set. So, you move the duration to three hours each week and finally settle on two.

The next anchoring technique manipulators often use is called bracketing. It is particularly popular in sales and becomes a means to prepare potential customers for higher price points. The salesperson makes two brackets of options with the implication that the customers do not have any other options except for choosing from these options.

To do this, they will frame their question as, "Is your budget in the eight to twelve thousand range, or above twelve thousand?" The customer becomes swindled into thinking they cannot choose a lower option, so they choose the lowest bracket, that is, the eight thousand dollar range. This technique is used by manipulators to increase the maximum budget points without needing to go into serious discussions.

The third, and most subtle, anchoring technique is the high-low reference point. So, if you are shopping for antiques, let us say you have kept aside a budget of $2000. You go to a shop, and the seller asks you, "is your budget lower or higher than $7700?" This figure, you think, represents the beginning of prices for their high-end products. The $700 is probably a marker for specificity. This sly little trick helps the salesperson set an anchor without needing to say it. Most people will feel compelled to increase their budget, even if it is only by five hundred dollars. Without even needing to go too hard on their words or convincing tactics, the seller still managed to get you to spend more than what you originally intended to.

Another kind of anchoring works a bit differently, but with the same intent of making the target conform to a particular feeling, thought, or pattern of action. This involves a series of steps, so let's take a look at each of them.

The manipulator will start the process by figuring out the feeling they wish to instill in the target. If their purpose is to raise confidence in the target (something of positive value), then this is what they will be focusing their attention on. On the other hand, they could also make the target more subservient. The feeling is subjective and depends on their intentions and could be anxiety, relaxation, sadness, happiness—anything the manipulator wants.

Next, the manipulator will choose a trigger. This is basically the means through which they will instill the feeling in their target. They can use storytelling or tell them of a time that makes them feel what the manipulator wants them to. For instance, if the manipulator wants their target to feel more confident, they may reminisce over a time when the target was assured of the decisions she made. The manipulator will describe the moment so the target will relive the feeling they had back then.

The third part is the identification of the anchor. In this stage of the process, the manipulator may make use of the senses, including sight, smell, sound, and taste, as well as anything else that induces a sense of comfort and familiarity in the target or causes them to think in the manner that the manipulator wants them to think.

For instance, if the manipulator wants to remind the target of something or get them to think a certain way using touch, they will have an accurate understanding of the body parts where the target is most sensitive to the tactile perception. Using this knowledge, they will touch the target in those locations to elicit favorable responses. At this time, they will work to actively trigger the anchoring feeling.

To anchor, the manipulator will tell the relevant story to the target. In this case, they will take their attention back to the time they felt self-assured. They will amplify this with statements targeting their target's confidence upliftment, like offering praise for a good deed they did or an opinion they made. Throughout different points of time in the course of the day over several days, they will make their partner feel more and more confident about different aspects of their existence.

Finally, when the target feels the intended emotion, they begin using the anchor. So, if the anchor is a quick touch on the target's shoulder or the inside of their wrist, they begin to do it. If it is a facial expression or a word, they use it. Over time, the manipulator will ensure that their target makes an association between the anchoring instrument they employ and the confidence levels of the target.

Whenever they want to boost the target's confidence, they will use this anchor, and the target will respond favorably. So yes, this will take a long time. But if done for good causes, it can turn out to be something very fruitful.

Pacing And Leading

You have no doubt heard the old saying, "never bring a knife if you are going to a gunfight." If I were to say this to you, you'd immediately reply, "Of course, I wouldn't. Who would do that?" So, how is it that successful business owners can market their products as ruthlessly as they can without the more dangerous tools of persuasion? We've all been there.

Have you ever had an interaction with a client, a customer, or a friend who has pushed you so close to the edge that you've thought *I'll either persuade them or die trying*? Not all of us succeed, but with pacing and leading, there is an increased chance that your persuasive efforts will not be in vain. This manipulation technique continues to be one of the most powerful tools of persuasion in marketing.

Pacing and leading can be used in areas like copywriting to influence readers or listeners of audiobooks, where the audience will feel as if the writer is speaking directly to them. To do this, the writer has to thoroughly understand the target market on an emotional level and lead the audience to a conclusion that is most favorable to the company.

Pacing and leading is a linguistic style that we use in normal conversational exchanges as well, and its seemingly innocuous nature means that it is usually hard to recognize. Often it becomes visible only through body language, by mirroring, for example. A person engaging in pacing and leading will take on the posture of the target to make them feel more at ease.

A core component of NLP is enhancing persuasion and influencing behavior in others. NLP includes a hybrid of different models and techniques, all centered on different aspects of human behavior and personality. Bandler and Grinder, the people responsible for giving a voice and name to NLP, found that pacing and leading could convince people to go into a kind of trance. Once in this trance, these people could be influenced to make decisions or do things they normally wouldn't do.

Take hypnosis, for example. A hypnotist uses the power of suggestion to put a person in a trance-like state by using words such as, "as you listen to my voice, you begin to feel sleepy." Often the word "sleepy" is repeated several times. Imagine you are sitting in that therapist's chair, relaxed and with your eyes closed. As the word "sleepy" drifts softly across your mind, you find yourself feeling drowsy.

It's almost impossible to resist the suggestion, and, eventually, you fall into a hypnotic state. You're not asleep but in a state of heightened concentration where you are aware of your surroundings and yet feel disconnected in some way. You haven't lost control, but you are open to being controlled by the therapist.

Pacing and leading work in the same way. In any situation where pacing and leading are in effect, the target is compelled to carry out a set of actions that will make them feel, think, or further act in a certain premeditated way.

Do something for me. Sit quietly somewhere with no distractions around you, and read the following lines as carefully as possible.

> "Today, we are going to learn all about a technique that will change the future of everything for you. When you master this technique, the world will become your oyster, and you will find that there is nothing out there, no human being who will not be convinced to do what you ask them to. Now, I normally offer this technique for $170, but you and I are not here by chance, but rather providence. I instinctively know you deserve and need my help. So, for the next 24 hours, I will be offering you the full course on learning this magic technique for only $30! You read that right!"

As you mull over these words, you may get more and more curious about what this technique is, and how it can be used to earn as much power as the statements unequivocally say. If you are even minutely curious at this stage, you have been paced and led to a state of being favorable to the seller of the course materials.

So, the course seller knows—whether by searching algorithms or going through your internet history, or simply the magic which makes a hundred saucepan advertisements appear all over social media sites the moment you search for one "big saucepan" online. The seller has acknowledged your desire to learn the technique of convincing others, and now, they are pacing and leading you into a situation where you will be curious enough to buy their product. They also add a sprinkling of scarcity principle along the way—*this is a one-time offer, only for you.*

The act of pacing begins with acknowledging the target's state before going on to discussing the topic on which you want to lead them. It disarms the target's mind immediately after letting them know that the manipulator is aware of the truth of their situation. Their mind will no longer consider that the rest of the information feels a little dubious, simply because the first bit—the acknowledgment—was so believable. Once the pace is ideal, the target is lured into a decision that may not be something they would agree with or resort to if they were in control of their full consciousness.

How do you use this to diffuse situations for good causes, though? Let me explain. Imagine that you and your partner are having an argument. There is a noticeable increase in your partner's volume. Your rage is understandable, but you don't want it to get out of hand. You know that your partner experiences blackouts if they become too angry, so you want to lead them out of this state and into a calmer state of being. To do this, you must match the pace of your partner.

However, this does not include shouting at your partner. Instead of shouting, you tell them firmly, "Look, I'm thirsty". You keep saying this, while slowly reducing your own vocal intensity and pace and simultaneously allowing your partner to do the same. Initially, your partner may be surprised by the abrupt change in tone, but you will notice they will generally follow your lead in de-escalating the situation.

You may use this in a variety of contexts, such as at a business meeting, where you can listen to your colleagues, match their speed, and then move on to your own agenda. This is used in advertising to acknowledge what customers are doing and then lead them to place an order for your products or services. You may even use it to pique someone's curiosity about a subject.

Body Language

The last technique we will discuss with regard to NLP is reading and using the target's body language. In this instance, the manipulator takes time to comprehend different nonverbal cues so that they can form a clear conception as to how the target is planning to act in or respond to a certain circumstance. Since reading body language is basically a window into understanding the target's mind, it gives the manipulator a clean and powerful tool to control and influence all situations involving the target's decision-making abilities.

In the cult classic *Scarface*, Tony Montana, played to perfection by Al Pacino, famously says, *"The eyes, Chico. They never lie."* If I had a dollar for how overused this term has become to reference moments of young adult romance and passion, I'd... well, let's say I'd be quite endowed. However, there is a lot of sense to what Montana said. We do like to believe that words are the most important things when it comes to exerting influence. To an extent, we'd be right. But in communicating with others, what we do is also as important as what we say.

Body language is a powerful nonverbal communication tool comprising hand and arm gestures, body movements and positions, facial expressions and eye mannerisms. So today, if I offer you my condolences for a period of grief you are being subjected to, but do it while laughing, you will probably never speak to me again. This is because the manner in which our bodies move and act provides clues to what we are thinking, which ends up getting interpreted by those we are communicating with.

The study of body language dates back to the 1940s. Albert Mehrabian, a leading researcher on the topic, found that four minutes of meeting someone for the first time is all it takes for fifty-five percent of our facial expressions to give away what we are thinking or feeling about the person we are meeting. To compare, he discerns that only seven percent of the impressions we form come from the words we speak. The remainder is decided by our tone of speaking.

The manner in which we portray our body language is usually inadvertent. People interpret nonverbal cues without being aware of what they are doing. In other words, we may not consciously know our nonverbal cues are leaving any impact on the people around us. But, the thousands of micro-expressions we make each point towards something and people read all of them, even if the reading and translating happens at levels of the subconscious.

Intuitive learned and hybrid motions, postures, and expressions make up body language. Blinking and blushing, for example, are inborn abilities, but forming a curtsy or raising the hand in greeting are acquired ones. In spite of the fact that these motions are natural, we are instructed how and when to tie them to specific circumstances. Body language may have a wide variety of meanings depending on where you are and what language you speak or write in. While in the U. S., a smile conveys delight, in Asia, it may be seen as an expression of concurrence. In certain Asian and African cultures, eye contact is seen as rude, however, in the United States, it is seen as a sign of attention or self-confidence. While waving one's arms to emphasize one's speech is typical in Italy, it is considered disrespectful by Japanese speakers.

Since body language does not come with a set of "codes" and is not typified via speech or written language, it can be seen as a less formal thing in terms of communication. But the skilled manipulator knows that body language encompasses a definite structure in each of us. Emblems, for instance, include nonverbal acts like shaking the head. Regulators indicate the other person should start speaking via the use of gestures like nodding the head or turning the fingers of opposite hands in a clockwise motion, a sign that the speaker should wind up.

Adaptors are gestures used to make the audience feel more comfortable, such as shifting positions to a more neutral stance while interacting with them. Affect display is a general category that covers movements and postures which convey different unspoken thoughts and emotions and is possibly the most important of all nonverbal cues out there.

Experts in psychology, intelligence, and law enforcement often believe that a person's body language can be interpreted like reading a book, particularly by the analysis of tiny variations in facial expressions, also known as micro-expressions. While going through every possible way the human facial muscles can be configured, Paul Ekman and Wallace Friesen identified three thousand different configurations, some entirely involuntary. All of them have a form of nonverbal meaning attached.

With this in mind, they made the FACS (Facial Action Coding System) to serve as a tool for drawing out meanings from expressions. Their seminal findings have important implications for modern-day criminology as well. Many contemporary FBI agents and investigators undergo training in analyzing micro-expressions before they can reach the level of questioning suspects.

With this being said, it is important to note that just as one can interpret body language, so also it is extremely easy to misinterpret it by taking things out of context. An expression that may seem very odd to us may come naturally to the one who is wielding it. A real-life example of this lies in a presentation given by consultant Carol Kinsey Goman.

The presentation was delivered to the chief executive of a financial services company. While Goman delivered her vision, the executive simply sat with his arms crossed and bore no smile on his austere face. Neither did he offer any words of encouragement.

Once Goman had finished speaking, the only thing he said was a "thank you." He did this without making eye contact and then left the room. Goman naturally thought the meeting had been a debacle, so when the executive's secretary informed her of him being impressed by what she had said, she was very surprised. The secretary explained that these nonverbal cues were normal for the CEO, and if he would have been displeased, the nonverbal cue to look out for would have been him walking out in the middle of her presentation.

Now, manipulators can definitely adjust their body language and read the body language of their targets to get what they want. But did you know that if you take time to become aware of your own nonverbal cues, you can increase your communication prowess?

To do this, begin by recording yourself giving a presentation to an audience or speaking with a group of friends. When you are alone, watch the recording without the sound to identify telltale nonverbal cues you use in interacting with others. You can also lean back on breathing exercises before stressful meetings so that when the time comes, you are more aware of your various nonverbal cues.

At times, manipulators will deliberately alter their body language to connect more meaningfully with another person. If the manipulator is trying to persuade someone to buy something, they may nod their head as they explain the various positives of the item of interest while also matching the potential buyer's facial expressions.

The buyer, as a consequence, feels stimulated into making a choice that will favor the manipulator's intentions. This becomes an extension of mirroring, where they carefully study voice tone, facial expressions, posture, and other micro-expressions of the target and then mimic them. This reduces the scope of misinterpretation and also makes the manipulator come across as someone intrinsically charming.

Now that we know how different mind control techniques can be used to get people to think, feel, and behave in predictable ways, my next question is—which professionals, according to you, must include an element of mind control in their working patterns if they are to succeed or make a name for themselves? Let's take a look.

ATTORNEYS AND MIND CONTROL

Making a good first impression on prospective clients and winning or losing cases may sometimes come down to how convincing the attorney's arguments are. And when we speak of convincing, an element of mind control will always come into play. The mere definition of the adjective is being capable of making someone believe something is real or true.

Whenever we use the phrase "making" someone believe, it is necessary for us to comprehend that the person in question may not have believed "something" to be real or true before they were persuaded of its authenticity by another person. Unless this someone is able to appeal to the audience's conscious mind and reinforce their faith in the existence of this "something" via mind control, we are looking at the losing end of a deal.

While attorneys rely on a mix of verbal and nonverbal cues for making convincing arguments, the power of their success rests upon their ability to choose the right legal language that is pertinent to each case. Let me give you a seemingly unrelated example before tying it together. Two college students, Hilda and Mary, are discussing their likes and dislikes when it comes to their professors. Hilda discusses one of their teachers, called Professor Boyd. Mary indicates she isn't planning to take any more of Boyd's classes despite Hilda's unequivocal statement of Boyd being "gold." This is because Mary finds Boyd to be a tad biased in her judgments about the students.

Hilda counters Mary's misgivings by declaring that no professor can be anything other than who they are, and the reason Boyd is gold is that she knows she is a *good* teacher. Only bad teachers go ahead and credit all students randomly without looking at their real merits.

There is nothing seemingly unusual about this discussion—such squabbles between students are pretty routine. The subtle technique of manipulation in play here is associating the definitive term "good" with "teacher." While Mary may have her misgivings, human beings are wired to react a certain way when they hear some terms being thrown around.

If I tell you Professor Boyd is a criminal enough times, you may actually believe me without me needing to make a strong argument. In the same way, if I tell you Professor Boyd is a caring and compassionate professor with appropriate nonverbal cues, you may find yourself getting swayed into believing me.

For attorneys, the most important element to success lies in controlling perspectives and the narrative of their cases. The way they open before judges, jurors, and clients can be the key to determining how the remainder of their interactions will flow.

They will have to study the art of making proper opening statements so they remain in the dominant position during exchanges because the proof of the persuasion pudding lies in convincing half the courtroom or half the mind of the potential client with a strong opening statement.

So, it is only natural that building rapport is one of the most important mind control tools the attorneys have at their disposal. To be able to convince someone to change their minds or form an opinion, there has to be an element of trust and rapport. When the human brain is confronted with a slew of new ideas or information which we do not intrinsically agree with, our natural biological response lies in shutting down the frontal cortex and going into sheer survival mode, also known as the fight-or-flight response. In other words, if the potential clients or the courtroom does not or cannot relate to the attorney's image or what they are saying or their nonverbal cues, their case is lost before it can even begin.

On the other hand, when people feel safe around someone else and are naturally curious to learn more about what they have to say, they are unlikely to rush to survival mode. This is why attorneys focus on building rapport regardless of their personal perceptions of a case, client, judge, or audience. And this goes beyond their own image.

They will also look to establish solid common ground between their client and the audience so that the courtroom can look at the client as someone "likable" or "relatable" and feel safe around them. At home, they may be suffering major rage issues, but in the professional scene, an attorney will be understanding, calm, humble, and respectful. If the case deems some light humor, they will use enough instances to keep the audience piqued while also establishing their client's innocence.

Another thing that attorneys are acutely aware of is any kind of objection or counterargument that may arise in the course of their trial. Yes, some things will be given to chance, but a successful attorney will spend hours prepping for all eventualities and happenstances. Based on their understanding of likely scenarios that may arise, they will prepare their arguments and standpoints in a manner that remains convincing against all the stances that may be adopted against them.

They will not leave any stone unturned until they are confident they have answered every question and objection in an appropriate manner. By learning to appreciate potential arguments, a successful attorney will persist over all tricky situations simply because they know how to manipulate the situations to suit their ends.

The best lawyers make a conscious effort to do background investigations on the prospective jurors and judges with whom they may have to interact, and they do all in their power to ensure that they have some say in the individuals who are appointed to sit in on their cases. If they have any say in the matter, they tailor their lines of reasoning, the evidence they give, and the manner in which they communicate in general to the people who will be listening to their presentation. It is impossible to predict when you will be put in a circumstance in which you will need to communicate clearly with those who are unfamiliar with the manner in which you typically do things.

Attorneys understand this and know that if they want the support of the individuals they are talking to, it is imperative for them to have as much information on them as they possibly can. So, they acquire the skill of communicating with people on their level to prevent the possibility of failing to achieve their desired ends owing to simple misunderstandings and miscommunications.

Attorneys may lean on storytelling to appeal to their audience's emotions. The mind is likelier to prefer a story when it comes to absorbing a point than it will be if it gets inundated with statistics and facts. Stories go beyond the logical aspects of the brain and encourage people to think with their emotions—which is ideal when your profession lies in winning the hearts (and favor) of others.

The imagination is more easily engaged by narratives and images than it is by the straightforward presentation of facts alone. Dates, research, and statistics are often less intriguing and more difficult for the brain to process compared to these things.

The most skilled lawyers are aware of this fact to a greater extent than anybody else and leverage it to their advantage. They won't just make a passing reference to the evidence; instead, they will offer it in its entirety as a physical, palatable, presentable entity whenever feasible.

They will keep referring back to it, despite the fact that the audience is aware that it is present, in order to keep reinforcing the 'truthfulness' of their case scenarios and re-establishing themselves as the agency in that particular scenario as they have visual proof of the truth that cannot be disputed.

Just as they know how to use storytelling to build their own cases, attorneys understand if someone is trying to use storytelling against them to make the audience fall for a point that will not be in their favor. Their capabilities lie in moving beyond this boundary and ensuring that they have responses that will return things to how they want them to be. Certain nonverbal cues like digging in the heels, locking the jaw, or putting up a very defensive stance can work against you, even if you are right. They make you seem vulnerable and prone to being excited, which is the last thing you want to make others think of if the case is something that demands seriousness.

Attorneys know this for a fact and they can recalibrate their methods depending on what individual encounters necessitate. This increases the chances of them getting what they want.

Attorneys look for small instances which will make their audiences lower their defenses. Once their guard is marginally low, they will make the logic of their argument so believable that it will become hard to dispute anything they say. Plus, attorneys understand that in certain cases, appealing to people's emotions is the surest way to victory.

They do this by saying things to the witnesses that make them fumble or get angry, so they slip up during their testimonies—if this is something the attorney needs to happen. They can make a jury feel bad for a defendant irrespective of the guilt factor. They can appeal to the trust of their potential clients, whatever their end intentions may be.

SALESPEOPLE AND MIND CONTROL

The most effective salespeople never give the impression that they are attempting to sell you anything as soon as they make their first contact with you. They approach you as if they were your counselor, directing you to locate the product that is most suitable for your needs. The idea is to get the customer to a stage where they will feel so on edge they become compelled to buy the product being sold.

The salesperson who wishes to persuade a prospective client to consider their product will know that the generic sales script is never enough for closing a deal. Repeating often-quoted words can make people sound overly rehearsed. If the salesperson is not sharing messages or information that feels personable while being very relevant to the client's needs, all their efforts (regardless of whether the product is actually good or bad) will go in one ear and straight out the other.

Consider how many phone calls we hang up on abruptly when we know it's a seller on the other end of the line. Sometimes, we don't even wait to hear what they have to offer. As soon as we hear the drone of "I am so and so from so and so," and especially if they call during hours when we are frantically busy, we curse the entire profession and hang up before they get a chance to say anything else.

So, the clever salesperson will not entirely wing their calls, but they will know the timings that work best for their target audiences, and they will also know how to adjust their messages depending on what the core interests of the prospective audience are.

During interactions with prospective clients, intuitive salespeople will listen closely for minor details, which will help them close an important deal. This could be anything—a sign of hesitation, a remark, a long pause—anything that will tell them the client is worth spending time on.

Say, for instance, a salesperson is selling payroll software to some small businesses. An inbound lead writes to the salesperson letting them know their company boasts: employees from multiple states, due to which they need a uniform all-in-one solution. This is key information to the salesperson and will form the basis of their pitch.

They know they now have to highlight their software's ability to determine tax rates for all fifty states simply at the click of one button. This is a feature that is most relevant to the company's concerns. Then, they can use a free tool to automate the process and rapidly personalize their messages depending on what each buyer is interested in.

This will work far better than simply calling up the heads and droning on about who the salesperson is and which company they are from and why they do what they do and why their product is so great. Our attention spans are categorically short when it comes to monotonous messages. We feel a greater impact when we can see things in action in front of us. A salesperson who is intent on success will know how to manipulate this knowledge to their advantage.

Efficient manipulators can mask their self-serving agendas by asserting their cause to be inherently selfless and noble. If they can use the right words, the selfishness behind their actions can be incredibly hard to identify. Many salespeople know and believe this to be true and apply this rule when trying to sell a service or product. They explain to potential consumers that their only mission is to fulfill their needs, and that, given how much effort individuals put into bringing pleasure to others, it brings them delight just to see the joy experienced by others.

They manipulate their words to make it seem as if they exist to serve the customer and their needs. In many instances, customers will do one of two things. They will either pity the salespeople and think, "How would they ever make sales if they are so timid? Best I buy something. It may be the only sale they make today." And voila, they are in the trap. The other reaction is the customer gets genuinely moved by what they perceive as the salespeople's kindness and compassion and ends up making the purchase of the product or service.

Manipulation is all about doing what is necessary to get what you want. It includes aspects of transparency and bearing a positive attitude alongside engaging in the occasional subtle trickery. Salespeople often manipulate prospective clients by luring them into buying products with the content that they have on their websites. They become a veritable online resource in their domain of function.

Instead of expecting people to simply buy their product or use their service, they work to give them something back in return. For instance, they can offer a well-made and highly strategic content marketing plan. This plan can include industry tips, marketing wisdom, advice, and other useful items while advertising the core products and services in a palatable form. Or they can also offer free products along with the products which they are selling.

Part of the content marketing strategy also involves storytelling about the salespeople's work ethics and everything they have achieved in their years of operation. The customers find these stories inspirational and can often form relationships with them.

A successful salesperson will always give their customers the illusion of control. They will not be bothered with throwing random product specifications and boring statistics in the customer's tired face. Rather, they will only share relevant information and then exhort them to ask additional questions.

This will make the customers feel an element of being in control, although it is the salesperson who is actually steering the conversation. The sales representative will instinctively know if a customer has even a tiny bit of interest. They will understand what aspects of their products or services interest them and increase emphasis on the effectiveness of these aspects rather than boring or confusing them with unnecessary information loads.

Keeping the strategy simple will also help the salesperson ensure their customer is on the same page as them. The more they go into technicalities and tricky information, the less likely this will be to happen. On the other hand, some customers may actually be interested in the technicalities. The key here is in understanding the customer's individual specifications and altering strategies to suit them.

A sales representative intent on a positive outcome will move beyond simply rattling off all the reasons why a customer should buy their product. Instead, they will explain why the product or service can help in solving the problems the customer may be facing. Since their concerns constitute the front, core, and end of the item being offered. The customers are likely to feel validated and therefore be more interested in buying the product.

For instance, if a sales representative sells expense and reporting software to entrepreneurs and the salesperson's lead lets them know the entrepreneurs are struggling with how cumbersome the manual logging of expenses feels, they will mention the different automated features of their software and how much time the customers will save on an average. This will also show they are actively listening and interested in solving the prospective client's concerns through viable solutions.

Often, salespeople will let past customers do the key business of selling for them. In other words, they will use social proof to their advantage. And we all know how powerful social proof can be as a persuasion tactic. Now, regardless of how genuine the salesperson's words are, or how persuasive they may be, buyers will always approach them with a grain of salt because they know that at the end of the day, the most important thing for them is to make the sale.

On the other hand, if a past buyer leaves behind a story or a testimonial with real experience on how the product or service being sold has alleviated their issues, it may be a plausible selling point. A salesperson who understands how persuasion works will know that if a client is showing resistance, sharing one such testimonial may clinch the deal.

At all times, the sales representative will anticipate different objections. They may have a solid understanding of their prospective clients and what these clients desire. Their notes may be foolproof, and everything may be going fine right up to the moment they feel ready to close the deal. Then, all of a sudden, they may find the prospect asking them several difficult questions and raising objections that they did not account for.

The rookie salesperson may give up immediately. But the seasoned one will know this is a learning experience. They will steer the conversation, via carefully constructed words and appropriate pauses, to a place where the client unequivocally believes the product is going to help them. This will be because the experienced salesperson has probably spent hours brainstorming different objections a prospect may throw their way, and they are likely to be prepared with all the necessary answers.

The capacity to manipulate the facts is only one of the numerous strategies that legal professionals and salesmen have in common. They are skilled at leaving out some realities or merely bending the truth in appropriate places so that you view the big picture in the manner that they want you to perceive it.

When it is convenient for them to do so, they will speak the truth, but when it is not, they will not. With a feeling of plausible deniability, they will continue to mess with the truth as long as it serves their interests. They may get experience in deceit this way without having to lie.

The most successful salesman you will ever meet will often exhibit chameleon-like behaviors. They will watch you and alter whatever aspects of themselves that they feel are necessary to draw you in. They tailor their sales speech specifically to fit your needs. The time-honored method of salesmanship known as "getting you to feel comfortable enough to listen and giving them more and more of your time" ensures that nothing will prevent them from getting what they want, which is your faith in their product and purchase from you.

The strategy known as "escalating" is one that is often used by salespeople. The use of escalation as a technique is quite effective in easing the transition from the sales floor to the office, where the documents are waiting for your signature. It entails gradually loading your hands with stuff or carefully organizing the trip so that you ultimately arrive at the workplace, where you may be alone and at ease. This also works well after the sale, when someone may phone you to follow up or maybe even attempt to generate new leads via you. When things are increased gradually, the consumer is put at rest to the point where they do not realize that the speed of the situation is not what they had anticipated.

At the end of the day, the sale must be made because the customer will really want to buy the product and not because they feel forced into making a decision. Nobody likes to feel they are being pressurized into saying a yes, so effective salespeople will never be too direct in their approaches.

They will give enough reminders to make the prospect feel that the ultimate purchasing power will be in their hands and a matter of their personal choice. This is an essential element to forming a personal connection that will make the customers believe and engage on a deeper level with the seller.

Buyers may like the brand and even the product, but if they find the sales rep to be a genuinely lovely person who makes them feel valued, there is nothing like it. If a salesman is able to put themselves in the shoes of a potential customer, they have a far greater chance of closing more deals. This is because they are able to develop a stronger connection with the individuals they speak to and convince them that they are in a safe and secure environment.

People are much more motivated to purchase with their feelings than with their heads. A confident salesperson can be very efficacious because people are more likely to want to respect them simply because of their self-assured demeanor. It's only logical to want to move in the same direction as someone else when they give off the impression that they know what they're doing. The salesperson makes the most of this knowledge by beginning the sale with confident mannerisms that engage customers well before any words have been said. This is an effective use of the information.

PUBLIC SPEAKERS AND MIND CONTROL

A powerful instrument that may be used for a variety of purposes lies in the art of public discourse. Speeches are often used to narrate a narrative or convey a message. As a result, if the speaker isn't cautious, the speech might come out as monotonous. It is not uncommon for speakers to use persuasion as a means of influencing their audience, or "receiver of the message," in a speech. This style of speech may be anything from a political discussion to a commercial pitch. Any speech intended to persuade others has as its primary purpose the goal of altering the minds of the listeners or at the very least reinforcing an existing viewpoint.

As a result, speakers use a range of arguments and methods that are best described as the three persuasive techniques: ethos, logos, and pathos. Each of these three arguments has the potential to be a very effective means of persuasion if used correctly.

Every public speaker has to remember that human beings come with an abysmally low attention span, so they have only sixty seconds at the onset to make their first and lasting impressions. It becomes crucial to engage the audience as early on as possible, and during this process, the speaker also has to assert their credibility. The way to do this is through *ethos*.

Ethos is related to the speaker's persona and reputation, which, in turn, are built on their reliability and credentials. Before we go to attend a speaker's workshop, we often make our decisions about whether it is worth our time, depending on how well we know the speaker's popular appeal. Ethos becomes a way of legitimizing this. It is the same for a lot of other professions.

For instance, when we go to a healthcare professional, we may want to run a background check to know their credentials. If we go to an investing company, we will need to do our homework to ensure they have a history of client support and good practices. This is basically a way of ensuring our money is going to someone who has done their research and isn't blabbering just about anything on stage.

Of course, every great speaker has to begin somewhere. If the speaker is new to the profession, the best way to go about it is to ensure they know what they are talking about, even if there are only five people in the audience. These five people should be able to go home and say "wow, that was a life-changing experience, I can't wait to tell others about it." They should know the front and end and all the possible arguments against their beliefs and be able to justify them nonetheless.

This will tell your audience that you not only know what you are saying, but you also deeply believe in it. No one wants to trust a person who has no faith in themselves or stumbles trying to explain why their words make sense. The speaker has to understand their audience, so some amount of interaction and background knowledge becomes essential. Many speakers do this by getting one or two lines from members of their audience about who they are and why they are attending their sessions. This helps tailor their messages in a way suitable to specific audiences.

Public speakers know referencing reliable sources is critical. For instance, a speaker highlighting the benefits of definite pharmaceutical products will often give references or quotes from well-known medical professionals, even if they aren't one themselves.

The fact that they are not a qualified expert on the issue is something that an audience may accept and even applaud if the speaker presents it from the perspective of a story including an expert's opinion. Nevertheless, they may not excuse the speaker if they just parrot something they have read or heard without crediting the expert whose opinion it is in the first place.

Clever speakers will share a personable story on how a particular pharma drug has helped them, in what ways, and to recover from which issues. Then, they will go on to highlight the expert opinion in a way that will make the audience resonate with the topic even more, such as saying something like, "I came across the work of X when I was at my lowest. What I am about to tell you is entirely what I learned from them—and you will know why it is so life-changing."

As a corollary to *logos,* effective public speakers will always justify the things they say with ample reasoning—it should not be overpowering, but it also should not be scant. I think many of us will have been in a situation where we emphatically know what we are saying to be right, but because we become overpowered by our need to prove it to our audience (and therefore, become angry in the process) we find it just about impossible to convince them.

Not only do they end up not believing us, but they also label us as "argumentative" and "unreasonable" in the process. To ensure their emotions don't get the better of their mind, public speakers use the principle of *logos,* which is a logical appeal derived from evidence-based facts to fortify their stories to appeal to both the audience's emotions and their logic. Now, logos often goes hand in hand with the next principle, *pathos.* Pathos is concerned with appealing to emotions.

The strategy behind using logos and pathos does not lie in merely spitting out a number or a fact and making that the primary argument. Rather, the speaker's success lies in using facts and proven information as a foundation for the argument—something to return to from time to time to reinforce the core of what the speaker is sharing with the audience. If the primary message for the speaker is to convince the audience to join a motivational speaking course, they will probably share a life-changing personal experience that catapulted them into the life of a motivational speaker. I've been there and heard all of them.

Devastating near-death experiences, life in prison, Ivy league dropouts—somehow, great speakers have experienced all of these things. And they are able to make most people in the audience believe the credibility behind these events because they fortify them with just enough facts and reasoning. Then, they share the foundations of motivation and why it has made their life so brilliant.

From flying in private jets to being invited to premier events, motivational speaking has done it all for them. And then comes the clincher. *You can enjoy all of it too.* This pattern of speaking is a curiously balanced mix of emotions, reason, appeal, and endorsement that simply leaves the audience craving for more.

The greatest of all public speakers never have to "try" to be excellent at what they do. We perceive them that way, but when they speak, they do so almost as if they are having out-of-body experiences. They are not bothered by who the audience is, where they are, or if their surroundings experience any malfunctions. In an environment that is amplified by the magnetic power of their words, the only thing that matters is that everything feels impossibly natural.

This is how they win over the toughest of audiences who cannot see the hours that have been spent in checking and fixing the venue and the technology to ensure nothing goes wrong, the days spent rehearsing all verbal and nonverbal cues that seem so spontaneous and "relatable" when done on stage, or the months spent in ensuring that the affirmations and stories used in the speech are configured to the wants and desires of the relevant audience. In the end, when they are facing the audience with the power of their words and their nonverbal cues, the only thing the audience will see, and indeed, the only thing that the speakers want them to see, is the human being making history on a stage.

Great speakers intrinsically know two things. First, they understand the audience is on their side, and that they want to be influenced and motivated into a course of action. Second, the mistakes made while speaking on stage are never as memorable, embarrassing, noticeable, or as big as they seem at the onset. They know that human beings are not supposed to be infallible, and if anything, owning up to the slight errors here and there and laughing it off will only increase their rating.

The audience is not expecting a God. They are expecting someone aspirational—which isn't the definition of a person who does not make mistakes, but rather, who treats their mistakes as natural happenings that can be used as a roadmap to future learnings and bigger victories.

Once they have finished their preparation, outstanding public speakers no longer feel the need to think about delivering an effective speech. They are aware that eventually, their muscle memory will kick in, and everything will become second nature, as if they were operating on autopilot.

A portion of this takes place during the preparation stages, but it is very important to keep this in mind prior to entering the performance area. The most effective public presenters are able to make their observations seem like they are just part of a natural discussion. The parts of the speech that involve preparation and practice are when the most outstanding aspects of the speech are developed.

The best speeches—the ones that we end up remembering for our entire lifetimes—are the ones that involve personal stories which come across as authentic. People love stories highlighting struggles. They don't want to know a speaker was born to a life of luxury. Rather, they want to be told that the speaker has faced intense hurdles and undergone life-changing experiences before they have reached the place where they are today. Nothing communicates the message of a speech better than the "there is a reason why I am here, and why you can be where I am too" story.

Not only are the stories easier to remember, but they are also more emotionally driven than a speech that gives a run-down of facts after facts. Now, this is an element of public speaking that needs the speaker to tread carefully. If they can frame the story well enough, most people won't think to go back and look for the name of the hospital where they experienced their "I saw God" moment or the point in their life where poverty made them decide they would never go without food again.

These personal accounts can be notoriously difficult to cross-verify at times, and if the speaker is able to make the stories emotional enough—while also showing that they have done sound research on others who have gone through the same process and the solutions that exist—they will not need to worry. This is what separates a persuasive speaker from one who stumbles and fumbles through their personal account and makes everything seem "too unrealistic" or "too good to be true."

Also, efficient public speakers won't beat around the bush for too long. There are few things more frustrating than listening to lectures that take what seems like an eternity to deliver the key purpose. Regardless of how compelling the argument presented in the speech truly was, it is very difficult to win back the attention of the audience after it has been lost, and the risk is sometimes not worth taking.

To counter this, speakers often begin by making the core elements of their speech known before delving into the personable aspects. Later, they will return to these elements at different points in the speech and tie them to the personable elements. They will always make sure that the audience never faces the possibility of missing the purpose of the speech at any moment.

Finally, if the purpose of the speaker is to engage the audience right up till the end when they offer them the tools they need to sign up for a further course, they will do it in a way that makes the audience crave for more. It's simple, really. If you put out all your cards on the table, people around you will be inclined to feel there's nothing more they can take from interacting with you.

On the other hand, if you place four out of six cards, and keep the two best ones hidden until the very end, and then you say, "so, you enjoyed these four, you want to see the best two that I haven't revealed yet." Then, the speaker goes on to share the details—how the audience can sign up for the detailed course, the monetary aspects, and so on. The key here is to leave the people listening to you with a sense of wonderment that makes them think, "I really need to learn more of this."

With the techniques and methods you have learned in this chapter, you can use what feels relevant in your personal life and see improvements with your own eyes. Every professional wants to get to a point in their lives where they can be in control of their actions and decisions.

It helps to be able to identify a manipulator—almost as much as it also helps to know what persuasion tactics you can use to stay ahead of the game yourself. Keeping this in mind, we will move on to the next chapter, which is all about hypnosis.

CHAPTER 6
HYPNOSIS

HYPNOSIS, at the end of the day, is only as real as the wielder will have it be. It is a genuine tool used in psychological therapy, although dark triad manipulators also employ it to unscrupulous ends. We will get to these ends in a while, but for now, let us begin by understanding how hypnosis began.

The earliest references to hypnosis date back to ancient Greece and Egypt. Although we now know that being in a state of hypnosis is much different from what we experience when we are sleeping, the name "hypnosis" originates from the Greek word that means "sleep."

Greek and Egyptian cultures were home to religious centers where people came to find solutions to various problems. Healers employed hypnosis to induce a steady state of dreaming, during which time the patients would be questioned to arrive at the root of their issues. In 2600 BC, Wong Tai, the father of Chinese medicine, wrote about techniques that used incantations and hand gestures.

The Hindu Vedas, which were written around 1500 BC, carry mention of hypnotic procedures. Likewise, trance-like states are known to have been a part of various yogic, druidic, shamanistic, and voodoo religious practices.

The father of contemporary hypnosis was Franz Mesmer, an Austrian physician. The word "mesmerism" and its variations have been inspired by his name. Mesmer developed the theory known as animal magnetism. The philosophy behind this was that disease occurred as a result of blockages obstructing the flow of magnetic forces within the human body. He believed he could store this animal magnetism and transfer it to patients via rods or "mesmeric passes".

The mesmeric pass was a long-winded way of putting someone in a trance. Mesmer would ask his subjects to stand still as he swept his hands across their bodies, at times for hours. He was a prolific showman and could manipulate his patients by virtue of his confidence and eccentricity that something was about to happen to them.

As a form of indirect suggestion, the mesmeric pass was undoubtedly powerful. Mesmer also portrayed himself as a hypnotist with magnetic eyes, a goatee, and a cape. His showbiz persona and his magnetic nature brought him many enemies who were jealous of the ease with which he could persuade people to believe in something so apparently ridiculous.

Eventually, his contemporaries maligned him to the extent of causing him great public humiliation. For a long time afterward, the future of hypnosis was deemed uncertain since the medical world was so unequivocally opposed to it.

John Elliotson (1791—1868), a forward thinker and professor at the London University, was credited with introducing the stethoscope in England. He tried championing the notions behind mesmerism, but his colleagues forced him to resign. However, he continued providing demonstrations of how mesmerism could impact patients to interested parties in his own home—and if not anything else, this led to an increase of literature on the topic.

Four years after the birth of Elliotson, the world made room for a tiny baby called James Braid. He would go on to become a Scottish eye doctor. One day, Braid was late for his appointment and found his patient staring into an old lamp in the waiting room, his eyes glazed over. Braid was fascinated. He instructed the patient to close his eyes and go to sleep. The patient apparently complied, and Braid's interest in the subject grew. With time, he found that getting patients to fixate on something before beginning the process of inducing them into a trance was essential.

In the early days, the swinging watch worked as a popular object for inducing fixation on patients. Braid went on to publish a book where he labeled the phenomena he had witnessed and was now studying as "hypnotism." Around this time, James Esdaile, a British surgeon working in India, found that hypnotism had enormous benefits for relieving pain. He performed many major operations with hypnotism as the only anesthetic.

Upon returning to England, when he tried to convince the medical world of what he had found, he was subjected to laughter and ridicule. With time, hypnosis became, and continues to be, an alternative form of medicine.

Émile Coué, a Frenchman, moved away from conventional ways of looking at hypnosis with his emphasis on auto-suggestion. He coined a famous term that goes on the lines of day by day, in every way, I am becoming better, and better. This led to an early notion of the use of affirmations as a tool of motivation, and today, affirmations continue to be one of the most influential ways of getting people to look over their limitations and get things done.

Coué believed he was responsible for helping people heal themselves. One of his most beloved notions was that the imagination of a human being is far more prolific than their will. For illustration purposes, if you challenge someone to walk steadily over a piece of wood laid out on the floor, in most cases they will be able to do it. They will, however, begin to wobble when you advise them to shut their eyes and assume that the board is hanging between two buildings several hundred feet above the ground.

Now, Coué was a practical man. As a result of this practicality, he understood there was an inherent placebo effect involved in hypnosis. In other words, people want to believe something beautiful and transcendental is happening to them. When the patient who is on the verge of giving up is told, "I have something that will cure you," they cannot help but be optimistic.

People who seek to manipulate for dark ends can use the power of this placebo effect to enormous advantage. For a time period, Freud himself was interested in hypnosis—but he wasn't particularly good at it. This meant that his early rejection of the concept further delayed the development of hypnotherapy—given that Freud was one of the biggest names in psychological literature. Things picked up again in the 1930s when Clark Hull published his work "Hypnosis And Suggestibility."

The contemporary theory of hypnosis owes many thanks to the work of Milton Erickson, who was a highly efficient psychotherapist. Stricken by polio and eventually paralyzed as a child, he remobilized himself. He found that his unordinary circumstances gave him the opportunity to spend time observing people.

In the course of his observations, he noted there was a remarkable difference in what people said they would do, and what they actually did. This formed the basis of his interest in human psychology, and he devised innumerable creative routes to healing people. These included the use of confusion, surprise, metaphors, and of course, hypnosis. Over the years, hypnosis has gained considerable credence—which of course, brings us to an important question. When does hypnosis become dark?

MAKING SENSE OF HYPNOSIS AND DARK HYPNOSIS

The use of hypnosis can cover many purposes. It is only when the hypnotist begins making suggestions that will make their subjects do things that are harmful that it becomes an act of dark manipulation. When we hear the word "hypnosis," the conventional norm still remains to jump to the conclusion of a man with a thin beard and a long cylindrical hat, waving a pendulum watch in front of a patient's face while the latter reclines in a chair. More often than not, we also visualize a kind of verbiage that goes along with it, for instance, "now you are falling asleep," "you are so tired," and so on.

The real aspect of going through hypnosis, however, is vastly different. As a matter of fact, the hypnosis isn't really "hypnotizing" the individual in front of them. Rather, with the use of subtle mind control techniques and a number of clever words, they are getting the individual to induce *themselves* into a trance.

In other words, the hypnotist alters the individual's state of mind so that they become more absorbing to whatever suggestions are being offered. While the individual is hypnotized, they can experience vivid fantasies and altered realities, be more open to manipulation, or experience increased attention to only specific objects.

Now, a version of hypnosis, much like a version of manipulation, can be used to do good. Using this procedure can bring about powerful therapeutic results which can help individuals. On the other hand, it can also be just as harmful, depending on what ideas are fed to the individual when they are in a trance.

It is important to use hypnosis judiciously because there is so much about it that we don't understand. Although it has been around for centuries and has even been the subject of scientific discourse for over two hundred years, there is a widespread misunderstanding about what it is and what it can do.

A search on the internet will give you the impression that hypnosis is a wide number of things. They will either make you believe that it lies in the realm between sleeping and waking as a state of existence that is cataleptic and unconscious. Within this state, all you experience is an apparent dissociation where you are dazed, lost, or bewildered. The other line of belief is that hypnosis takes you into a place where your attention is amplified to exorbitant levels, and within it, you are able to give your full focus to the tasks you have at hand, or are asked to do.

However, hypnosis deserves a better quantification. It is supposed to be separate from a stage of consciousness. It is an artificial means of accessing your internal REM stage. Under natural circumstances, REM is a stage of sleeping that happens within an hour to an hour and a half of falling asleep. It is characterized by the occurrence of vivid dreams.

Therefore, rather than being a separate entity unto itself, hypnosis is a process that is separate from the state of trance that you experience while being in it. Hypnotherapists often assure their clients that this is an entirely safe process, given that we go in and out of trance all the time. They aren't wrong.

We enter a trance-like state at all times when our attention is focused on something very specific. But this also means that whenever we enter this trance, our viewpoint becomes limited to only the tiny little realm within which the object of our attention is focused on one narrow aspect of existence.

For instance, if I am in a trance-like state of concentration about a topic I am studying, I will probably forget to eat for hours. I may even forget to drink water. My sole focus may only lie in what I am studying, which means I have no time or inclination to consider anything else out there. Therein lies the danger of hypnosis. It isn't about what it is, rather, *the risk lies in what it can make you do.*

Anyone with the capability of focusing their attention for a period, or anyone who can experience emotional arousal and has a good imagination, will enter a trance-like state on occasion. Even if we're indoctrinated by religions, cults, or politicians, we can't see beyond our own blind spots.

Regardless of how exciting it may be to support a team to victory, feel swept away by the music, be moved by literature, art, or theater, fall madly in love or make passionate love, or experience an incredible marvel that takes our breath away, exciting events are no less restricting in contexts of our ability to look beyond the immediate occurrence and consider the bigger picture.

Whenever we become highly aroused, for instance, when we feel so angry, furious, hateful, frightened, anxious, worried, or depressed to the extent that we cannot think of anything else except for the emotion that is consuming us, we begin operating as individuals cut off from our capacities to think logically. Our perception of reality becomes limited and locked in.

The state of being in a trance can also happen when we employ day-to-day living skills. For example, when driving or looking through the window of a moving car, our thoughts may be entirely incognizant of the roads we pass through or even the landmarks that we cross along the way.

When we are engaged in something creative, for instance, cooking, gardening, painting, writing, singing, or dancing, we enter a trance for the extent of the time that we are performing the activity. This is why you will often hear that maestros of a particular craft can go for hours, even days, without being bothered to eat, drink, or even take a shower.

When creative geniuses feel that they are on the brink of creating their next masterpiece, the world external to this masterpiece may seem like a hazy fog that they will not focus on. The term "flow" refers to a trance-like condition that occurs when we know how to perform something so well that our feeling of separate self fades while we are engaged in the action.

When we're in this state of joyful trance, it's as if we've become the experience we're creating. Some psychologists call this "peak experience" or "being in the zone," and it adds much to a feeling of purpose and meaning in life if it can be used for good.

On the other hand, trance can also be the result of inducement through drugs, rituals, shocks, sexual activities, prayers, reflection, being compelled to remember certain memories, altering breathing patterns, and hypnotic language. Any stimulus which can invoke a strong emotion and cause the human mind to slow down and enter a deep state of relaxation along with lowering emotional arousal can cause a trance. Once the state has been induced, it is expected that the individual will dream, become focused, and be receptive to learning new things.

The manner of inducing the focused state in which attention is only on one thing can impact the kind of trance experienced by the individual, as well as its duration and depth. A reason why so many places of religious worship are designed so beautifully and ornately is to induce people to enter into a state of dreamlike awe the second they enter, which would assuredly make them more receptive to what is being taught or preached within the walls of the religious institute.

The manner in which religious officials speak in these institutes, carrying a tone that is often quiet and reverential, often gives off a feeling that helps in the retention of this induced stupor. The idea is to give the participants the feeling of being in a very holy place, a place that is magnified by only one divine entity and his chosen people. The presence of this entity should be felt in such ways that makes the people obey each and every command.

Joe Griffin discerned that the deepest hypnotic state comes from dreaming. A basic form of trance, human beings begin to dream right from the time they are in the womb in a fetal form and can manifest REM sleep. Michel Jouvet, a sleep research pioneer, gave the insight that during REM sleep, human instincts are programmed within us from our genes.

We keep returning to these instincts whenever we dream, and they, in turn, maintain the integrity of these instincts. Our dreams, in themselves, are nothing save for metaphorical translations comprising expectations emotionally aroused and not acted upon during the time that we are awake. Dreams work to deactivate emotional arousal and free the brain to respond to every new day as it comes.

A trance resembles the REM (Rapid Eye Movement) state because of how similar it is to REM sleep. When we go into a state of trance induced by hypnosis, our minds and bodies undergo many similar experiences to REM sleep, like not being receptive to sensory information from the outside, low pain sensitivity, paralysis of the muscles, and so forth.

Many hypnotherapists employ rhythmic movements to help induce a stupor, including making repetitive hand movements or making their patients continuously stare at something in motion. The level of profound relaxation that serves as the gateway into the trancelike state is analogous to what occurs to our bodies when we start to drift off to sleep. Once the target is relaxed, guided imagery is used to enable them to see things from a different perspective. This could be used for good, or bad.

Metaphors are a very important part of therapy, and dreams are nothing save for an act of residing in metaphors. Trance-like experiences often involve hallucinations. Targets may "feel" something they were imagining. So, if they are imagining pain, there is a chance they will feel it too. Phenomena can be induced during these stupors, like amnesia, dissociation, body illusions, and catalepsy.

The REM stage constitutes the core of being in this tranced state. It is very much an active stage of functioning where you can learn, daydream, and solve issues. When you undergo a difficult situation, the REM stage is the medium via which the traumatic occurrence gets captured by your brain. It then serves as a template for you to be prepared the next time you encounter something extraordinarily difficult.

With hypnosis, part of the confusion also stems from the proliferation of half-truths about the topic. Many of these half-truths are considered believable, and often, the sanest of targets will feel there is an aspect of truth in them.

For instance, there is a widely-held belief that hypnosis constitutes a natural state of concentration and relaxation where there is a high level of awareness that gets amplified by suggestions from an external source. Hypnosis is not a natural state. It is artificially induced and can even be the result of a violent event like a loud noise or a sudden movement that causes us to go into a state of trance.

Next, there is conception hypnosis, which is safe and does not come with any side effects. Hypnosis is extremely powerful. Some people can feel uneasy or dizzy because of its impact. There is a widely prevalent sense of feeling "out of control," and extremely divorced from one's surroundings and inner voice, especially if they are acting on suggestions that defy the core of who they are.

Hypnosis has been linked to a slew of unsettling or even hazardous side effects, as documented in a wealth of literature. There is a wide range of symptoms, which include chronic fatigue, antisocial behavior and distress, panic attacks, attention deficit disorder, self-image obfuscations, and more.

Another misconception a manipulator will tell their targets before ensnaring them is that they will be aware of everything being said to them. On the other hand, do we remember all the things we dream of? When people go into a deep trance, it is very unlikely they will remember anything the manipulator says or makes them do.

Later, once they wake up, it is highly possible they will have no memory of what they did. The same manipulators will also say that hypnosis is entirely different from sleep. It is nothing more than a state of heightened relaxation.

In reality, hypnosis is deeply connected to sleep and dreaming. Plus, a dark manipulator will convince their target that the human unconscious is very wise and will not do anything wrong. However, nothing could be further from the truth.

The unconscious depends on many variables, including the manner in which we have been brought up, our culture and socio-economic backgrounds, and our overall conditioning. Our moral codes are not that simple. In fact, there is a plethora of data demonstrating that individuals often act against their own interests if they can be convinced to do so. There are no hard and fast rules when it comes to morality.

Finally, and perhaps the most erroneous belief of all, is that a hypnotist cannot influence a target to act against their will. There are enough examples of unwanted influence. To cite one of the direst examples, in 2015, two students with underlying mental health issues, Wesley McKinley and Brittany Palumbo took their lives after being hypnotized by their principal (who was also a self-appointed healer). You can be influenced to make careless mistakes and do things so dire they could cost you your entire life. That is how dangerous hypnosis is.

When it comes to the dark side of hypnosis, perhaps one of the most important concerns is that it can take away the target's sense of control and independent ability to think, judge, and act. Having an iota of control over our own lives is nothing if not a right. A manipulator is wrong to assume they have the reins over what a target can possibly need, but in their minds, they are most likely not operating from a place of concern for you. So, when they take their targets to a zone where they have no control over their sense of self, they won't care so long as it gets the target to do what they desire from them.

Second, one can never know the intentions of the manipulator. While they may be acting out of concern for the target, it can also be they want to induce hypnosis to achieve something extremely dangerous.

It was 1894, and Anderson Gray was a rich farmer who lived just outside of Sumner County, Kansas. He was embroiled in a lawsuit and Thomas Patton, who lived next door to him, was aware of what had taken place. On May 5, Gray went to the farmhand Thomas McDonald's house in order to permanently stop Patton. In response to Gray's claim that Patton was making up stories about McDonald's wife, McDonald and Patton had a furious verbal exchange. McDonald went back to his house after the altercation.

The next time Gray came to see McDonald, he hypnotized him, telling him that unless he killed Patton, Patton would murder him. Gray's magnetic effect was too powerful for McDonald to resist. As a consequence of this, Gray was able to hypnotize McDonald into having outstanding rifle aim, despite the fact that McDonald had a terrible aim in the past. Gray then informed McDonald of Patton's whereabouts in the woods.

As Patton rode past, McDonald waited until he was in range, then fired at him. Gray and McDonald got taken into custody. Gray was tried and convicted first, and he was given the death penalty. McDonald was ruled not culpable because Gray's trance had put him in a stupor, even though he had confessed to murdering Gray. This is one of the earliest known accounts of what hypnosis can do when the manipulator's intentions are wrong.

Third, hypnosis can lead to false memories. We discussed some experiments in the earlier chapters, where we talked about how students were compelled to act against their will, or how a whole war-like scenario was induced through the power of a few words. During the 1980s and 90s, entire families were ripped apart because of false memories being fed into patients about suffering sexual abuse at the hands of their caregivers.

In one such horrific instance, a young woman was made to believe she had been subjected to repeated counts of rape by a

Satanist cult that included her family members besides people in the local community. Later on, the truth came out that these induced memories were all false. Manipulators can indeed induce hallucinations which may cause entire psychotic breakdowns. That, of course, is the specialty of the stage hypnotist. It is very risky since a person who is spellbound is unable to differentiate between the actual world and the world of their dreams.

Hypnosis can often be used by manipulators to con their targets into believing something. When politicians use abstract words along the lines of "positive changes," "principles," "upstanding society," "revolutionary," or "values," they induce their audiences to go into a collective stupor where the search for the meanings behind these words is very one-dimensional.

Indeed, many times, the politicians have very warped notions of what "progressive change" can encapsulate. So, if you think hypnosis is silly, Hitler himself studied it in great detail after he professed to get cured from hysterical blindness at the end of World War I. The hypnotist told him he was special and possessed great powers which he could use to cure his own blindness.

Hitler took this as a sign that he had the powers to induce hypnotic states in entire crowds. He would bombard them with emotionally charged dialogues, including the adoption of the stylized Nazi salute. It is therefore important to remember how power can be abused, and how there can be terrible consequences when hypnotic language is flung around casually.

Dark hypnosis can be dangerous to the point of destroying the target's entire essence. When a manipulator uses hypnosis to get the target to enter a REM state, they are effectively tapping into the target's unique individual essence for their own gain. In other words, they are trespassing into the private mental space of the target, a space where they do not belong.

Using hypnosis on repeated counts can not just weaken the targets, but also leave them increasingly vulnerable to suggestions. Extreme hypnosis can derange the brain and make targets behave not as thinking, conscious beings, but rather as objects or play toys in the hands of their manipulators. All dangerous mass movements constitute an element of hypnosis and have worked by programming people after arousing them to dangerous levels of emotional turmoil.

THE STAGES OF HYPNOSIS

At this stage, I am going to assume that if you want to learn the stages of hypnosis, there is an element of personal curiosity about it for you. You have a concept of what can happen if hypnosis goes wrong. Knowing these precautions, let us take a look at what hypnosis can mean in terms of the stages it encapsulates.

Getting someone's undivided attention is the first stage in changing their conscious state. This initial stage of hypnosis may take place in both vocal and nonverbal ways. Consider, for example, how a person might get so engrossed in their task that they lose sight of the world around them. Nonverbal hypnosis is an excellent illustration of how our psychological states change when we are focused on something with all of our concentration. Of course, it is simpler to get someone's full attention if you use words.

When someone is describing imagery or presenting a prospective tale, people tend to clutch more tightly at their words. How some individuals prefer mental imagery as a guide to learning over conventional textual learning is a lot like this. In other words, it is easier for the human mind to follow along when there are visual and mental cues.

This first step of concentration absorption is something that may be practiced via regular conversation. Try telling a friend or colleague that you have a narrative for them when you are out with them and notice how much more attention they pay to you as a result. You may tell them a tale that's based on real events or one that you've made up, but be certain to provide a lot of specifics.

Create a vivid image in the listeners' minds by filling it with your words and using a wide variety of descriptive details to elucidate the entire setting. It is to your advantage to make use of as many of your senses as possible. You should provide something for their intellect and creativity to work with. When you have effectively captured their attention and led them into the second stage of hypnosis, you will know that you have succeeded when you have them caught up in your story.

In itself, the conscious mind is more limited than we'd think it to be. You are inundated with new information on a daily basis, and your brain processes all of it in a logical manner. Unconscious thoughts often have a much more casual and relaxed quality to them than your conscious patterns of thinking.

Things like the facts of existence do not always play a role in our unconscious minds. When you dream, for instance, your unconscious mind is operating at full capacity. This is something to keep in mind. Even if you've never really witnessed a unicorn with a rainbow mane in real life, your subconscious mind is free to assume that such a creature does, in fact, exist. Practical concerns dominate the majority of the attention paid by the conscious mind.

In the context of hypnosis, this concept is referred to and regarded as the "critical faculty." Think of the critical faculty as a sentry standing at the threshold of the subconscious, and you'll have a good idea of what it does. Your critical faculties will alert you to things that are inconsistent with logic and reason, as well as those that are unlikely to be true.

When you are attempting to hypnotize someone, the most difficult obstacle you will face is the critical faculty. You may get someone's undivided attention by just keeping their gaze and conversing more slowly and quietly than is typical. This will assist you before you attempt to control their critical faculties. It's possible that adopting a hypnotic tone of voice might assist you to enter a trance state and bypass the target's critical faculties.

While you are hypnotizing your target, you should be on the watch for any signs that they are entering a trance state. Before providing any hypnotic recommendations to your subject, you should at all times wait until you are very certain that they have entered the altered state of consciousness. If you bypass this and begin verbalizing random hypnotic statements, there is a very high chance the critical faculties of your target will reject everything you say.

Next, you will be working on generating an unconscious response. Getting this response does not necessarily have to be a wild thing. You are, after all, not doing it to get your target to run around in circles or quack like a duck. It may be as subtle as making the target laugh or frown or get them to gasp in shock. Any reaction that takes place while the target is not obviously aware of what is going on is considered an unconscious response.

The target may have to be told they performed this action to understand it happened. To simplify, an unconscious response is something that the human body does when the conscious mind is not involved.

Have you ever faced a situation where you are just waking up and trying to get out of bed, but your body acts before your mind can program what is happening and you stumble? This is an example of an unconscious response when your body is working on autopilot.

Getting a target to give an unconscious response is easy once they have entered a hypnotic state. You need to look for signs like the pupils become dilated, the breathing rate changing, or the skin changing color and flushing. These are all signals that point to your target being in a vulnerable state. In other words, your target has let their guard down. When this happens, try to garner an unconscious response from them. You can describe something you know they love in their waking state.

For example, if they are huge fans of salted pecan ice cream, you may use this time to give them a rundown of the salted pecan ice cream that is considered to be the tastiest. Talk about the texture, the perfect balance of flavors, how the dessert looks, and how it makes the target feel. Or, you could go along another trajectory and describe something they are really scared of, like a ghost or a horror story. Go into vivid imagery, and see how they react.

Slowly lead the target towards your outcome of choice through metaphors. At this stage, you are directly communicating with their unconscious mind and taking advantage of their altered state of consciousness to either help them arrive at an outcome, conclusion, or decision that will benefit you. An example of this stage is known as priming.

For example, if you want to go on a trek, and you want them to accompany you, illustrate a story of snow-capped peaks, adventure trails, hot meals in unknown locations, and the cool flow of hidden fountains. This could generate a post-hypnotic reaction which will help you get to your desired outcome of making the target *need* to go on a trek with you.

HYPNOSIS VIA PATTERN INTERRUPTING

Once you enter a guided hypnotic trance, you will get suggestions from the hypnotist that will be directed only to your unconscious mind. In other words, your conscious state of existence will no longer be at play, and all decisions you make will only be the result of your unconscious mind's processing of the hypnotist's dictates.

These dictates often include ways via which you can change your life through altering habits, mental patterns, and beliefs. In many cases, the hypnotist will work to change something or alter a thought pattern that is harming you. However, a dark hypnotist will probably use forms of hypnosis as a tool to get you to do what they want, regardless of whether it is good or bad for you.

While trance-based hypnosis measures are among the commonest ways to induce a stupor in the target's minds, there are occasions that call for a more indirect approach. This is when conversational hypnosis becomes a usable tactic. It is also called indirect hypnosis, and it works via the relaying of allegories and stories rather than relying on direct hypnotic suggestions which will program the mind to behave in certain ways.

These stories are meant to aid the unconscious mind in forming conclusions of its own. A key difference between conversational hypnosis and other forms of hypnotism lies in its ability to trance the target with the eyes open. Unlike other hypnosis forms, this one doesn't need you to have your eyes closed.

An altered state of consciousness is what is meant by the term "state of hypnosis." What this means is you have the individual's entire attention at all levels of awareness so that you may affect them almost completely. To do this, all you need to do is use conversational hypnosis.

When a thought pattern is disrupted, a new one takes its place. Within this state, the target will not be able to come up with a rational explanation on their own and will be looking to you for help. In this way, you have the best chance of making an embedded command. Include the specific action you want them to perform in this command contained in the text.

Using pattern interrupts is among one of the most popular ways to carry out conversational hypnosis. Pattern interrupts can be used easily and are very effective in inducing the state of trance. A pattern interrupt is used to refer to any event which leads to the disruption of an existing and habitual pattern someone possesses.

Pattern interrupts can be very powerful because they momentarily shock the target's system so that their critical faculty gets consumed by what is happening. The manipulator uses this shock as a gateway to interject hypnotic suggestions of their choosing, including those which can send the target into a hazy state of mind.

Let me illustrate. All of us learn to tie our shoelaces when we are little children. Since we have gone to school after tying our shoelaces, we can safely assume that this is an activity we have done every day over many, many years. So, over the course of our lives, we end up tying our shoelaces so frequently that by the time we reach a certain age, mostly during our teenage years, the way in which we tie our shoelaces becomes a well-formed habit. So, by this time, tying our shoelaces is something that happens as a reflex.

We do not need to think about anything extra when it comes to tying these shoelaces any longer; it has just become part and parcel of our daily routine. Before going to school, we slip our shoes on, understand that they need to be tied, do the laces, and leave.

Now, let's say that one day, we are tying our shoelaces, and someone interrupts us with a story at that very moment. We are momentarily stumped, and our concentration becomes muddied for a second. It takes us more thought than it normally would to complete tying the shoelaces.

However, with time, it becomes just as it was, easy and simple. This is the power of habits to work on autopilot. Once the pattern interrupt stage is over, we will likely go back to what we were doing without even remembering we ever thought, felt, or did anything else for that short time.

Whenever a habitual pattern gets interrupted, we are left with two choices. We can either start the pattern all over again, or we can recover the concentration we lost and think our way through completing the pattern. The more complex habits will likely be the sum of smaller habits.

We should be able to go back to start the step we left off at before something interrupted our pattern. The bottom line? Our brains like to work on a resource conservation basis. Thinking our way through patterns can often take up more time and resources, so the brain may ask you to simply start what you were doing all over again.

In hypnosis and neuro-language processing, habits that we interrupt are known as patterns. The example I just illustrated is simply one of the many habits we employ in the course of our lives. When we sit back and think about everything we do in the course of a day, it becomes more and more apparent that most of what we act out occurs through a perpetual cycle of habitual processes.

As much as ninety-five percent of the things we say, think, and act out are the result of habits imposed over time. We don't really notice most of our habitual behaviors since they are so automated. They don't require us to think consciously or invest extra time in doing them. To use a pattern interrupt, the manipulator will make a note of any habit that the target is performing, then disrupt it with the use of some tactic or the other. As the manipulator disrupts the habit, they will deliver a hypnotic suggestion.

For instance, let us go back to the instance of tying shoelaces. Let's imagine we are on autopilot, and our mind is pretty much non-operational since we are acting on the reflex of habits. The manipulator suddenly asks us a question that disrupts the tying process. We get thrown off kilter.

Even though we have memorized what we are doing, it takes us time to return our thoughts back to where we are in the process of tying the shoelaces, and how we are supposed to move ahead. This is just what the manipulator wants. The moment of confusion resulting from disrupting the target's habit means they will have to use their mental resources to deal with the sudden slew of information.

This moves their critical faculty to the side, and they become open to hypnotic suggestions. Timing is the most important element when pattern interruptions are happening. The disruption may not last for more than a second, so the suggestion the manipulator makes has to be sharp, short, and full of intention. There are times they will use just one word to clinch the deal.

They will use a pattern interrupt to break a habitual process and give a hypnotic suggestion, for example, asking the target to "sleep." They will move on to using a hypnotic deepener. Once the subject is in a state of hypnosis, they will give some positive suggestions or use hypnotic triggers and cause them to act in specific ways of their choosing.

In the course of our lives, unconscious habits make up a large portion of everything we do. There are, therefore, countless examples of pattern interrupts at play. One such method is the handshake induction. The manipulator greets their target with an extended hand as if they are trying to shake their target's hand to greet them. However, they do something else entirely, and this disrupts what the target anticipated or thought would happen, which allows the manipulator the opportunity to generate hypnosis.

To induce this kind of hypnosis, the manipulator will begin by reaching out to shake the target's hand as if performing a normal greeting gesture. As soon as the hands meet, they will abruptly pull their hand down and say a word like "sleep." Then, they will move on to using any hypnotic deepener of their choosing. They can add in many more gestures.

For instance, instead of using one pattern interrupt, they can increase their success rate by layering multiple pattern interrupts. They can position a very confusing and vague question as they reach for the target's hand, and pull the hand down as the target attempts to answer. This is just an illustration of what could happen if the target is susceptible to this pattern. Of course, the manipulator will need to have a clear

268

idea of what patterns the target is most comfortable with and used to.

Sometimes, the manipulator will say something you disagree with. This will inevitably lead to a form of argument or disagreement in most situations. However, while you may be trying to convince the manipulator to see why you are right and they are mistaken, they will use the time to understand what your core perspectives are.

Then suddenly, they will agree with what you say. You will be caught off guard and experience some kind of validation. The momentary confusion that ensues will loosen the strength of your critical faculties. They will use this moment to begin feeding you something to deepen the trance even further. Once the trance is in place, they will employ hypnotic commands to get you to do what they want from you.

Sometimes, it can be as simple as saying something unexpected or out of turn. It's as simple as cutting someone off in the middle of their thought process. It may be a narrative about something like a run-in they had at the grocery store or a disagreement with someone who crashed into them on the sidewalk.

Use a non-related sentence like, "I have often pondered what renders the sky so bright" to stop them mid-story. Your acquaintance was engrossed in his or her narrative, and may even have been on autopilot if it had been a story they had previously recounted. You shattered their train of thought when you interjected with a remark about the sky.

As a result, you now have their whole attention. In order to receive the information they need, they are now tethered to your every word. Because of this, they are susceptible to hypnotic suggestions. It's not clear where these solutions will originate. That would be, of course, via you.

As soon as hypnotists are in this position, they may implant their hypnotic suggestions, which may or may not have anything to do with what the subject was saying or thinking. This works because the brain is completely committed to pursuing the pattern to its rational end while it is engaged in a pattern.

Once the pattern is successfully disrupted, the brain tries to find a new pattern or attempt to complete the previous one. If you were to envision someone strolling down a meandering hallway, imagine that you could turn the lights off and plunge the hallway into darkness. When the lights go out, the individual has no means of finding their way through this maze of a hallway. They are hoping for someone to switch the lights on again so that they may navigate their way.

All of a sudden, you turn the lights back on, and they are able to see everything. When someone is groping about in the dark looking for a source of light, they are in their most vulnerable state. They are analogous to the sensations that occur in the brain whenever the normal flow of cognition is interrupted. It is searching for the switch that will turn the habitual patterns of thinking back on so the individual may resume following the established patterns of behavior.

Now let's imagine that you don't turn the lights on until you observe that the person who is walking down this hallway has fully twisted themself around in a desperate attempt to find a light switch. What would happen in this scenario? They continue going in the incorrect way because they are oblivious to the fact that their position has changed and they are now facing the reverse way that they were traveling in.

When you have effectively disrupted an individual's thinking pattern, you may implant a hypnotic suggestion. You cause their brains to wander in a new direction than they were before, much as you confused the individual in the hallway with darkness to the extent that they began wandering in the wrong direction.

The person's route, which they were following, served as the pattern, and the darkness in this scenario served as an example of an interruption to the pattern. This is how a trained hypnotist may regulate how a person talks after inducing a pattern to interrupt.

With conversational hypnosis, it's preferable to use pattern interrupts that are relevant to the embedded command for optimal effects. Because it will help you finish the newly discovered pattern, the embedded command is more useful this way. Let's say you're a salesman trying to overcome a customer complaint about the product's excessive cost. In light of the product's high price, he's worried that it would severely cut into his spending power.

"How much are you willing to spend in order to attain your goals?" is the appropriate pattern to interrupt in this scenario. This automatically encourages the individual to consider investment returns rather than outright cash expenditures. You may use this to persuade a potential customer to buy your goods by highlighting their positive attributes. As a result, you have a better understanding of how to use pattern interrupts effectively during conversational hypnosis. If you want to become a master of hypnosis, the best way to do so is to keep learning and practicing.

Now that we have an understanding of what hypnosis is, and what it can do, it is time to look at one of the darkest aspects of hypnotizing someone. This, of course, is brainwashing. When it comes to the practice of indoctrination, it's important to note that the term "brainwashing" encompasses a wide range of psychological tactics used to influence or change a person's thoughts and behavior.

Those who are brainwashed are considered to be unable to think critically or autonomously, allowing undesirable concepts and ideas to enter their brains, and changing their behaviors, values, and principles.

In 1950, Edward Hunter used the word "brainwashing" in English to describe how the Chinese government seemed to coerce its citizens. Some criminal proceedings in the United States and the behavior of people traffickers were also examined as part of the research on the idea.

For a long time, scientists and lawyers debated whether the use of LSD (lysergic acid diethylamide) or joining so-called cults may lead to brainwashing. The media also covered this issue extensively in the late 1960s and early 1970s. In the next chapter, we will go into deeper details about what it is, and how it has been used time and again to delude whole civilizations into acting out of turn.

CHAPTER 7
BRAINWASHING AND THE LESSER KNOWN DARK TACTICS

WHEN IT COMES to the history of what we have now come to understand as "brainwashing," Edward Hunter, a journalist, was probably the first to sound an alarm when he penned the headline for a scoop in the Miami Daily News, September 1950. The headline read, *"Brainwashing Tactics Force Chinese Into Ranks Of Communist Party."*

Within this political article, as well as in a book he would publish, later on, Hunter illustrated how the founder of the People's Republic Of China (PRC) Mao Zedong, through his Red Army, had used horrifying ancient tactics to compel the Chinese population into becoming Communist-conforming.

This, to him, was a hypnotic process, a brainwashing. He likened the tactic to *xi-nao*, the mandarin words xi denoting "wash" and nao denoting "brain." He warned the world about how dangerous the real-life applications of this technique could be. At the time, the process was used to signify the ability to alter a mind so radically that its owner would be nothing but a living, breathing puppet, parroting the words which would be fed to it by the master manipulator.

Fears of Communism and mind control had already entered the minds of the American public. In 1946, the United States Chamber of Commerce was so paranoid about Communism spreading that it considered removing all proponents of socialists, liberals, and communists from schools, newspapers, entertainment mediums, and news broadcasts.

The inflammatory rhetoric stirred by Hunter did not cause a shattering impact right at the onset. But three years into one of the worst wars, the Korean war, American prisoners of war began saying they had committed strange acts which they professed to have done under external influences.

When Colonel Frank Schwable was captured in Korean territory in 1952, he was among the highest-ranking military officials. By February 1953, he, along with other war prisoners, had apparently "falsely" acknowledged that they had used germ warfare to destroy the Koreans, by which they had dropped all manner of germs from anthrax to the plague on unsuspecting Korean civilians. Five thousand of the prisoners of war either signed their confessions or petitioned the United States government, appealing to them to end the war. Twenty-0ne of them refused to be repatriated.

Suddenly, it felt as if brainwashing had become a genuine threat that was about to destroy the entire nation. The United States military, while denying the confessions made by the prisoners of war, could find no way to explain why on earth the soldiers had made such fantastical claims in the first place. To them, nothing could explain the odd behavior of the soldiers except that they were brainwashed.

Pop culture became awash with the concepts of mind control. Films like The Manchurian Candidate started doing the rounds, capturing the attention of audiences whose minds were essentially wiped and "controlled" by external forces. J. Edgar Hoover, the FBI director, referred to mind control on repeated occasions in his book *Masters of Deceit*. By 1980, the American Psychiatric Association had recognized brainwashing by including it under the dissociative disorders section in the third edition of the DSM (Diagnostic and Statistical Manual of Mental Disorders).

Now, there were different connotations attached to the understanding of what brainwashing entailed at the time. Hunter was actually an agent of the propaganda wing of the Central Intelligence Agency (CIA). Therefore, he had a lot of political motivations behind attaching a racial connotation to the concept of brainwashing as a mystical Oriental practice that the West could not fathom.

However, scientists had a whole simpler understanding as to how people were forced into acting in ways that they would normally never consider. Essentially, the route was through torture. One of the psychiatrists who had worked with the veterans of war and also studied doctors who aided and abetted Nazi war crimes found eight criteria for brainwashing, also known as thought reform.

These included having complete and total power over the target's surroundings, forcing the target to confess to some crimes repeatedly, even if there were high chances the targets were not culpable. For the American prisoners of war who had been brainwashed in the Korean prison camps, brainwashing involved depriving the men of sleep and food, confining them to solitary quarters, keeping them standing up for extended durations of time, and repeatedly blaring Communist propaganda in close proximity to them. Essentially, the prisoners of war were traumatized enough to the point where they could not process anything save for what their captors were feeding into their minds.

With the onset of the 1950s, there was an increasing interest in military studies regarding the topic of psychological torture. Military directors had a mind of their own, and the workings of this mind would be far more sinister, at times inhumanly so, when we compare it to how we would normally think. To the extent, rather than concluding the American soldiers deserved and needed rehabilitation, the directors formed the opinion that these men were nothing but weak.

They were not interested in the topic of brainwashing at all. To them, it was a kind of hogwash; a cover-up of their purported reality that American soldiers could not stand up to torture. They came up with the SERE (Survival, Evasion, Resistance, and Escape program) to "educate" their men against all future attempts that would be made to change their minds via psychological torture. Ironically enough, to bring this change about, *they employed the very same torture tactics on their own men.*

On the other hand, the popular American culture was still mesmerized by what they understood to be hypnotic brainwashing. This was in part due to the work of psychologists Joost Meerloo and William Sargant. They self-proclaimed themselves as "public intellectuals" and began drawing similarities between their understanding of brainwashing and manipulative tactics used by the Communist supporters as well as American capitalist marketers.

Meerlo was of the opinion that dictatorship-ridden societies such as the Soviet Union, Communist China, or Nazi Germany had been very successful in brainwashing total populations into states of hypnotic subservience. In the same breath, they also believed modern techniques of manipulation and brainwashing were far more subtle and, therefore, doubly dangerous.

At the time, part of the conception as to what brainwashing truly meant was influenced by the tenets of behaviorism. The notion was that humans, and indeed all animals, who could be trained to do something by the use of a certain stimulus, would continue to do it even if the reward is not present. For instance, if you teach a dog that the sound of the bell means they need to come for food, they will respond by salivating whenever you ring this bell, even if you do not have food for them. According to the behaviorist school of thought, our brains are born as nothing more than blank canvases, and as we get older, they are gradually molded by a variety of conditioning variables, both from the outside and the inside.

As the American society became more and more awash with concepts of brainwashing and everything it was supposedly capable of, they grew increasingly afraid their minds were being controlled by those who claimed mastery over this manipulation tool.

Throughout the twentieth century, the American people continued to fear the effects of mind-control. Allen Dulles, the director of the CIA, legitimized a number of psychological experiments which were nothing short of horrifying. For one, he allowed the use of hallucinogens like LSD. For another, he also encouraged biological manipulation tactics like sleep deprivation.

His interest was in finding out if brainwashing could result from these techniques. The research results garnered from his experiments could serve as propaganda tools to be used against the Soviet Union.

The beginning of Project MK-Ultra may be traced back to 1953, and its activities would continue over the next decade. But with the Watergate scandal tearing the nation apart, the CIA had to destroy all evidence existing of the program. Twenty thousand documents were recovered via a Freedom of Information Act mandate launched in 1977. These files bore testimony to everything the CIA had done.

From drugs, sensory deception, and hypnotism to electroshock, they had tested the technique of brainwashing on pretty much everyone they could, including agency operatives, recovering drug addicts, prostitutes, and prisoners. Even their consent or lack thereof had not stopped them.

While the public outrage was natural, the Government would continue to employ such torture tactics to elicit pieces of information from fundamentalists and civilians in Iraq, Abu Gharib, and Guantanamo Bay.

All the things that had happened until this point gave birth to the essential history of brainwashing within the United States. The concept, at the start, was no more than a fledgling Orientalist propaganda made by the CIA to enlist domestic support. It proved to be so effective that the operations directorate ended up believing it and began the hunt for an actual weapon of mind control.

What resulted from this frenzied hunt was a simulated brainwashing program that was meant to be a precautionary tool against any form of torture, whether real or imagined, true or false, current or future, from the enemy front.

Since complete seclusion and dependency on the part of the patient are prerequisites for brainwashing, the term is most often associated with totalitarian cults and correctional facilities. Even essential human actions like resting, eating, and going to the restroom are susceptible to external directives since the brainwasher (the agent) has to have absolute control over the victim.

During the brainwashing process, the agent strives to destroy the target's sense of who they are and their place in the world. The agent will then begin to instill in the target a whole new collection of behaviors, attitudes, and beliefs that are uniquely suited to the circumstances in which they now find themselves.

Mental detachment is now a regular aspect of soldiers' training in many countries across the world. Meditative methods such as visualization and mantra recitation are used to help the subject disconnect from their environment, irrespective of how difficult this environment may be. Some regimens also instruct troops on how to perform brainwashing, because by their logic, if a subject is aware of the technique, it will be less successful for them.

So, I suppose we could all move on to wondering, does brainwashing really exist, then? I would unequivocally say, yes, it does. A program of isolation and inducing complete and total obedience via rigorous protocol can lead to absolute and total changes in people, especially if these people have already been subjected to a life of deprivation. This is one of the main reasons why Hitler was so successful in brainwashing an entire civilization into believing that the only way to achieve greatness was through mass genocide.

THE STEPS

We mentioned Robert Lifton and his notion of brainwashing involving eight essential steps. So, according to Lifton, the process of brainwashing encapsulated multiple steps, beginning with an attack on the prisoner's identity and sense of self. This would go on and on until the time came when the prisoner would experience a complete alteration in their belief systems.

To Lifton, the steps involved in this process started with an assault on the individual identity, followed by guilt and a sense of self-betrayal. The victim would naturally reach a breaking point. They would then experience leniency and the need to confess so that they could channel their guilt somehow. The final three stages would be guilt release, progress and harmony, and the final confession along with rebirth.

All of these stages would occur in an isolated environment. Normal social reference points are not available under these circumstances and the techniques used, like depriving the subjects of sleep or malnourishing them, work to cloud their minds. There is the constant fear of being harmed physically, which adds to the target's inability to think or act independently. The processes Lifton discerned can be broken down into three stages. These are a breakdown of the self, inculcating the possibility of retribution, and a rebuilding of the self.

The breakdown of the self begins with an assault on the target's identity, which forces them to think they are not the people they have known themselves to be this entire time. The target's entire sense of self, their ego and identity, and the sum total that makes up their core beliefs are vilified. The manipulator will make the target reach a place where they can no longer identify themselves as who they once were.

For instance, if the person being brainwashed used to be a woman and a doctor, the manipulator will say things along the lines of "you are not a woman," "you are not a healer," and "you are not helping anyone." The target will be subjected to constant verbal bashing until they grow disoriented, confused, and tired out of their mind. Their beliefs will cease to be operational.

Next, the manipulator will force the target to believe they are a terrible person. As the identity crisis settles in and the target feels more and more exposed, the manipulator will wreck them with guilt. They will amplify or make up any mistakes the target has made until it seems as if the entirety of the target's life has only been one mistake after another. The manipulator will criticize them for everything, from their nasty ideas to their sluggish eating habits. It becomes more difficult for the target to maintain their composure.

Once the target has been confused and overwhelmed by guilt, the manipulator drives them to renounce their family, friends, and peers who hold the same "destructive" set of beliefs by threatening physical violence or the continuation of the mental onslaught. This treachery of their own ideas and of those to whom they feel a feeling of devotion exacerbates the sense of humiliation and alienation that the victim is already going through.

The target may have a psychological breakdown as a result of their identity dilemma, tremendous guilt, and betrayal of the things they have always trusted in. The term "nervous breakdown" in psychology refers to a group of symptoms that may suggest a wide range of mental health issues. Sobbing uncontrollably and feeling depressed may be among the symptoms.

The individual may have lost their sense of reality and feel entirely alone. As soon as the target's psyche is shattered, they lose all sense of self and don't know who or what they are any longer. At this juncture, the manipulator prepares the target to succumb to the lure of converting to a different belief system that would free them from their suffering.

In the next stage, the brainwasher will make the show of being lenient. Now that the target has fully entered a state of crisis, the manipulator will show them the way out. This will be in the form of a tiny little kindness, just a sliver of hope from all the abuse and berating they have suffered.

For example, if they have been withholding food from the target or giving them inadequate nutrition, they may now give them a glass of water or a bite to eat as a peace offering. They may go down the emotional salvation route and ask what the target misses about their home. Since the target has been constantly subjected to a situation where they have only been indoctrinated about the darkness within and around them, now, this will feel like a small light at the end of the tunnel. A sense of relief and gratitude will result, and this will often be far in excess of the meager kindness that has been offered to them.

The brainwasher will then seek to earn their loyalty. They will give the target the opportunity to confess. For the first time in the entire process of brainwashing them, the target will find that they have the option to make a choice. They can either continue to exist and face the guilt, pain, and shame of their current state, or they can choose leniency.

The target may, and most likely will, want to reciprocate the small kindnesses the manipulator offers them. In their addled minds, this kindness is the route to their salvation. Just when this happens, the manipulator will present the idea of a confession and tell them that this is their route to salvation from all the guilt and pain they have suffered.

Guilt is likely the most important reason why the target is in so much pain. Following the period of them being under assault, their minds are now only programmed with anger for the betrayals they have faced from the ones they held close, and the shame they have built about their own identities. They are no longer sure why everything feels so wrong at the moment, but all they know is that everything needs to change.

This means that they have become a blank canvas looking for solutions. Aka, the manipulator, now has a canvas to work on. They can take this "emptiness" and make them do whatever they want. The manipulator will take the target's lack of meaning and attach whatever meaning they want to it. They will attach the guilt to whatever belief system they want it to encapsulate.

The target will come to believe that it is because of their faulty belief systems and all the people they have trusted in the past that they have accrued so much shame in their lives. So, the only way to salvation now is to choose the new and abandon the old. Staying back with the old will not yield anything except psychological agony. The new belief system will present the opportunity to escape that agony and build a new life.

The next key step will be releasing the guilt. The target will be relieved to learn that the cause of their issues is all an external source. So, they will believe they can escape all their wrongness if they can shun the wrong belief system that has been holding them back. All that they need to do is denounce the institutions and people who "forced" them to conform to the wrong belief system. So long as they do that, they will no longer be in any pain.

The target earns the power to release themselves from all they have suffered so long as they shun all of these bad, older influences. So, they confess and complete the psychological rejection of everything that formed the core of their former identity. Now, it is the manipulator who will offer them their new identity.

The time is now ripe for the target to enter a relationship that will be defined by complete allegiance to the manipulator. The manipulator presents the target with a path, which, according to them, will be their route to harmony and progress. They will amp it up by saying that if the target chooses, they can still bring about good, both within and around them.

The manipulator also cuts back on the abuse and offers physical comforts and reassurance to the target, along with the promise of everything the new belief system will apparently do for them. So, the target starts feeling they must choose between the old and the new. In other words, although the choice has already been made for them by the manipulator, they will be deluded into thinking they are the ones making the choice and that they have their fate in their hands.

At this stage, the choice is not difficult. In contrast to their previous persona, which contributed to eventual mental collapse, the new identity seems secure and desired. For those who have already renounced their former beliefs, making the "conscious decision" in favor of the opposing system of belief helps to alleviate their guilt: If they sincerely believe, then they didn't betray anybody.

The ultimate confession and rebirth is next, and it is this: "I choose good." When the target considers the misery of the old identity in comparison to the tranquility of the new identity, they choose the new identity and cling to it like a life raft. Rather than clinging to their old beliefs, they abandon them in anticipation of the current ones that promise to improve their lots in life.

At this point, rituals and ceremonies are typically used to officially welcome the newly converted target into the new group. Some brainwashed individuals have characterized this stage as one of resurrection.

Lifton based this description on all the accounts he heard of what techniques the American prisoners of war in Korea were exposed to. By all accounts, he believed that variations in the degree to which different people became brainwashed depended on their inherent suggestibility and how they responded to the different mediums of psychological and physical torture inflicted upon them. Of course, there are personality traits that influence the extent to which brainwashing a target is possible.

Individuals who are likely to break under pressure and suffer from a lack of self-esteem or have a weak notion of what their character is can be easily led into lines of shame, guilt, and a penchant for autarchy. This includes people who have a long history of suffering abuse at the hands of their families or larger environment or have experienced some form of childhood trauma.

A strong sense of identity and a healthy level of self-confidence will make a target far less susceptible to becoming brainwashed. Plus, some targets may also have unequivocal faith in a power higher than themselves. For them, salvation can only occur through this higher power and not via any ideology that is man-made. It would be notoriously difficult to brainwash such targets as well.

UNRAVELING THE CORE OF BRAINWASHING

Let's take a look at the meaning of the phrase "brainwashing" now that we've established its historical context. One way to explain brainwashing is to think of it as a process in which one person or a group of individuals uses deceptive or crafty strategies to convince another person to change their will so that it aligns with that of the manipulator.

Because there are many methods that individuals might convince one another in today's world, particularly in the realm of politics, it is essential to make a distinction between genuine persuasion and brainwashing whenever this issue is brought up for discussion.

People have an easier time getting others to comply with their will when they state a few items in their argument that are likely to elicit a positive reaction from the subject of their argument. They round off their argument with a factual assertion that serves as the cherry on top. At the very end, they will express whatever it is that they want individuals to do in response to what they have spoken.

Consider, for instance, the following excerpt from a speech: "Are you sick and tired of shelling out expensive fees for your children's schooling? What should we do about the steadily increasing costs of gas and electricity? Are you troubled by the repeated outbreaks of violence and labor action?"

It is important to keep in mind that the government has stated that the nation is inching closer and closer to entering a recession and that the cost of fuel will continue to increase because they are experiencing the biggest decline in the economic system since the time of the civil war. So, the solution is to vote for Democratic candidates if you want to see positive change come to the nation. The fact of the matter is that you most likely do not want to admit the idea that these techniques are used for brainwashing.

Now that you know how brainwashing happens, let us look at some of the most common techniques through which brainwashing is induced.

Brainwashing Through Isolation

One of the first things that happen when trying to brainwash someone is the complete isolation of the victim from their near and dear ones. This is done to make sure that the target will not have any chance of reconnecting with their previous self. Every time the target gets in touch with people who are essentially their well-wishers, they will experience a break in their reformation.

This means that there will be constant breaks in the process of being manipulated, and if the loved one is concerned enough, they will ensure that the manipulator will not have any further contact with the brainwasher. The more isolated the brainwashed target is, the more susceptible they will be to whatever indoctrinations they receive from the manipulator. The victim will acquire all new information and ideas from the manipulator and form their new ideologies based on these, without any third party stepping in to ask as to what is going on.

Brainwashing Through Self-Esteem Onslaught

Let me take you back to Germany after the First World War. The country was facing an all-time low, both politically and economically. The Germans were suffering from nationwide recession and unemployment, and the government was pretty much defunct. There was an overall feeling of hopelessness. Inflation played a large role in Germany's issues. The nation had acquired a huge debt from the World War. Authorities were struggling to repay this debt, and they formed the wrong notion they could repay the debt if they printed more money.

Too much of the international economy was dependent on the counterproductive passing of paper from the United States to Germany in the form of loans, from Germany to the Allies in the form of reparations, and from the Allies to the United States in the form of payment of war debts. In addition, the United States increased its tariffs in 1922 and again in 1930 to levels that made it very difficult for Europeans to earn money by selling to Americans.

The resultant effect was that people from all sections of the country were unemployed, homeless, and starving. The welfare system in Germany crashed because they could not handle all the people who were in need of assistance. There were only a few soup kitchens available and all of them had very long lines, making it essentially impossible to feed everyone who needed help.

People slept on the alleys, sidewalks, and wherever they could find some amount of warmth. In 1932, a German writer described his experience of spending a night in the Berlin municipal lodging house. He wrote of men standing in long rows, dressed in nightshirts huge enough to reach the ground. They took what little steam they could get from the food to warm themselves and asked for a "real helping," or a little more. They were so terribly hungry.

The answer lay, apparently, with Hitler. He posed as a moral crusader who had all the solutions that would work against deceit, corruption, and inequality. The Germans were long-suffering, and with the collapse of their moral standards following the World War, they became duped by all the promises that he made. They felt he would bring about the moral rejuvenation they were craving.

His ideologies resonated with the Germans, who were already disgusted with what they had become. Rampant hedonism of the Weimar high society and modern cultural norms had reduced them to wondering how things had become so loose and immoral. The notion of a "Fatherland," of returning Germany to the greatness from which it once came was a promise they wanted to be fulfilled. In other words, they wanted an answer, a real answer that would bolster their failing self-worth.

When Hitler began his verbal brainwashing, he made sure to remind the people of just how much they had lost. He made repeated references to all their sufferings and how much they had reduced from the great nation they once were. So, he constantly brought forward instances highlighting their need to rebuild their broken self-esteem. Nazism came as an awakening of the German people, a promise to revive the culture that was once so great, but now had nothing save decay and degeneration.

Once a manipulator has said and done what needs to be said and done to break the self-esteem of their targets, they will use their tactics to rebuild the target's image however they wish to. This can include reminders, indoctrination tactics, or plain ridicule. The target will go through a constant phase of mental torture and be reminded of everything they have lost.

They will accomplish this by deceiving the victim with falsehoods and then causing the victim to feel humiliated by revealing the truth about themselves to other individuals. They are also able to harass their victims and not allow them any type of personal space, which is another form of bullying that they may engage in.

Brainwashing Through Music

Just as music has the power to heal the soul and uplift us from the vagaries of life, so also it can manipulate and destroy us. Which is surprising, considering how many of us turn to music as a form of healing when we are sad or depressed. On the other hand, the majority of objects in the world have two aspects to them. One that can bring about immense good, and the other that can cause a lot of destruction.

Under normal circumstances, music works as a powerful tool to inspire powerfully pleasurable feelings. It releases something alchemical in our minds when we listen to or perform it. For a second, think of the many ways in which we use music, other than hearing it to comfort ourselves. We make playlists to communicate with and seduce others. We have those special songs that we need to listen to when we are working out, and then there are those extra blue ones for the times we feel low.

Stores and supermarkets use various kinds of songs to entice customers to spend longer hours amidst aisles, mindlessly purchasing items as part of their consciousness is solely focused on the familiarity of the tunes and words blaring through the loudspeakers. Restaurants feature ambient tunes that work to whet the appetite.

Films use scores to stir emotions in us, and these emotions can range from pure joy to absolute, terrifying fear. Most of the scary movies we are so hooked on would be nothing without sudden bursts of ominous music that made me want to melt into my sofa when I was a kid. And, whether we'd like to acknowledge it or not, legitimate authorities like the CIA have weaponized sound to torture and extract information from detainees.

Time and again, cult leaders have utilized the negative potentialities of music to influence their followers. They use different forms of chanting to relax the human mind to a state where all guards are down, and then they focus the group's energy as they please.

Sometimes, these groups of vulnerable people will be instructed to chant if they are facing difficulties or feeling low. This generates an inability to think about solutions or process emotions because of the euphoria resulting from merely chanting and thinking about how their leader would save them without their needing to so much as bat an eyelash.

Cult leaders are known for alienating their followers and commanding their absolute loyalty. They use the feelings of subservience within these groups with singing and dancing routines to exercise brainwashing. Religious ceremonies comprising holy chants become tools to direct physiological and emotional attention to a place where they become the messengers of God or a divine entity unto themselves.

This absolute state of being brainwashed rewires how the human brain works, and the targets become isolated from the world existing outside the narrow boundaries of their cult.

You may wonder how music does this, but the truth is, your guess is as good as mine. What I can tell you is music activates the biological reward systems in the brain, pretty much in the same way as eating something we love, having pleasurable intercourse, drugs and wealth would. While no one can dispute the clear biological motivations supporting our penchant for good food, procreation, and drugs, it is difficult to rationalize why something that is all tunes can produce such chemical pleasure within the reward centers of the brain.

Consider The Moonies *(The Family Federation for World Peace and Unification)*, a cult that would go down in history for their arranged mass marriages, and for how Reverend Moon owned absolute sexual control over all women who were part of the cult.

Reverend Moon rose to the heights of being considered a reincarnation of the Messiah. He taxed his followers in amounts that equaled their life's savings. And he believed in the power of music. He founded the Universal Ballet Foundation and installed one of his own daughters as the prima ballerina. He was also a major sponsor of the New York Symphony Orchestra. So powerful were their tactics (which included the use of music) that they were able to apparently brainwash young recruits into leaving their families to join their cult.

Perhaps one of the reasons why music is so immersive is because it gives us something akin to a deep sense of pleasure, from both the sensory perspective and the "emotional" perspective. It alters our hormonal makeup and affects vital signs like heart rate, breathing, and blood pressure. It can make us feel exalted and break down in tears. It can immerse us for hours. And the brainwasher knows this. They know they can employ music to destroy the mental makeup of their targets and get them to conform to everything they want.

Brainwashing Through Selective Association

When a manipulator is brainwashing a person, they make sure their target is not going to come in contact with any person or people other than those who are also members of the same group of brainwashed individuals. This leaves room for peer pressure. Since everyone wants to be desired and accepted, the brainwashed individual is made to feel at home among those "of their kind." They will come to believe that others outside their group are not as reformed or superior as them.

The brainwashed group is completely isolated and then exposed to selective techniques that will only allow them to relate to people who have been subjected to the same brainwashing techniques. This is one of the reasons why members of a cult are recruited from a very early age. The idea is that the sooner they can be recruited and made to conform to the group's doctrines, the better. Once the indoctrination is complete, they will serve as the new recruiters who will help bring in more young people to be brainwashed.

The manipulator makes the victim believe that there is a "us" and a "them," and they provide the victim the apparent opportunity to pick which group they desire to belong to. But then again, when faced with absolute redemption and a higher form of living, which the victim will only gain if they choose "us," against a life of complete drudgery and desolation that will result from choosing "them," what choice do they have? This causes the victim to feel as if they have a choice between the two groups. This is done in order to win the victim's undivided allegiance and complete obedience.

Brainwashing Through Love Bombing Or Gaslighting

Love bombing is possibly one of the most dangerous tools to brainwash and influence people to the point of no return. It is a grooming process where the predator employs excessively careful flattery, praise, and promises of a beautiful alliance, all designed in ways that will help them fulfill their own manipulative agendas. When predators love bomb their victims, they can persuade them to fulfill any desires they have. This is also a tool used in cults to ensure unquestioned loyalty to the cult leader.

Love bombing often works like gaslighting. Gaslighting is the emotional blackmail of a person, typically over a longer length of time, that causes the victim to doubt the legitimacy of their own thoughts, understanding of reality, or recollections and typically results in ambiguity, a crisis of trust and self-esteem, unpredictability of one's underlying mental stability, and heavy reliance on the perpetrator.

Gaslighting is a kind of psychological manipulation in which an individual's perspective of reality is intentionally distorted. When someone is trying to make you doubt yourself, your recollections, current events, and perceptions, they are engaging in a tactic known as gaslighting. After having a conversation with the individual who is gaslighting you, you may find that you are left feeling confused and question if there is anything wrong with you. It's possible that you'll be led to believe that you're the one at fault for anything, or that you're simply being too sensitive to the situation.

Anyone can become a victim of love bombing, but it can particularly destroy children of narcissistic parents since they become programmed to seek approval from an external source rather than finding it within themselves. These children also grow up with the wrong notion that they must act to please others and constantly look for sources of external validation so they can survive the destructive effects of their turbulent childhoods.

The term "love bombing" isn't inherently a new concept. As a matter of fact, it has existed since the 1970s. In traditional lingo, it has always been viewed as a practice resorted to by cults and religious organizations as a way to indoctrinate new recruits. A number of people believe that it was the Unification Church of the United States (the Moonies) who coined the term. In a 1984 issue of the *Social Analysis* journal, Thomas Robbins discerned that there were numerous controversial elements surrounding the concept of brainwashing in cults.

Traditionally, potential and new converts would be showered with affection, that is love bombed, to influence their belief that their fledgling relationships to divine love and spiritual honesty were the result of the deep and divine love and truth reflected by senior members of the cult. This form of coercive love was used to make the new recruits believe that if they conformed to the cult practices, they would only know and feel a higher power and a supreme love being showered over them.

Dennis Tourish and Ashly Pinnington would, in 2002, write that love bombing is drawn from inter-personal literature on perception and founded on the concept of ingratiation. The psychology operating behind this is surprisingly simple. We always prefer to be around people who agree with us and have nice things to say about us. We want to be in the presence of humans who radiate attributes such as compassion, wholesomeness, warmth, and empathy, or in other words, people who would give of themselves to help save us from the "tragedies" of the world.

Cults make a big show of showing how considerate they are of their constituent members. They shower prospective recruits with complete attention and affection, which eventually extends to a show of deep love. They take people who are already troubled with interpersonal relationships and make them feel as if they will be able to love them back to life. This is like a dangerous courtship where the cult leaders seduce new recruits into the umbrella of the organization and slowly but surely habituate them to the cult's native rituals and complicated belief systems.

They understand that it is only during the early stages, the stages where potential recruits will still have their doubts about what the cult can do for them, resistance will be the highest. Paying consideration to each and every individual cult member is a perfect tool to break this barrier of resistance and get them to conform. Once the recruit is in, and believes that "this cult is my home," there is hardly ever any turning back.

The practice of love bombing is not limited to cults or religious leaders alone. It has been used by pimps and gang leaders to establish coercive control over their victims, and also in relationships that thrive on complete obedience to the alpha partner.

Love bombing works through different contexts because human beings experience a natural need to experience feeling worthy about who they are. When it comes to feeling good about ourselves, we often find that self-appreciation doesn't quite cut it. This is when we become more susceptible to love bombing. The manipulators who specialize in this brainwashing technique know when someone's self-esteem is low and strike while the iron is hot.

The irony is that love bombing is often done by people who are very insecure and need complete subservience. So, while they require submission, they themselves may be suffering from low self-worth. They are generally insecure individuals looking to boost their egos. So, the more victims or the more positive attributes they have, the more validated they will feel.

They single out the needy and the vulnerable and shower them with what seems like genuine attention and affection. The victim naturally feels a massive dopamine rush that fills the void in the context of their self-validity.

When a person is in a relationship with a psychopathic predator, love bombing and intermittent reinforcement are used together to produce feelings of insecurity and yearning in the victim of the relationship. In the context of mental abuse, the pattern of harsh, callous behavior mixed in with occasional affection is referred to as intermittent reinforcement.

Throughout the course of the abusive cycle, the abuser will sometimes and unexpectedly provide the victim with positive reinforcement in the form of love, praise, or presents. The result of this is that the victim will never stop trying to get their favor, even if it means accepting the scraps that come in the form of their rare bouts of affection.

When the predator works to build a fear in the victim that they can lose the relationship at any time, and then suddenly intersperses it with a lot of affection and attention, the victim enters a muddied zone where they feel they cannot do anything except try harder. It's like a gambler plowing away at a slot machine because he hopes there will be a potential winner even after losing multiple rounds.

The victim in the cycle of abuse and reinforcement can form the idea that the only way they can get any return is to keep doing, keep giving, and keep being subservient. Plus, intermittent reinforcement makes the target bond deeply with their manipulators and they become desperate to earn those little acts of kindness.

People belonging to the dark triad can point out the deepest desirable attributes each target possesses. They can make a great show of how worthy the target is by commenting on their positives, like their personality traits, accomplishments, and charm. This is the phase of hooking the target in, based on the correct assumption that we want to be recognized and admired. They also fixate on these traits to fulfill their devious agendas, not because they really care about the target.

Abusers dig as deep as they can to get what they want but the target is never able to understand that their affection will come and go as the rain, and be interspersed with contempt, jealousy, and hate that is so profound it will break the target into tiny fragments so they can do nothing except depend on their abuser.

In other words, the target employs toxic affection. A poisonous attachment is one that has a hidden agenda if love and fondness are to be defined as the basis for it. As a way of expressing my feelings, I may declare that I love you. Alternatively, maybe it's only because I want to hook up with you, get funds from you, or simply want you to repeat it back to me. Affection as a kind of persuasion is typically effective since we desire and therefore need to be loved, much as with love bombing.

When human beings are confronted with a threat or danger that poses an immediate risk to their preconceived ideals of safety and security, they want to hear that there is at least a glimmer of hope that things could turn out better for them in the future. Abusers make use of this human psyche to show the victim an iota of kindness after subjecting them to extended spells of cold treatment.

The victim takes this to mean that not all hope is lost. So, even a tiny card or a gift or a treat or "I promise I am trying to change" may not just be interpreted as a massively positive sign, but also a form of evidence that the abuser isn't all bad, and that most importantly, they still "feel something" for the victim.

The victim reads this as the opportunity to try harder to please them so that the cold treatment does not come back. Even while they are being devalued and rejected by their abusers, victims of psychological and emotional violence still desire the love bombing that was so comforting during the idealization period. Intermittent reinforcement and the effects of trauma all collaborate to create a strong link between both the victim and the abuser, so this is not surprising.

Targets of love bombing tend to mistake superficial bonds characterized by over affection for meaningful relationships that are meant to last for a lifetime. They make the issue of believing that they have found themselves an exceptional love. In most cases, the problem is that the manipulators know how to play this role at the onset. They will be the perfect partner, everything the target had ever dreamed of.

They will never make it feel as if they are only playing at the onset. It is only once the target has fallen that they will show their true colors, and even then, they will infrequently change back to show a tiny bit of love to remind them of what they could regain if they "tried a little harder" to be obedient.

The most susceptible, as I mentioned before, are the children of narcissistic parents. Children of dark triad parents often navigate the world alone, and they run the risk of repeatedly encountering such manipulators. They do not have any "supportive" caretakers who will heal their troubles, whether in childhood or during adulthood. They look for what solace they can get, and when a manipulator comes along with the promise of a home, they don't notice the red flags as quickly as they should.

The hunger for love and a sense of connection is too deep and too much. They stay focused on those tiny leeways—the occasional kiss or gift, the kind word, the dreamy night out. All the abuse becomes "okay" so long as these once-in-a-blue-moon occasions pop up.

While love-bombing relationships may be fast-paced and passionate, they can also be addictive due to their fast-paced nature and the excitement of finally being acknowledged. Due to their misinterpretation of attention, they develop an addiction to the feeling of genuine connection.

Narcissistic parents frequently use their children as a pawn in a power struggle between them and their own siblings, making them vulnerable prey for predators who want to exploit their sense of self-worth. Children of narcissists have almost always sought this kind of attention, and an emotional predator who nurtures them gives them enough of it.

Their pain is exacerbated when they are placed in a triangle involving their primary abuser and other people who will also be part of the relationship they have—for an abuser will never be content with just one target. As a result, those who are the victims of malignant narcissists begin to feel even more inferior and unworthy, as if they must compete with others who may be better than them in order to be taken seriously.

Children of narcissists grow up being diminished and made to feel like the source of all their parents' problems. So, alternating between bouts of excessive criticism and the occasional praise, they go from being on high alert to feeling disarmed. This causes chemical turmoil. They want love, desire, and the feeling that comes from being heard, cared for, and seen for who they are.

So, in their minds, the question remains—do they love me, or do they not? They feel that there are times when they belong and there is a sense of kinship. On the other hand, there is also the predominant worry that they are only outcasts to their own family, which probably means the larger society will cast them out too.

Safeguards

The way out of this kind of love bombing, and any form of brainwashing in general, lies in trying to seek internal validation for the traits that targets have been love bombed with for so long. They must believe that they already embody these traits, and not because the predator feels so, *but because they inherently need them and have them.* The effort must be made to surround themselves with people who can recognize and appreciate good qualities rather than make a huge pomp and show about how great they are.

Remember, genuine compliments cost nothing. They do not *need you* to do something so that you earn them. Be on the lookout for flattery that goes above and beyond what is normal and is accompanied by a request or unjustified praise. Just be mindful that even if the praise seems to be justified, there may be a hidden motive behind it.

Another thing you can do to avoid becoming a victim of love bombing is focus on all the traits that make you unique and resist all impulses to compare yourself to other people. You have to remember that when you are being subjected to praise from a target; they are doing nothing except looking at you as a new toy that they get to play with.

Rather than running to seek this kind of attention, again and again, make it a point to look inwards and consider what you would praise about yourself if you were the outsider. What are your qualities? Are you a kind, compassionate, empathetic, creative soul? Think of everything that has brought you to a place of sustenance, because you have been doing it for yourself. Look how far you have come, and continue to focus on everything that has made you keep going.

Avoid putting your trust in individuals who are nothing but superficial well-wishers by learning to tell the difference between genuine connection and superficial flattery from the get-go. Make a list of the connections and alliances in your life that have the potential to evolve into deeper partnerships and those that don't.

When it comes to building a long-term relationship, trust, honesty, and reliability are essential. A quick fix will only last as long as the abuser is "interested enough."

Build an authentic relationship that bases itself on healthy feedback rather than one focused on punishment and trauma. Understand that there is no one out there with the potential to replace who you are and everything you contribute to the world. You remain unique with or without reinforcement from an external source.

This will help you to become selective about who you open the gates to. Manipulators and toxic people will no longer have access to your inner soul and instead, you will attract people who *actually care.*

At the end of the day, you have to make a choice between only living through lies and half-truths and being the subject of endless counts of abuse interspersed with occasional flattery; and building genuine connections. You see, a connection that is meant to last will make exceptions for you, even on your lowest days.

The people who genuinely care will attempt to show you the light more than once, or at least until they know there is still some hope. They will not abandon you on a whim. And they will certainly not be in a relationship with you simply so that you can fulfill a certain end for them, with no foreseeable benefit for you.

With this, we are nearing the close of the book. I hope that by now, you feel sufficiently equipped to understand different dark tactics and manipulative practices that may be employed against you, and what you can do to steer clear of each of them, or, if possible, turn the tables so that you stay in the driver's seat so far as the control in the relationship is concerned.

Always keep in mind that manipulation is only inherently dishonest when individuals choose to use it in an unethical manner. The concepts of what constitutes morality, and what is otherwise immoral, can differ from society to society and individual to individual. However, all of us can agree on the basics of what makes up something that is inherently evil.

Hurting, killing, maiming, or injuring for nothing but personal gain or pleasure becomes evil, and if the act of manipulation is only concerned with this, then you should know how to defend yourself and your loved ones.

EPILOGUE

ANYONE WHO HAS BEEN the subject of an act of coercion or manipulation for the wrong reasons will have known a world of pain. For most of us, spotting manipulators is very difficult because they are individuals who know how to hide in plain sight and appeal to the aspects of us which are most in need of attention.

If we have known abusive relationships for the greater part of our lives, we will also intrinsically form a connection that sets off a response whenever we meet someone who seems too good to be true. A part of us may end up feeling this is our dues getting returned to us, or conversely, we may also feel we need to hang on to this relationship with everything we have.

When we try to do this, when we decide that attachment has to be something permanent, the dangers are real because the manipulator who is only concerned with inflicting hurt will always know when their target is ripe.

It is difficult for the majority of individuals to recognize the telltale signals of manipulators. This is particularly true for those individuals who are vulnerable to manipulation at the hands of their romantic partners. In general, it might be difficult to recognize certain indicators of manipulation.

In addition, it is sometimes more difficult to recognize these behaviors in individuals whom you love and who you feel love you in return. In romantic partnerships, individuals often "turn a blind eye" to the manipulative behaviors of their significant other because they consider such behaviors to represent flaws in themselves.

When we are in partnerships, we make an effort to comprehend the shortcomings of one another. When it comes to relationships, there are indeed a lot of different indicators that point to the presence of manipulation, and although you should be aware of the personality qualities of a deceiver, there are also a lot of additional symptoms.

This is due to the fact that people who are skilled at manipulation often relax their guard because they're at home or in familiar territory. They are operating from a place of ease and confidence, certain that they are capable of doing anything, while you are too helpless to defend yourself or make an effort to alter the situation.

Society and history are rife with instances of people who have been manipulated into doing terrible things. We talked about how cults operate, and how puny men became dictators of such mark and terror that the world will essentially never forgive them. How else do you explain convincing people to commit heinous crimes, crimes no soul should ever be able to justify?

The thing is, when you are only concerned with influence, persuasion, and manipulation as words, as tools to simply achieve something without causing harm to or destroying other people, you are not likely to be the source of damage. On the other hand, if your primary intention is to use manipulation to hurt and kill, then, the terms become bad unto themselves.

At the end of the day, you have to ask yourself what your purpose is. You have to want to be safe and to keep those you love and care about protected, and for doing this, it will be important for you to be able to use manipulation and influence from time to time.

When seen from a more favorable perspective, manipulation may become a helpful influence; nonetheless, manipulation itself is inherently risky if you are new to it. Take time to learn what it entails, and also to understand your core motivations.

If you can be a persuasive person who can not only get what you want but also fulfill the needs of others, then it will be much simpler for you to be able to have the things that you want most in life. You may become just as influential while keeping yourself safe from those who have abused your good nature and willingness to be useful in the past.

I hope you feel sufficiently prepared to step out and see how you can use the knowledge and tools now at your disposal. Remember that no one in this world should get to force you to do things against your ethics and values. After all, the manipulator who chooses to hurt is only showing their deepest insecurities and hoping that hurting you will act as a balm for them. Keep your head intact, and all will be well.

BIBLIOGRAPHY

Beer, David. 2021. "How Netflix Affects What We Watch and Who We Are – and It's Not Just the Algorithm." The Conversation: Https://Theconversation.Com/How-Netflix-Affects-What-We-Watch-and-Who-We-Are-and-Its-Not-Just-the-Algorithm-169897. October 14, 2021.

Berman, Sanford. 2019. "Where Have All the Moonies Gone?" In Reference Services and Technical Services, 133–44. Routledge. https://doi.org/10.4324/9780367808303-12.

Burns, Peter. 2021. "5 Psychological Experiments That Show The Dark Side Of Human Nature." Medium: Https://Medium.Com/Lessons-from-History/5-Psychological-Experiments-That-Show-the-Dark-Side-of-Human-Nature-10aedf864bd5. June 21, 2021.

Chartrand, Tanya L., and John A. Bargh. 1999. "The Chameleon Effect: The Perception–Behavior Link and Social Interaction." Journal of Personality and Social Psychology 76 (6): 893–910. https://doi.org/10.1037/0022-3514.76.6.893.

Dębska, Małgorzata, Paweł Dębski, Jacek Polechoński, Michał Rozpara, and Rajmund Tomik. 2021. "The Dark Triad of Personality in the Context of Health Behaviors: Ally or Enemy?" International Journal of Environmental Research and Public Health 18 (8): 4113. https://doi.org/10.3390/ijerph18084113.

Elizabeth Griffith. 1761. The Memoirs of Ninon de L'Enclos, with Her Letters to Monsr de St Evremond and to the Marquis de Sevigné.

Elnahla, Nada. 2020. "Black Mirror: Bandersnatch and How Netflix Manipulates Us, the New Gods." Consumption Markets & Culture 23 (5): 506–11. https://doi.org/10.1080/10253866.2019.1653288.

Goldstein, Noah J., Robert B. Cialdini, Vladas Griskevicius, and John Deighton served as editor and Mary Frances Luce served as associate editor for this article. "A Room with a Viewpoint: Using Social Norms to Motivate Environmental Conservation in Hotels." Journal of Consumer Research 35, no. 3 (2008): 472–82. https://doi.org/10.1086/586910.

Goman, Carol Kinsey. 2011. "The Mistakes People Make Reading Your Body Language ." Forbes: Https://Www.Forbes.Com/Sites/Carolkinseygoman/2011/03/01/the-Mistakes-People-Make-Reading-Your-Body-Language/?Sh=4f2fbaa19c0f. 2011.

Haden, Jeff. 2020. "9 Secrets of Incredibly Persuasive People (That You Should Steal)." Https://Www.Themuse.Com/Advice/9-Secrets-of-Incredibly-Persuasive-People-That-You-Should-Steal. 2020.

Hajjat, Fatima. 2016. "Is There Such a Thing as Reverse Psychology?" In , 721–22. https://doi.org/10.1007/978-3-319-11815-4_218.

Hood, Ralph W., and Eileen Barker. 1986. "The Making of a Moonie." Review of Religious Research 27 (3): 270. https://doi.org/10.2307/3511427.

James, Oliver. 2018. "All about Love Bombing." In Love Bombing, 1–24. Routledge. https://doi.org/10.4324/9780429476914-1.

Jauk, Emanuel, and Raoul Dieterich. 2019. "Addiction and the Dark Triad of Personality." Frontiers in Psychiatry 10 (September). https://doi.org/10.3389/fpsyt.2019.00662.

Jay, Phyllida, Elizabeth Paton, and Kai Schultz. 2020. "Luxury's Hidden Indian Supply Chain ." Forbes: Https://Www.Nytimes.Com/2020/03/11/Style/Dior-Saint-Laurent-Indian-Labor-Exploitation.Html. March 11, 2020.

Liu, Yaqian, Na Zhao, and Min Ma. 2021. "The Dark Triad Traits and the Prediction of Eudaimonic Wellbeing." Frontiers in Psychology 12 (November). https://doi.org/10.3389/fpsyg.2021.693778.

"Market Manipulation." 2022. Corporate Finance: Https://Corporatefinanceinstitute.Com/Resources/Knowledge/Trading-Investing/Market-Manipulation/. 2022.

Noah J. Goldstein, Steve J. Martin, and Robert Cialdini. 2009. "Yes!: 50 Scientifically Proven Ways to Be Persuasive Paperback." December 29, 2009.

Petrone, Paul. 2018. "How to Turn a No Into a Yes: 3 Phrases You Should Use." LinkedIn: Https://Www.Linkedin.Com/Business/Learning/Blog/Productivity-Tips/How-to-Turn-a-No-into-a-Yes. 2018.

Rauthmann, John F., and Gerald P. Kolar. 2012. "How 'Dark' Are the Dark Triad Traits? Examining the Perceived Darkness of Narcissism, Machiavellianism, and Psychopathy." Personality and Individual Differences 53 (7): 884–89. https://doi.org/10.1016/j.paid.2012.06.020.

Reynolds, Gretchen. 2003. "The Stuttering Doctor's 'Monster Study.'" NY Times: Https://Www.Nytimes.Com/2003/03/16/Magazine/the-Stuttering-Doctor-s-Monster-Study.Html. March 16, 2003.

Sinha, Indrajit, and Thomas Foscht. 2007. Reverse Psychology Marketing. London: Palgrave Macmillan UK. https://doi.org/10.1057/9780230625068.

Tourish, Dennis, and Ashly Pinnington. "Transformational Leadership, Corporate Cultism and the Spirituality Paradigm: An Unholy Trinity in the Workplace?" Human Relations 55, no. 2 (February 2002): 147–72. https://doi.org/10.1177/0018726702055002181.

Tversky, Amos, and Daniel Kahneman. "Judgment under Uncertainty: Heuristics and Biases." Science 185, no. 4157 (1974): 1124–31. http://www.jstor.org/stable/1738360.

Wissing, Benno Gerrit, and Marc-André Reinhard. 2019. "The Dark Triad and Deception Perceptions." Frontiers in Psychology 10 (August). https://doi.org/10.3389/fpsyg.2019.01811.